Europe's Digital Revolution

Europe's Digital Revolution focuses on the increasingly urgent issue of the broadcasting policies of the European Union and its member states, and the challenges posed by digital broadcasting. Examining the European Union's record in the field of broadcasting policy and its desire to become a more central actor in the regulation of the converging communications sector, this book analyses the extent to which technological change and globalisation are aiding those ambitions, as they have already done in related areas such as telecommunications.

David Levy explores the particular problem that broadcasting poses for European policy makers. The economic, political and cultural importance of broadcasting has fuelled attempts to develop an EU broadcasting policy, but it also explains the determination of key governments to retain control on a national level. The range of EU regulatory initiatives and approaches are examined and set in the context of widely differing national regulatory traditions and policy styles. *Europe's Digital Revolution* explores the latest thinking to emerge from the EU in response to digital broadcasting, including the recent attempt to promote 'regulatory convergence' or a common approach at the EU level to the regulation of telecoms, IT and broadcasting. While in other areas technological change has been cited as justifying the transfer of regulatory responsibility to the EU level, digital broadcasting is unlikely to lead to a rapid 'Europeanisation' of broadcasting policy. David Levy argues that EU-wide approaches should focus on anti-competitive practices rather than on matters of cultural and content regulation.

This book provides an insider's analysis of a particularly complex area of EU and national policy making. It is the most up-to-date personal assessment of the impact of digital broadcasting in the UK, France and Germany, and on EU regulatory approaches. It will interest students of the EU policy making process as well as those involved in the regulation of the media. *Europe's Digital Revolution* throws new light on the wider debate about how technological change and 'convergence' affect public policy.

Dr David Levy works on European broadcasting policy and digital regulation at the BBC but is writing here in a personal capacity. He has recently published in *West European Politics* and *Telecommunications Policy* and is a regular speaker at industry and academic conferences.

Routledge Research in European Public Policy
Edited by Jeremy Richardson
Nuffield College, University of Oxford

Europe's Digital Revolution

Broadcasting regulation, the EU
and the nation state

David A. L. Levy

London and New York

First published 1999
by Routledge
11 New Fetter Lane, London EC4P 4EE

Simultaneously published in the USA and Canada
by Routledge
29 West 35th Street, New York, NY 10001

Routledge is an imprint of the Taylor & Francis Group

© 1999 David A. L. Levy

Typeset in Baskerville by Curran Publishing Services
Printed and bound in Great Britain by
St Edmundsbury Press, Bury St Edmunds, Suffolk.

British Library Cataloguing in Publication Data
A catalogue record for this book is available
from the British Library

Library of Congress Cataloguing in Publication Data
Levy, David A.
  Europe's digital revolution: broadcasting regulation, the EU, and
the nation state / David A. Levy
224 p. 23.4 x 15.6 cm – (Routledge research in European public
policy: 5)
Includes bibliographical references and index
1. Broadcasting policy – European Union countries. 2. Digital
communications – European Union countries. 3. Technological
innovationis – European Union countries. I. Title. II. Series.
HE8689.9.E9L48 1999   99–17496
                                          CIP

ISBN 0–415–17196–2

Contents

Tables

Preface and acknowledgements

My interest in European policy making goes back to 1990–1 when I was reporting for the BBC's *Newsnight* programme on the run-up to and the aftermath of the Maastricht Treaty negotiations. At the time hardly a week went by without another presumed assault on British sovereignty where first Margaret Thatcher, and then John Major, was called in to bat for Britain against the triumvirate of Delors, Kohl and Mitterrand. And yet even the most casual observer could not but be struck by the curious mismatch between the arguments of high principle dominating the European Debate, and the often highly technical issues that filled the constant rounds of meetings between national and EU officials. What was it, I wondered, that could suddenly turn a debate over food additives into an assault by 'Brussels' on the British sovereign right to eat prawn-flavoured crisps?

Since Maastricht the mood towards Europe has become more sceptical, but the amount of essentially technical problem-solving in Council working groups, the Commission and Parliament has continued to grow. Indeed, perhaps in response to this scepticism, rallying calls for Europe tend now to be couched in largely pragmatic rather than idealistic terms. In this new climate, technological change and globalisation are cited as requiring a Europe-wide response, whether because of the 'Information Society', 'convergence', the need for Internet Governance, or just in the name of creating a more competitive Europe. This book sets out to explain why broadcasting has been relatively resistant to such rallying cries, and to examine how far digitalisation is likely to change the balance between national and EU level regulation. In answering those questions, I also hope to throw some light on the nature of the EU policy process, the pressures at work within the EU policy community, and the ways in which differing national regulatory traditions and policy styles continue to exert a determining influence on broadcasting policy outcomes within the EU, when much conventional wisdom might have expected them to be smoothed over by technological change.

In writing this book I owe a great debt to many people from different walks of life. My series editor, Jeremy Richardson, encouraged me to write the book, was enthusiastic about the proposal, maintained a diplomatic silence about the overlong delay before delivery, and then provided extremely useful feedback on the manuscript. Countless conversations with my friend Anthony Teasdale have helped increase my knowledge and understanding of the EU. Vincent Wright, and the Warden and Fellows of Nuffield College welcomed me into their midst for the academic year 1996–7, and provided a stimulating and congenial working environment. The Trustees of the Anglo-German Foundation supported several research trips during which I tried to get to grips with the ways in which fifteen different Länder authorities approach media regulation. That task was made immensely easier and more successful thanks to the help of Katharina Grimme, Professor Hoffmann-Riem, Peter Humphreys, Emannuelle Machet, Runar Woldt, those media regulators and government officials who were kind enough to be interviewed, and the hospitality of the European Institute for the Media in Düsseldorf and of the Hans Bredow Institute in Hamburg.

Thanks are due also to the BBC: to Patricia Hodgson for releasing me from my job to do the research and to Dominic Morris for his understanding as I saw the book through to completion. Both supported my decision to undertake this as a personal project, and the end result should be read in that light, as a statement purely of my own views, and not those of my employers.

Over the last two years many academics and practitioners here and elsewhere in Western Europe have shared their knowledge and ideas with me, helped me to track down key regulators and references, and given me the benefit of their wisdom. Most will disagree with some parts of this book and none bear responsibility for its contents, but I owe thanks to them all; above all to Stefaan Verhulst and Campbell Cowie for their very helpful comments on the manuscript of this book, and to the late Vincent Wright, a valued friend and mentor over more than two decades.

The biggest debt is to my family. To my mother and sister for their support, encouragement and forbearance. To Jo for putting up with an absent partner for so much time, for her comments on an early version of the manuscript, and for her support in many different ways. Also to Patrick and Lydia for understanding that a project of this kind takes more time than most children can contemplate, and for reminding me, at moments when I might have thought otherwise, that life is not only about writing books.

David Levy

Abbreviations

API	applications programming interface
ATVS	Advanced Television Standards Directive
BSC	Broadcasting Standards Commission
CSA	Conseil Supérieur de l'audiovisuel
DCMS	Department of Culture, Media and Sport
DLM	German Conference of the Directors of State Media Authorities
DNH	Department of National Heritage
DT	Deutsche Telekom
DTI	Department of Trade and Industry
DTT	digital terrestrial television
DVB	Digital Video Broadcasting Group
EBU	European Broadcasting Union
EC	European Commission
ECJ	European Court of Justice
EP	European Parliament
EPG	electronic programme guide
EU	European Union
ICT	information and communications technologies
IS	information society
ITC	Independent Television Commission
LMA	State Media Authority (Germany)
MTF	Merger Task Force
PSB	public service broadcasting/broadcaster
OFT	Office of Fair Trading
TVWF	Television Without Frontiers Directive
VOD	video on demand

Introduction by the series editor

It has become conventional wisdom to argue that rapid technological change and, especially, the convergence of technologies, are important exogenous causes of policy change. Public policy, particularly public regulation, so the theory goes, is constantly trying to catch up with changing technology and with the associated changes in market structure. Moreover, it is also argued that the march of technology will erode the importance of *national* regulation (and even its very rationale) and reinforce existing trends for greater Europeanisation and globalisation of the regulatory process.

David Levy's detailed analysis of the processes of policy change at the national and European level in the field of digital broadcasting presents fascinating insights into the validity of these claims. As he points out, the arrival of digital broadcasting, accompanied by changes in market and consumer behaviour, raises new regulatory issues and calls into question some of the existing approaches to broadcasting regulation. Others suggest that the diversity of existing public policy at the national level is an impediment to the successful convergence of IT, broadcasting and telecommunications technologies and that regulatory reform at both the national and EU levels is a necessary condition of successful convergence. A third argument is that technological and market changes will lead to the erosion of national differences in regulatory styles. A related, but equally important public policy issue, is, of course, the question of monopolistic or oligopolistic behaviour by firms in the new markets which technology creates. These, and many other issues (such as the practicality of regulating such technologies as the Internet), confront governments at both the national and European levels. Thus, as David Levy suggests, national governments face a central dilemma. They wish to retain the traditional controls over television, as a politically and culturally sensitive sector, yet fear the consequences of international competition if neighbouring countries introduce a more relaxed regulatory regime, which is more attractive to the big media companies.

The central focus of this study, illuminated by the author's direct personal involvement in the policy process under discussion, is the European Union's record in the field of broadcasting regulation; its desire to become a more central actor in the regulation of the converging communications sector; and the degree to which broadcasting has witnessed the same degree of Europeanisation (by which we generally mean the shift from the national to the European level seen in such sectors as telecoms or environmental policy). In analysing the events and the contrasting role of different institutions and actors in this process, David Levy does much more than write a political history of an important policy area. He also sheds much light on the central questions which occupy the attention of those scholars interested in the European policy process more generally. Thus, his study passes the most difficult test of any case study of a policy area, namely that one need have no particular interest in the policy area, however important it might be, in order to learn much that is of wider interest. For example, his study is rich in analysis of the role of the European Commission as a policy entrepreneur and the differing constraints which it faces; of the internal competition within the Commission; and the Commission's evolving approach towards European regulation. Similarly, there is much here on the role of the European Parliament, and the role of different interest organisations and competing advocacy coalitions in the European policy process and the ways in which the European consultation process works.

His study is not, however, confined to the European level. The interrelationship between the European level and the national level plays a central role in the trajectory of policy development. For example, the willingness of national governments to cede power to the European level is limited; national traditions, cultures and policy styles remain very important and have acted as rather effective constraints on policy convergence across national boundaries. Thus, a key finding of great interest to students of the European policy process is the resistance of national policy styles to European erosion, notwithstanding the fact that the reform *agenda* was often similar across the member states. As policy style theory would predict, the solutions adopted to a common problem certainly varied across Europe.

A further insight into the nature of the EU and national policy processes is provided by the contrast in the policy reform trajectories of the three converging policy areas (IT, telecoms, and broadcasting). In telecoms and IT policy, he argues, the Commission has been much more successful as a policy entrepreneur than in broadcasting. In practice, though the Commission has had an important impact on the broadcasting policy area (especially though not exclusively through competition policy), Levy's broad conclusion is that regulatory reform is more likely to occur at the national rather than the EU level. Thus, the Commission's earlier successes in establishing itself as a key actor and agenda setter in the regulation of convergence across the communications sector, now seem to be on the wane, and it may have a more limited impact on broadcasting than originally seemed likely.

Reform and policy change are, however, not impossible The book concludes with a forward look at how further change might occur and asks what shape that change might take. Here, as throughout the book, David Levy brings a perceptive eye to the dynamics of policy-making which reflects his own experiences of the processes being analysed. He has performed that most difficult task of combining the knowledge of an insider with the ability to stand back from what he has experienced, in order to focus on the key issues of European policy-making.

Jeremy Richardson
Centre for European Politics, Economics and Society
University of Oxford
November 1998

Introduction by the author

This book is about technological change and public policy in the European broadcasting market. Broadcasting in Europe started as a highly regulated industry, where the primary focus of regulation was decidedly national, the objectives and instruments of these national approaches differed wildly, and where in every case the regulation of broadcasting was treated very differently to that of other sections of the communications sector such as telecommunications or newspapers and publishing. Here we set out to assess the pressures for change in these distinctive aspects of broadcasting regulation, and the way in which European Union (EU) approaches to broadcasting policy for the analogue and digital environments, can help throw light on wider questions about the European policy-making process.

The book combines study of EU policy towards broadcasting with detailed accounts of broadcasting regulation in three of the key member states; the UK, France and Germany. There are several reasons for choosing these three countries as national case studies. The UK, France and Germany are the three largest broadcasting markets in the EU, yet their differing regulatory traditions means they might be expected to react in different ways to EU regulatory ambitions. Germany's federal structure and decentralised responsibility for broadcasting is particularly interesting in this light. In addition, as the three key national players within the EU, these three countries offer some of the most interesting material for examination of the interplay between the national and the EU policy process, and of the extent to which technological change, in the shape of digital broadcasting, created pressures for changes in the balance of regulation between the national, the sub-national, and the supra-national levels.

Much of the European discussion of the impact of digital technology on broadcasting has been dominated by debates over 'convergence', a term which has many meanings. Digitalisation is bringing about undoubted technological convergence between the previously distinct technologies of broadcasting, computing and telecommunications. But other aspects of convergence are far less certain. How far will technological convergence lead to a convergence of consumer behaviour? Will 'broadcasting' give way to 'narrowcasting', where the very concept of TV channels or indeed TV itself die, to be subsumed into an all purpose multimedia delivery system, used for everything from retrieving e-mails, to reading the 'newspaper', to accessing video material literally on demand? And how far should techno-logical convergence be accompanied by convergence in the regulatory field too, where regulatory distinctions between broadcasting and telecom-munications are removed? If regulation is remodelled should this occur purely at the national level, or should the EU play an increased role in reg-ulating an industry that is internationalising as well as converging?

Many of these questions are currently being addressed both by national governments and by the EU. The mid to late 1990s will be remembered as a period when the profound technological changes represented by digital-isation of broadcasting were accompanied by a wave of regulatory reform and rethinking at the national and EU levels. In 1996–7 major new broad-casting reforms were launched in the UK, France, Germany and Italy. In December 1997 the European Commission produced a Green Paper looking at the regulatory implications of Convergence and in July 1998 the UK Government published their own Green Paper on the same subject. The new French broadcasting law was due to be discussed in the French parliament in May 1999, after this book went to press.

Amidst this flurry of activity this book takes a cool assessment of how much the traditional paradigm for regulating broadcasting is under chal-lenge, and the likelihood of a fundamental shift in regulatory responsibili-ties from the nation state to the European Union. These questions are approached in the four sections of the book. In the first section, Part One, we examine the technological changes that are underway, and the nature and consequences of the move to digital broadcasting. Part Two focuses on the approaches adopted to date to the regulation of analogue broadcast-ing, by the EU and the Member States, analysing the ways in which policy-makers at both levels have come to terms with a sector which has such an important cultural and political as well as economic role. In the third section we turn to examine the range of national and EU responses to the regulatory challenges posed by digital broadcasting and convergence, with an overview of national regulatory reform, and detailed studies covering the role of EU competition policy in digital TV, the EU's involvement in technical standards setting, and the way in which early Commission efforts in favour of telecoms liberalisation and the creation of a European Information Society developed into proposals for regulatory convergence across the entire communications sector.

The fourth and final section of the book draws conclusions about the nature of EU policy-making – in particular why broadcasting proved so much more resistant to Commission policy leadership and activism than many other sectors – and proposes an alternative agenda and division of responsibilities between the nation state and the EU for the future regulation of digital TV. While recognising the enormity of the technological changes that are underway, this final section scrutinises the argument that technological change and globalisation must inevitably lead to deregulation of national broadcasting markets and re-regulation at the European level. Two key conclusions emerge. The first is that in many areas of economic and infrastructure regulation a greater EU role could be useful. The second is that the continuing specificity and political and cultural significance of broadcasting means that arguments for true regulatory convergence, where a single communications regulation framework deals in an undifferentiated manner with the delivery and consumption of all digitally transmitted material, are still far from persuasive.

For readers whose primary interest is in the EU policy-making process there is much here on the way that EU policy is made, the tensions between the different policy actors, and the influence of national policy styles and traditions on the framing of EU regulation and policy. For those who are primarily interested in European broadcasting, it is also hoped that this book will provide a helpful overview of national and EU regulation to date, an assessment of the ways in which digital TV and concerns with the Information Society have impacted on regulation at both the national and EU levels, and a set of proposals which might guide future regulation of broadcasting within the much larger converging communications sector.

Part I

The impact of convergence

1 Converging technologies, changing markets

The European media industry is in a period of change. What were previously national markets are becoming international in nature. Single sector media companies are merging into multi sector conglomerates. The industry is becoming more competitive, as companies from the IT and telecommunications markets, and new media specialists, enter the fray.

(McGarvey 1997: 1)

The fast rate of technological change characterising the communications industry, the rapid emergence of new services and new market opportunities, and in particular the convergence between broadcasting and telecommunications, is continuously calling for new policy initiatives.

(OECD, 1997c: 19)

Introduction

Analogue broadcasting was characterised by limited channel choice, the need for the viewer to fit in with the schedulers, and a clear understanding that the television was simply a device for watching broadcast programmes. Digitalisation will create the possibility of hundreds of channels, convert the television set into a multipurpose/multimedia terminal, and allow viewers to become their own schedulers, watching programmes when they want and, in time, even interacting with the programmes themselves. Two forces are driving broadcasters and other media companies to invest in digital technology and new programme rights. The first is the belief that viewers can be persuaded to pay much more for television: through increased channel choice, charging for programmes currently viewed free-to-air, and using live sport, first release films and 'adult' programming to drive the take-up of pay-TV. Second is the conviction that the television, as the most ubiquitous household consumer device, will become the conduit through which an ever increasing variety of information will be conveyed and transactions conducted. No one can be certain about the degree to which these predictions will be realised. Indeed, one of the greatest commercial risks within the current enthusiasm for digital technology is that company strategies will be driven by a technological push rather than a consumer pull. As with most new technologies the uncertainties about the true extent of consumer demand are even greater than those surrounding the technology itself. Most observers agree, however, that in time the technological and commercial possibilities of digital television will transform the broadcasting markets of Europe's major countries. This chapter looks first at the technological bases of the 'digital revolution' before moving on to examine some of the ways in which that technology seems likely to be applied in the market.

A technological revolution

At its most basic, digital technology involves converting sound and pictures into binary digits – a series of ones and noughts – rather than the variations in amplitude and frequency that carry the information in analogue broadcasting. Once audio-visual material is created and transmitted digitally it can benefit from the vast increases in computing, processing and storage power that are currently taking place. Moore's law suggests a doubling of computer power for the same cost every eighteen months and a doubling of computer storage capacity every twelve months.[1] The speed and capacity of transmission networks is now beginning to increase at a similar rate, through the creation of new digital satellite and cable networks, through the upgrading of existing telecoms networks, and perhaps most dramatically, with the application of new technologies such as ADSL (Asymetric Digital Subscriber Loop) that allow fast transmission of data and video over existing telephone lines. Digital television combines a common digital coding system and this increased processing power with three other key technological changes: first digital compression; second technological and commercial convergence between hitherto discrete technologies and sectors; and third the spread of the conditional access technologies which are necessary both for the success of pay television and for the growth of new TV-based transactional services.

Compression and the end of spectrum scarcity

Digital compression technologies – which currently allow up to ten digital channels to be squeezed into the space previously occupied by one analogue channel – are reducing the impact of spectrum scarcity in limiting the number of broadcast TV channels. There will shortly be enough capacity for 500 digital satellite channels to be broadcast to the UK, digitalisation of the cable system will make space for up to 1,000 cable channels, and nearly thirty channels are initially available on the six multiplexes (or frequency blocks) that the UK Government has released for digital terrestrial television.[2] Continued improvements in compression technologies, and the eventual release of the spectrum when analogue satellite and (in the very long term) terrestrial transmissions are switched off, will mean that the number of available channels will be much higher. Conventional broadcast channels and their relatively high budget programmes are likely to dominate viewers' preferences for some time to come, but much of the additional capacity will be put to new uses.[3] New 'narrowcast' channels, targeting small communities of interest, or offering specialist services – such as rolling weather, financial or news services – will develop. The largest number of channels, however, are likely to be used for pay services – ranging from the simultaneous transmission of all the first division football matches being played on a Saturday afternoon, to a near video-on-demand service (NVOD) offering perhaps the top ten films, with each of them starting at, say, fifteen-minute intervals, throughout the evening.[4] The rush to acquire content for these new digital outlets has already been reflected in dramatically increased prices for key film and sports rights.

Convergence

Technological convergence is made possible by a common digital coding system, compression and increased transmission capacity. It has been described as a multi-faceted phenomenon covering the 'convergence of the *content* of media or media forms, convergence of *delivery channels* and convergence of customer interfaces' such as the telephone, the computer and the TV (Prosser *et al.* 1996: 3). One study conducted for the European Commission portrays convergence as the coming together of:

- the 'logical' convergence of physical information distribution infra-structures (such as broadcast television and telecommunications) to carry similar sorts of information at increasingly lower costs;
- the interactive information storage and processing capabilities of the computer world;
- the ubiquity and ease of use of consumer electronics; and
- content from the audio-visual and publishing worlds.

(KPMG 1996 vol. 2: 87)

Convergence could potentially have a dramatic impact on consumers as transmission systems to the home, and domestic electronic equipment such as the telephone, the computer and the TV, begin to operate inter-changeably. UK cable operators already provide telephony. Digital satellite and terrestrial transmission systems transmit data and graphics alongside TV programmes. Increasingly e-mails, web pages and audio and video (initially in poor quality) will be accessed on the Internet via satellite and cable more often and much more rapidly than through current telephone systems. Convergence will also be evident through the development of add-on units or set-top boxes allowing viewers to see TV programmes on their PC or use their TV as an Internet terminal. There will no doubt be some integrated PC/TVs but they will be more common in offices than in the home, since consumers wanting TV entertainment will continue to prefer a larger size screen in the living room rather than the desktop PC approach. Within five to seven years widescreen digital televisions will include large computer hard-disk drives capable of storing hundreds of hours of TV programmes.

Convergence could also change the structure of the communications market. Past market structures were defined by the method of delivery. They will begin to merge and new distribution methods will

> allow the creation of new products and services which may or may not be close substitutes for established ones. CDs replace vinyl records; on-line news services replace . . . press cuttings services; and video-on-demand (or near video-on-demand), once introduced, may replace video rental through video rental shops.
>
> (Hoehn *et al.* 1997: 4)

The key question for those trying to regulate the information industries (a question to which we will return in Chapter 8) is the extent to which the impact of convergence will undermine the specificity of the broadcasting, publishing and telecommunications sectors, and whether that will demand a radical re-evaluation of existing regulatory categories and intentions.

Conditional access

Increasingly common and ever more sophisticated conditional access technologies will be another key feature of digital broadcasting. Conditional access operates like an electronic turnstile. Through encrypting programmes on transmission and their decryption via a set-top box in the customer's household, only those viewers who have paid their subscription can view a pay TV service (Cruickshank 1997). Every household using digital TV will be equipped with a conditional access system with far more computer memory and 'intelligence' than its analogue counterpart, together with a 'return path' which will allow the consumer to communicate with the broadcaster or service provider, to order subscription or pay per view (PPV) programmes from their remote control, and access a range of other transactional services through the TV set. As more and more transactions are conducted via the TV set, so the TV will combine the roles of an extremely powerful marketing tool and a department store. Conditional access systems will operate as the gateway through which all these programmes and services must pass.

Faced with a proliferation of channels and services, viewers will become increasingly dependent on complex navigation systems or electronic programme guides (EPGs), incorporated into the conditional access systems, to guide them around the programmes and services that are available.

These EPGs will become marketing tools in their own right, capable of influencing the ways in which consumers choose their programmes and services, according to the prominence, attractiveness or ease with which different options are presented. The ability that they will create for viewers to seek out material by programme category or to construct their own schedules and news bulletins could change the way that TV is used. Views differ on whether this combination of increased numbers of channels and sophisticated EPGs will lead to the Internet model, where channel identities disappear and relatively crude search engines supply a comprehensive listing of what is available, or whether instead the threat of information overload will lead viewers to become more dependent on their perception that quality is guaranteed either by a channel or a brand (Cruickshank 1997, Graham 1997a). What is clear, however, is that, in the new transactional world of television, there will be far greater opportunities to influence the choices of viewers and consumers and to gather information about customers' viewing and purchasing patterns. Important issues of privacy and data protection will be raised as the set-top box in the home supercedes the supermarket loyalty card as *the* key source of customer information.

New digital services and a changing market

The move towards greater charging and interactivity has the potential to change the way in which television is consumed, as well as the structure of the market and the regulatory issues raised by television. Technology will facilitate this transformation but it will be the commercial opportunities for pay television and the provision of a range of TV-based services, that will determine the pace of the development of digital television. For commercial TV companies, digital broadcasting offers the tantalising prospect of closing the current gap between the two-thirds of leisure time that the average British consumer spends watching television (or listening to radio) as opposed to the mere 11 per cent of their leisure spending which is devoted to TV and videos (Morgan 1998a: 28–9). Much of the investment currently being made in digital technology, in acquiring new programme rights, and in cross-media mergers is based on the hope that viewers will pay more for television programmes and that an increased number of transactions will be conducted through the television, as well as the fear that companies which don't move fast may be excluded forever from a potentially very profitable market.

✦ *Pay TV*

Pay television – primarily subscription and PPV (pay per view) sport and films – will dominate the development of digital TV. The high returns produced by pay TV companies such as Canal Plus and BSkyB from their analogue operations have spurred on others to emulate their success. Pay TV revenues already represented almost 50 per cent of those of the private TV sector in Western Europe in 1996 (Brown 1997: 14). UK subscription television revenues which accounted for 20 per cent of all industry funding in 1995 are expected to rise three or even fourfold in the decade to 2005, to a point where they represent between a third and a half of UK audio-visual industry income (BBC 1996: 23).

The development of UK analogue pay TV has been heavily dependent on BSkyB's exclusive live rights to Premier League and other key football rights. Rupert Murdoch has, with customary clarity, declared his intention to use sport as 'a battering ram' for News Corporation's global pay television services (*Guardian* 16 October 1996). The England–Italy World Cup qualifying match broadcast in February 1997 reached a record 3.6 million UK viewers out of a total of around six million BSkyB subscribers. BSkyB's first experiment with PPV sport on the night of 16–17 March 1996 – when 600,000 subscribers (14 per cent of their total) paid £10–£15 to watch a live boxing contest between Mike Tyson and Frank Bruno in the early hours – indicated the scale of PPV revenues that could be extracted from sports fans. Digital subscribers to Telepiu in Italy and Canal Satellite in France can already buy virtual 'season tickets' to premium football league matches, and BSkyB digital satellite service includes a similar facility (*Screen Digest* 1997c: 86).[5]

PPV soccer is likely to play a major part in the development of digital TV in the UK. One survey conducted in June 1997 found that nearly ten million UK households (41 per cent of the total) would be willing to pay for PPV events for one or more of the four major sports: Premier League football, world title boxing matches, Formula One motor racing and top golf tournaments (*New Media Markets* 12 June 1997, vol. 15 no. 21).[6] This suggests that even though currently only around 25 per cent of UK households have access to subscription sports channels, once digital conditional access systems are more widely deployed, more households are likely to opt for either subscription or PPV sport. Since pay TV companies can pass their programming costs on to a self-selected audience, they will usually be able to outbid free-to-air broadcasters for sports rights, thereby increasing the incentive for dedicated fans to subscribe to their services.

Films are likely to be the other key driver of digital pay TV. Revenues from cinema admissions – at 31 per cent of all EU consumer spending on films – are already less than those either from pay TV (34 per cent) or from video sales and rentals (34 per cent) (*Screen Digest* 1997a). The advent of digital NVOD and, in time, true video-on-demand services, will mean that much of the money currently spent in video shops will be spent in the home as the TV set is used to download films from a virtual video store either on a 'rental' basis, for single use, or for purchase.

Broadcasters in France, Germany and the UK have been engaged in a scramble to buy the film rights they believe will help them sustain their digital services. Leo Kirch in Germany almost bankrupted his company when his 9.3 billion DM expenditure to secure 'nearly all the TV rights to Hollywood output' for the German market was followed by the failure of his digital channel, DF1, to attract more than 40,000 subscribers in its first year (*Financial Times* 21 Oct. 1996, *Les Echos* 17 June 1997) UK broadcasters Carlton have been engaged in a similar, though smaller scale, exercise to build up their catalogue of film rights. In France, meanwhile, the two rival digital TV packages, TPS (Télévision par Satellite) and Canal Satellite (operated by Canal Plus) have been engaged in a bidding war for US film rights, where the exclusive long term rights Canal Plus has acquired to the output of Disney, Warner, MCA, Universal, Columbia and Twentieth Century Fox, have been cited in a complaint by TPS to the French competition authorities (*Canal+* 1997: 52, *Le Monde* 28 July 1997). Alongside their catalogues of Hollywood films, most digital operators will also offer specialist 'adult' channels which, given their relatively low production costs, can be very lucrative. In Germany, where pay channels face the obstacle of competing with the thirty free analogue channels that most households can receive via cable, the ability to offer adult pay channels may be particularly important in encouraging consumers to switch to digital TV.[7]

New services and commercial convergence

Digital television will be used to develop a wide range of other services in addition to conventional TV programmes and pay sport and film channels. One of the first new services introduced by Canal Satellite in France was enabling customers to download computer games through their digital decoder boxes. From the end of 1997 Internet access, e-mail and other interactive services such as home banking were also available via set-top boxes. In the UK the services planned by British Interactive Broadcasting Limited (BIB), the joint venture between British Telecom, BSkyB, Midland Bank, and Matsushita Electric, will also offer viewers access to services such as home shopping, banking, travel information and the Internet, and sending and receiving e-mails from their digital television via a telephone connection. Convergence will also work in the opposite direction. It is already possible to broadcast audio and poor quality moving images over the Internet. Within five to ten years it will be possible to broadcast something much closer to television over the World Wide Web.

Technological convergence is being mirrored by commercial convergence, as the opportunities offered by digital television lead to a major wave of new ventures, mergers and realignments which are crossing the traditional national and sectoral boundaries of the broadcasting industry. The first wave of 'digital' mergers started in the US media industry in the mid-1990s. News Corporation's purchase of Twentieth Century Fox and Sony's of Columbia Pictures were followed by Disney buying the broadcaster ABC, Time Warner spending $7.5 billion on a merger with Turner Broadcasting (owner of CNN) and Viacom acquiring Paramount Pictures and Blockbuster Entertainment. In 1996 Europe followed suit. Bertelsmann merged its TV interests in UFA with those of CLT, the Luxembourg-based European-wide broadcaster, to create CLT/UFA, a company with nineteen TV and twenty-three radio stations across ten different countries ('CLT-UFA: leader audiovisuel européen', *Le Monde* 16 Jan. 1997).[8] In the same year Canal Plus took over Nethold, a loss-making South African owned pay TV broadcaster, with interests in Benelux, Scandinavia, Greece and Central Europe. The merger not only created Europe's largest pay TV company, with over 8.5 million subscribers, it also gave Canal Plus control of the two leading conditional access technologies used in Europe, its own SECA Mediaguard system and the Irdeto system used by Kirch's DF1 station in Germany, and which Deutsche Telekom had intended to use for digital services on its cable networks.[9]

The creation of BIB referred to above provides one example of commercial convergence in practice as the broadcasting industry extends into new areas and attracts the participation of telecommunications companies and other new players. From BSkyB's perspective, the main function of the £700 million BIB joint venture is to provide a subsidy for digital set-top boxes, reducing their retail price from about £500 to £200, and thereby removing in the UK what has been found to be a significant cost obstacle to consumer take-up of digital TV in the US and Germany. BT and Midland Bank meanwhile are attracted by the prospect of a new way of accessing their customers, promoting their products, and sharing in the revenues of the various interactive services which will pass through the set-top box.

French and German telecommunications operators have also been breaking new ground. France Telecom is a shareholder in the digital television service – Télévision par Satellite (TPS) – that was launched at the end of 1996, with the participation of France Télévision, and TF1, and it has established France Telecom Multimedia, to produce CD ROMs and other content for the on-line service provider Wanadoo (which is itself jointly owned by France Telecom and the media conglomerate Havas). Deutsche Telekom, as the major operator of Germany's cable networks (reaching 16.7 million households in 1996), occupies a key position for the launch of digital television in Germany and harbours ambitions to provide technical services such as subscriber management and possibly content for digital TV in the future.[10] Bertelsmann and Kirch signed an alliance with Deutsche Telekom in June 1997 to give them the access to the digital cable channels of Deutsche Telekom which they require for any chance of commercial success, and at the same time agreed to co-operate in the launch of a single – rather than competing – digital TV package.[11] In Italy a similar alliance was under discussion between the public service television operator RAI and the State Telephone company to launch digital TV services.

The convergence of computing and television

The cross-sectoral alliances between telephone, film and TV companies have also been joined by the entrance of computing and software developers into content and hardware development. Microsoft, for example, started to build on its base as the world's largest software company by moving into multimedia and on-line publishing, with activities such as its CD ROM encyclopedia *Encarta*, the purchase of the rights to key art collections and the launch of the on-line newspaper *SLATE*. Then, in 1997, Microsoft also established an on-line news service MSNBC with the broadcaster NBC; moved into the US cable industry by acquiring the US's fourth-largest operator COMCAST for $1 billion; and bought the company Web TV, which had developed a device which gave viewers the ability to surf the Internet and send e-mails from their TV. From Microsoft's perspective the development of Internet-enhanced, and in time fully interactive, digital TV was of interest since it meant that TVs would increasingly require software-based operating systems, similar to those deployed in PCs. The opportunity for Microsoft – and the threat for established electronics manufacturers and indeed many pay TV operators who were developing their own operating systems – was that Microsoft might acquire the same dominance in TV operating systems, with their scaled down system Windows CE, as they had already established through Windows and MSDOS in the computer world.

The fear that Microsoft's PC standards might, in the end, predominate in the development of digital TV technology raised the broader question of whether the TV itself, and indeed the experience of watching TV, were about to be replaced by an entirely new entity and experience. There was uncertainty as to what the development of devices such as Web TV and Net Channel that allow Internet access via the TV, actually meant for the broadcasting industry. As one commentator put it:

> What we are witnessing is not the end of TV broadcasters, but it is the end of broadcast TV as we know it. Convergence between the Internet and emerging digital terrestrial and satellite broadcast systems, and between the PC and network devices that can access the network via a set-top box, is bringing about the delivery of new services as part of a multichannel offering that will arrive shortly.
>
> (Thompson 1997: 7)

Yet one should not confuse the arrival of new ways of enhancing the uses to which the TV screen can be put, or indeed of new ways of delivering TV services, with the death of TV itself. The mass access to the Internet that will become a possibility via a TV screen will increase pressures for the Internet and the World Wide Web to move beyond the ham radio phase and become more reliable and predictable environments, where ordinary consumers know what to expect, will be able to find what they want relatively speedily, and can assume a relatively high level of consumer protection and technical reliability: in short to become more like the TV experience. Moves in this direction include 'push technology' to deliver pre-selected information to users' screens, and the increasingly professional and commercial nature of the World Wide Web. The most frequently visited sites are those that are prepared and maintained in a reasonably professional way. In March 1998, of the top twenty most visited UK Web sites ten were provided by existing UK media companies. Many of the rest of the top twenty were accounted for by the search engines used to guide people around the Web. A similar trend is represented by the growth of so-called 'walled gardens' offered by on-line service providers such as America On Line or indeed Web TV itself, and proposed by British Interactive Broadcasting, which offer access to a limited pre-selected or specially produced range of material. These trends indicate a more general point: technological convergence between the computing and TV industries will not necessarily lead to a convergence in consumer behaviour, or to traditional models of TV consumption suddenly being replaced by those from the IT world and the Internet.

Convergence and a new regulatory agenda

Technological change on its own does not require a change in regulatory objectives. But technological change when accompanied by changes in the market and in consumer behaviour can raise new regulatory issues and call into question some of the existing approaches to broadcasting regulation. One increasingly influential school goes further, arguing that digital convergence undermines both the rationale for, and the feasibility of, most nationally based broadcast-specific regulation. Others suggest that regulatory reform is required to help facilitate the convergence process:

> One of the key policy challenges for information infrastructure is to eliminate restrictions preventing the convergence of broadcasting and communication services so as to stimulate the development of services as well as infrastructures. . . . Convergence is putting increased pressure on existing broadcast market structures and regulations which are constraining market opportunities and the diffusion of new services, and imposing obstacles to the convergence process itself.
>
> (OECD 1997c: 73)

The advocates of greater regulatory convergence between telecommunications and broadcasting regulation frequently proposed an accompanying narrowing of the differences between national regulatory approaches. Sometimes it was greater co-ordination between different states that was proposed. At other times it was suggested that national regulation might be replaced by a greater regulatory role for the EU or other supra-national organisations. These arguments will be examined in more detail in Chapters 7 and 8. The remainder of this chapter looks briefly at some of the new regulatory issues and approaches that arose in response to convergence.

New regulatory issues

Amidst the confusion of converging technologies several features stand out which distinguish the digital future from the existing pattern of television.

First, the digital gateway – the conditional access system, applications programming interface (API) and accompanying EPG – will increase the opportunities for monopoly control and anti-competitive behaviour.[12] Since every TV programme and transaction must pass through that gateway, the question of access to it raises regulatory issues more akin to those relating to access and interconnection in telecommunications than to those previously raised by television. The issues become even more complex and difficult to resolve when, as will increasingly be the case, the gateway controller is not a neutral third party network operator, but rather a vertically integrated company, which both controls the network and offers its own content and services through that network. Companies have already been seeking to consolidate their positions by buying the key programme rights and acquiring exclusive rights to the proprietary encryption technologies that will oblige third parties to rely on them for encryption and decoding of their programmes.

The second distinguishing feature of digital television also relates to the gateway and the issue of distribution. The growth of charging mechanisms for television is directly linked to the decline of universality. With analogue terrestrial TV (with the sole exception of Canal Plus in France) broadcasters were given access to scarce spectrum in return for making their service freely available to the entire population. As the TV became the single most unbiquitous consumer device, so television became a powerful potentially unifying force in increasingly individualised and fragmented societies. The advent of digital TV, and the accompanying growth of pay channels and rival distribution systems, will transform this near universal service to one where the range of material available will be dependent on the payments made and the distribution systems that are available. Digital television also seems likely to accelerate a fragmentation in distribution systems and cause a dramatic increase in the number of pay channels. Cable operators may come to have a monopoly over distribution in many homes where the alternatives – of satellite or terrestrial distribution – are either impractical because of geographical location or planning restrictions, or would give access to a more limited range of channels. Regulators will have to decide how to deal with these distribution monopolies. Policy makers, for their part, will need to reflect on the extent to which the move from a limited number of universally available channels to a much more fragmented picture of pay channels and of channels available in some homes but not in others, is something that they are prepared to accept or whether they feel that some form of intervention is required to sustain the common channel of information that television currently offers.

Third, as TV increasingly becomes a transactional service, so service providers and programme makers will learn more about their consumers and their audiences. Once again, policy-makers will need to decide whether to impose limits on this process or to allow it to continue unchecked.

Finally, as convergence blurs the boundaries between previously distinct communications sectors, so the boundaries between regulation of television and telecommunications will become blurred. It will no longer be adequate to define regulatory responsibilities in terms of the method of distribution, since increasingly the same distribution method will be used for a variety of different kinds of content: for example a cable TV connection will be used for anything from telephony, to sending e-mails, ordering video-on-demand films and watching conventional broadcast programmes. Television programmes will themselves be distributed in a wide variety of new ways – terrestrially, via cable and satellite, through the telephone network, and eventually even via the Internet. Regulators clearly need to confront the definitional problems that convergence raises, and to decide whether to define new regulatory responsibilities in terms of any particular technology – where the virtue of clarity may rapidly be negated by the pace of technological progress – or instead to adopt regulatory boundaries that are related to the nature of the material being transmitted.

Reconsidering existing regulatory arrangements

Digital television may also lead to moves to reconsider both the utility and practicality of existing broadcasting regulation and the continued value of nationally organised regulation.

Content regulation is one of the mainstays of broadcasting regulation to date. Countries that wish to continue with some forms of content regulation for broadcasting will face a variety of challenges. Among the practical problems will be those facing regulators used to recording and watching a few TV channels, who are unlikely to be given the resources for comprehensive monitoring of several hundred channels. But there are also questions of principle at stake in whether the same restrictive approach to content regulation would be appropriate with a much more fragmented TV market. In fact, most predictions suggest that a relatively small number of channels will still dominate viewers' preferences. But even if these predictions are proved correct, governments seeking to impose content regulation will still have to decide whether different standards should apply to encrypted pay services compared to free-to-air broadcast programmes, whether time-based rules on, for example, taste and decency make any sense with on-demand services, and whether, more generally, the move to a transactional rather than a broadcast model of television makes all forms of content regulation more difficult to justify.

Similarly, the growth of cross-frontier broadcasting, and the apparently borderless nature of many of the new communications networks, such as the Internet and satellite broadcasting, will lead states to review the practicality and desirability of purely national regulation and to contemplate more international approaches to regulation. This will be particularly problematic in broadcast services since their regulation traditionally reflects distinct national views on issues like taste and decency and also differing policies aimed at promoting national production, both for cultural and economic reasons. It also raises serious questions about the level at which such regulation could occur, and within Europe, the appropriateness of current EU institutions for dealing with this task. Governments may be torn between a desire to retain control of such a politically and culturally sensitive sector, and the fear that national regulation which is dramatically out of line with that of neighbouring countries may be difficult to enforce, and leave them exposed to media companies moving to more relaxed regulatory environments.

Conclusion

The technological and market changes accompanying the launch of digital television are, therefore, considerable and they are leading to widespread debate about the suitability of current regulatory arrangements. This debate should start from an assessment of the objectives for communications regulation, and be followed by an examination of the ways in which changes in technology and consumer behaviour either change the way in which those objectives might be accomplished, raise new regulatory issues, or alter the degree to which existing regulatory objectives require public intervention. Technological change is often cited in support of the expansionist ambitions of rival regulators and Government departments, of key directorates within the European Commission, and of the understandable desire of many commercial companies that regulatory reform will free them from irritating constraints.

This is a highly politicised debate, but it is also one in which the most technologically literate advocates of reform often seize the initiative early on. Their critics are easily depicted as failing to understand the nature of the technological change and of jeopardising future competitiveness. Whilst the first accusation is frequently true, the second is far more debatable. The following chapters focus on the EU's record in broadcasting regulation to date, and its claims to become more involved in regulation of the converging communications sector in the future. Attempts to move more regulation from the nation-state to the EU will inevitably be contentious, since the normal task of reaching agreement between

Member States is rendered more than usually complex by differences within each nation's approach to regulation of telecommunications and broadcasting and the intensely political nature of issues such as regulation of taste and decency, political impartiality and media ownership rules. The EU's record in broadcasting policy to date has not been particularly successful. Its rather better record in telecommunications regulation is not necessarily a particularly good guide to future moves in the more public and, literally, more visible area of broadcasting.

Part II
Regulating analogue broadcasting

2 National regulatory traditions in France, Germany and the UK

Introduction

It is easy to portray the rich diversity of the existing pattern of national broadcasting regulation in Europe's major member states as perverse and anachronistic. National regulators, with widely divergent aims and rules, predominate in an internationalising industry (Kuhn 1997: 275). Distinct broadcasting and telecommunications regulators persist in a converging communications sector. And as digital technology stands poised to offer huge increases in the number of channels and consumer choice, the dominant regulatory paradigm is one apparently designed for a period of spectrum scarcity and limited competition. Critics of the status quo have a strong argument. Broadcasting remains one of the most tightly regulated industries in Western Europe. No country has plans to roll back broadcasting regulation to a point where it resembles that applied either to newspapers or telephony. And whilst politicians everywhere have high hopes of the economic growth that may flow from the audio-visual sector, regulation is more commonly designed (if not always implemented) with cultural and political, rather than economic, concerns paramount.

For some, this characterisation of national regulation lends weight to the case for regulatory reform and for moves towards greater regulatory convergence and Europeanisation of communications regulation. (See Chapters 7 and 8.) But it is equally the case that this regulatory diversity stems from the very different political and cultural agendas of Europe's major states. As a result national administrators and politicians are more likely to resist EU policy leadership in the broadcasting sector than in many others. Chapters 2 and 3 explore the interaction between national and European level regulation in the analogue world, with Chapter 2 focusing on the national bases of regulation, and Chapter 3 looking at the impact of EU regulation to date. Later chapters examine how this interplay between national and European regulation is developing in response to digital broadcasting.

A common concern to regulate

Despite their contrasting approaches, successive French, German and British governments have shared the belief that broadcasting was too important to be left to the market. Regulatory intervention was justified in many different ways; both economically, in terms of spectrum scarcity and hence the limited competition in the broadcasting market, and culturally, because of broadcasting's role as an educational tool in terms of disseminating high, and popular, culture, and establishing many of the key tastes and reference points for the population. Finally, and perhaps most crucially, intervention was justified because of the enormous political influence of broadcasting; in creating the conditions for widespread political debate; as a vehicle for the presentation of diverse political views; and as a potentially dangerous tool in the hands of propagandists (Barendt 1995: 3–10 provides a useful discussion of the various rationales for regulation).

The political rationale for regulation has been expressed most clearly in Germany, where concerns to avoid any repeat of the Nazis' innovative use of broadcasting for propaganda weighed heavily on those involved in constructing the new post-war West German state. In practice all countries are aware of the political importance of broadcasting, and regulation of the political sphere is often a significant motivation for broadcasting law and policy. This has usually been justified in terms of the need to secure impartial coverage, but on occasions the instruments of political regulation – such as influence over, or control of, a public service broadcaster, or the power to allocate or refuse broadcasting licences to commercial stations – have been used for more partisan purposes. This was frequently the case in Gaullist, and to a lesser degree Mitterrand's France. It occurs within Germany's Federal system, and is rare, though not unknown, in the UK broadcasting industry.

The creation of commercial television, in Britain in 1954, and in Germany and France only in 1984, had surprisingly little impact on the basic assumption of policymakers about the need for regulation in broadcasting. In Britain, after some initial hesitation, a highly regulated commercial TV sector was created. The French and Germans followed suit by subjecting their commercial broadcasters to a range of different regulatory obligations. None of the three countries gave much serious thought to the idea that commercial TV companies should not be regulated any more heavily than, say, newspapers. Instead, in each case, the advent of commercial TV led to a dual system of regulation, with public service channels sometimes regulated more strictly than private ones, but where extensive regulatory constraints were imposed on all broadcasters.

The development of satellite and cable distribution in the 1980s prompted a more far-reaching debate about the continued need for broadcasting regulation – particularly in Germany and the UK – given the expectation that these new distribution technologies would reduce spectrum scarcity, Some, such as Peter Jay, argued that, with the reduction in scarcity, broadcasting could be treated more like publishing, with a consequent relaxation of regulation (Peacock 1986). These ideas accorded with the deregulatory climate of the 1980s but there were several reasons why their impact was far less substantial than might have been expected.

First, the rate at which new distribution technologies developed was, in Britain and France at least, much slower than earlier predictions. Cable, which had been the favoured technology in France, developed slowly, only reaching 10 per cent of homes by 1997. Similarly in Britain, not much more than a quarter of homes had either cable or satellite by 1997 (Morgan 1998a: 11). The result was that the vast majority of French and British households were still dependent on a relatively small number (four in the UK and six in France) of terrestrial channels by the late 1990s. In Germany, cable expanded much more rapidly, and by January 1997 68 per cent of German households had access to multichannel TV via either cable or satellite (European Audiovisual Observatory 1998). But this did not put an end to spectrum scarcity since the thirty- channel analogue cable network supplied by Deutsche Telekom soon became overloaded, with the result that regulatory authorities spent much of their time making decisions over the allocation of cable capacity.

Second, the advent of an increased number of channels did nothing to weaken the political arguments for regulation. Rather the reverse, since technological change was accompanied by the increased 'mediatisation' of politics (Kuhn 1997: 276–9). The move to a more competitive TV market occurred at the same time as political debate and electioneering increasingly moved away from the streets and the newspapers and into the TV studios. Instead of competition, as had been predicted, reducing television's influence, it appeared to increase it, thus reinforcing the rationale for political regulation. As a result, in spite of the substantial economic and technological change of the mid-1980s and early 1990s few politicians were persuaded that key regulatory instruments – controls on media ownership, licensing regimes, obligations to respect political balance in programmes or across a range of channels, and publicly funded public service broadcasters – should be relinquished.

Commercialisation and the advent of new distribution technologies also created new arguments for intervention. As the TV sector expanded so its importance for local and national economic development was recognised. Cable TV systems were seen as part of early attempts at creating 'wired cities', and technical standards for experiments such as High Definition TV (HDTV) were increasingly viewed as part of a wider battle for European competitiveness. Expansion, however, also awakened fears that an unregulated commercial sector would increasingly buy its programmes from the US. This led to calls for protectionist measures to reduce the cultural and economic impact of schedules dominated by foreign programming.

For all these reasons the move from monopoly to competition prompted regulatory reform and re-regulation rather than wholesale deregulation. By the mid-1990s, after more than a decade of increasing competition and the growth of new distribution systems, broadcasters in France, Germany and the UK were subject to a more onerous regulatory framework than that applied to almost any other private sector industry. Having said that, broadcasters were unusually adept at influencing the implementation, and often the design too, of 'their' regulatory regime. The following sections look in more detail at the key characteristic of the three national systems.

France

French broadcasting has been a key arena for political conflict and intervention ever since the creation of the Fifth Republic in 1958. This has been reflected in the constant changes to the legal and regulatory framework as successive ministers have developed their own broadcasting law, and in the changes of key personnel in France Television which traditionally accompanied the arrival of a new government.[1] In this politicised atmosphere, consensus has, however, reigned on the three defining objectives of French broadcasting policy:

• promoting and defending French culture and language
• sustaining a healthy French film industry
• assisting in the creation of competitive national media companies and the development of a successful French high technology sector.

Administrative structures

French broadcasting regulation is highly centralised and is devised and implemented by the Ministry of Culture, the Service Juridique et Technique de l'Information (attached to the Prime Minister's Office) and the regulator, the Conseil Supérieure de l'Audiovisuel (CSA).[2] France has not been immune from the interdepartmental rivalries that characterise broadcasting policy-making across Europe, but the relatively high degree of centralisation of policy has created greater coherence, if not always more success, than among her neighbours. The three goals noted above have been implemented in a way that has often been mutually reinforcing.

National and EU policy

France has engaged with EU broadcasting policy, and on occasions, been successful in helping to lead it. French campaigns for the recognition of 'l'exception culturelle' were important in preserving the provisions for production quotas in Television Without Frontiers, in the face of the 1993

GATT negotiations on the treatment of audio-visual services. In many ways this point represented the high-water mark of French influence within EU audio-visual policy, and this was aided by the conjunction of the Delors Presidency of the Commission and the presence of his mentor, Francois Mitterrand, in the Elysée Palace. But French intervention in EU broadcasting policy has often been defensive, aimed at keeping at bay the free market assumptions of EU policies. It has been seen by some as generally less successful than British attempts at preserving the status quo (Collins 1998). French influence over EU broadcasting policy started to decline with the end of the Delors Presidency and the expansion of the Community in 1995. At the same time the increasing move within the EU towards greater reliance on market mechanisms and the extension of the EU's programme of telecoms liberalisation into a new Information Society project both reflected and served further to diminish that influence.

Encouraging national production

France is the country where legislators and regulators probably devote more attention than anywhere else in Europe to the promotion of national programming and culture within the broadcasting system. Broadcasting regulation is also geared to sustaining the French film industry. This reflects a cultural belief in the importance of film, and the influence of the French cinema lobby, but it also derives from the fact that over the last decade the French film industry has been relatively much more important than that of Britain or Germany.[3] A recent Eurostat study shows that the number of films made in France regularly exceeds that of any other EU country, and while the average EU citizen only went to the cinema 1.9 times in 1996, in France the figure was 2.3 (as against 1.6 for Germany, 2.1 for the UK and 4.6 for the US) (Eurostat 1998: 3–7).

The result of this preoccupation with film, and nationally-produced programming, is a complex and highly detailed system of broadcast production quotas and investment obligations. Terrestrial TV stations must ensure that 60 per cent of their programming – as against the 50 per cent figure laid down in the EU Television Without Frontiers directive – is of European origin, and that this output includes a minimum of 40 per cent of French made material. The numbers and scheduling of feature films on TV are also strictly regulated, with the main free-to-air TV channels only being allowed to show 192 feature films a year, with no films shown on Wednesdays, Fridays and Saturdays, and a limitation on the numbers of films to be shown on other days between 20.30 and 22.30. The aim is to maximise cinema attendance. Programming quotas are complemented by investment quotas where TV stations must choose whether they prefer to invest:

• 15 per cent of their turnover in French audio-visual works productions and 20 per cent in European audio-visual works, or

- 15 per cent of their turnover in French audio-visual works and broad-cast a minimum of 120 hours of European/French audio-visual works in prime time.

In addition all TV stations are obliged to spend 3 per cent of turnover on European/French film production (KPMG *1996 Annexes, France*, 131).

Obligations on broadcasters are combined with direct support from the state to create what has been described as 'the most all-encompassing and ambitious audio-visual support system in the world'. Subsidy schemes also sustain a large number of film and TV production companies and determine much of the agenda for the French film industry, although this was not always the best way to create a commercially successful industry (Brown 1996: 69, 81).[4] Regulation was crucial to establishing Canal Plus as a major source of finance for the French film industry. In return for a very favourable regulatory regime, the channel is obliged to invest 25 per cent of its turnover in the acquisition of film rights, of which 60 per cent must be European-made films.[5] Canal Plus soon decided to make a virtue of necessity and in 1990 it established Le Studio Canal Plus, to ensure that it had a ready supply of high quality films for its subscribers, as well as to demonstrate its commitment to the French film industry (*Canal+* 1995, Kuhn 1995: 202).[6] Films made by Le Studio Canal Plus accounted for 30 per cent of all French film box office admissions in 1996. TV channels provide 42 per cent of total investment in the French film industry, of which more than half is accounted for by advance sales to, and productions by, Canal Plus (EC 1998d 17). The penalty for this success has been that Canal Plus's rivals have accused it of exercising unfair dominance within the industry.

A tradition of a high degree of political intervention and control

The creation of Canal Plus in 1984 reflected the high degree of political intervention in the French media industry as well as the extent to which media companies are seen as critical to French industrial, as well as cultural, policy. Canal Plus was run by Havas, a company in which the French state held over 50 per cent of the capital. The fact that the chairman of Havas and first chairman of Canal Plus, André Rousselet, was a close associate of President Mitterrand (having been director of the President's *Cabinet* until 1982) served to reinforce the links between the Government and France's first commercial channel. Canal Plus was given a terrestrial frequency which guaranteed it universal coverage within a year of start-up, an extraordinary privilege for a pay TV channel that has not been repeated anywhere else in the EU. The Government saw the channel as part of its broader industrial objectives of boosting the French electronics industry (through the production of decoders for the channel, and its anticipated impact in increasing demand for TVs), limiting the demand for foreign made video recorders and videos, and of helping France resist the threat represented by foreign satellite channels (Kuhn 1995: 178–81).[7] This strong interventionist streak meant that, in France, moves to introduce commercial competition in broadcasting were never synonymous with deregulation. According to one well-informed critic:

> The number, weight and detail of the obligations imposed on terrestrial broadcast channels (and . . . on cable channels) is unequalled anywhere in the world. It seems as though the legislator and even more so the regulatory authority, secretly remorseful about having freed the airwaves, were attempting to take back with one hand what had been given with the other.'
>
> (Cathodon 1995: 279)

But not all these obligations were enforced equally rigidly. When the main commercial channel, TF1, failed in 1995, for the third successive year, to meet its 60 per cent European quota, the CSA simply imposed what it termed a 'non-fine', under which TF1 was obliged to invest 45 million francs in original audio-visual production during the following year.[8]

The 1982 initiative to develop the cable industry (the Plan Câble) reflected a similar taste for interventionist solutions. French governments were persuaded that cable offered the way forward to a 'wired', and hence more modern and competitive, society. Cable was also attractive to government as it appeared to offer the prospect of multichannel TV under French control, in contrast to the difficulties that were anticipated in establishing national control over satellite channels (Kuhn 1995: 210–11). The plan was for a twenty year, 50 billion franc programme to connect French households to a high grade fibre-optic network.

But whereas Canal Plus moved into profit within two years of launch, the French cable industry has remained in the doldrums, and been the subject of repeated rescue plans (Michel 1994: 80–2). Vedel summed up the situation at the end of 1995: 'Almost 15 years after the launch of the cable plan and an overall investment of 35 billion FF, France has no more than 1.6 million cable subscribers'. Fibre-optic cabling had to be abandoned early on as too expensive and cable was ill prepared to compete with the challenge posed by the parallel expansion of the number of terrestrial stations in France:

> The programming offered at first on cable was not attractive: the major cable operators, which are subsidiaries of public utilities companies, tended to consider cable TV as another public utility and did not do any marketing effort. It is only when investments in specific programs for cable channels were made that consumers' interest for cable TV grew. Finally, numerous and heavy regulatory constraints apply to cable. For example, channels on cable have to be licensed. Since cable operators failed to get such licenses for Arabic channels,

they lost many subscribers among the French Muslim population (which has turned to satellite reception).

(Vedel 1996)

The experience of Plan Câble and the launch of Canal Plus reveal an important aspect of the way in which French audio-visual policy was made. From the outside it was often seen as obsessed with cultural issues, but there was a strong industrial element as well:

All too often, the only voices that the executive seemed to listen to were the technocrats and the engineers. As a result, policy tended to reflect a narrow mix of political and technocratic criteria; it also tended to be highly voluntaristic.

(Humphreys 1996: 136)

This closed political-administrative culture was reflected in the ownership structure of the French broadcasting industry which is dominated by a high degree of cross-ownership between relatively few firms, most of whom either have or have had close relations with highly placed political person-alities, are former nationalised companies, are highly dependent on government contracts, or bring together a combination of these elements. Utilities like Compagnie Générale des Eaux (CGE) and Lyonnaise des Eaux and former state companies such as Havas dominate the shareholding struc-tures. The ironic inquiry in 1997 of one independent producer turned satellite operator – 'Does one have to sell water to make television in France?' – seemed appropriate in a country where the construction company Bouygues controlled 39 per cent of the most popular TV station, TF1, where Lyonnaise des Eaux held 34 per cent of M6, and where the Compagnie Générale des Eaux owned 30 per cent of Havas, which in turn, was the main shareholder in Canal Plus (*Le Monde* 9 August 1997). This strong degree of cross-ownership, and the web of connections between companies dependent on government contracts and the broadcasting industry, ensured that even in a notionally liberalised sector, government influence extended well beyond the confines of the public broadcaster, France Télévision.

Germany

With thirty channels available to the majority of its thirty-seven million TV households, Germany is the largest, most competitive and most advanced multichannel broadcasting market in Western Europe. The complex inter-play of a law-based approach to policy, concerns for pluralism, the frequent interventions of the Constitutional Court, and the ever present fact of Federalism, together with fifteen different state media authorities, have combined to create the most detailed, complex and intrusive regulatory framework of any of the three countries studied here. In practice the apparently inflexible constitutional approach to the broadcasting sector, and the high degree of micro-management favoured by state media authorities, have often been nuanced by the tendency of national and state policy-makers to view commercial broadcasting as an arm of regional and national industrial policy. This conflict between the highly legalistic form of German broadcasting regulation, and its rather more pragmatic implementation, is one of the key features of the German broadcasting industry.

Law, pluralism and corporatist structures

Law plays a vital part in the treatment of broadcasting in Germany, both through the constitution (Basic Law) itself and through a wave of crucial decisions on the treatment of broadcasting which have been passed down by the Federal Constitutional Court. This 'broadcasting constitutionalism' derives from a recognition of the political and social importance of the media, at least in part in reaction to the way in which the Third Reich centralised power and used its control of the media to manipulate public opinion.[9] But the presence of so many constitutional guarantees means that decisions that elsewhere could be decided simply by administrative order or at most by legislation – for example, for the launch of commercial broadcasting – in Germany invariably have to be referred to the Constitutional Court, which can take years to produce a decision (Humphreys 1996: 137).[10]

The Nazi experience and the totalitarian media system of the GDR created a situation where:

> West German elites shared a deep-rooted, historically determined and highly self conscious concern legally to safeguard the free expression of opinion, information and culture against control or interference either by the state or by any dominant socio-economic interest. Concern to keep the state, in particular, at a safe distance has always informed much of media policy debate in the Federal Republic.
>
> (Humphreys 1994: 316)

These concerns were expressed both in Article 5 of the German Basic Law, the 1949 Bonn Constitution, which guarantees the freedom of communication, and in the ways that the Constitutional Court has interpreted that precept in the field of broadcasting. In a famous 1971 decision the Court argued that:

> broadcasting has become one of the most powerful means of mass communications, which, because of its wide-reaching effect and possibilities as well as the danger of misuse for one-sided propagandizing, cannot be left to the free play of market forces.
>
> (quoted in Noam 1991: 80)

The Court has argued that intervention is necessary to ensure that broadcasting is independent both of state and private interests. The aim is to:

> ensure that an overall range of broadcast material is available in which the plurality of opinion which is the hallmark of free democracy can find expression. . . . This cannot, of course, be guaranteed with absolute certainty, but there must at least be a sufficient likelihood that a balanced variety will prevail in the regulated broadcasting system.
>
> (Constitutional Court decision of 1981 – Third TV judgement –
> cited in Meyn 1994: 82)

This preoccupation with pluralism is reflected not just in the obligations imposed on broadcasters but also in the structures of the supervisory bodies established within the public and the private broadcasting sectors. The Broadcasting and Administrative Councils of German public broadcasters ARD and ZDF, for example, are made up from so called 'socially relevant groups' including representatives of political parties, trade unions, churches, employers' associations, and cultural organisations, precisely with the aim of ensuring pluralism.

In practice, since the Broadcasting Councils can exercise wide-ranging powers over senior appointments, programming, finance and organisational matters, these supposed guarantors of pluralism have become highly politicised. Many commentators have noted that the structures have not always produced the desired results. Hoffman-Riem points out how: 'Originally conceived as guarantors of independence from the state and other power holders, the Broadcasting and Administrative Councils have, however, in reality emerged as agents of political influence' (Hoffmann-Riem 1996: 124).

This influence is at its strongest in those states where the same ruling party has been in power for a long time. Even though political parties are not allowed to nominate more than a third of the membership of the broadcasting councils, according to some accounts they frequently 'appoint two out of three or, indeed, nearly all council members' (quoted in Meyn 1994: 89). Public service stations within the ARD network will often reflect the political control of their area; thus Bayerische Rundfunk in CSU-dominated Bavaria will adopt a more conservative tone than that of West Deutscher Rundfunk in Cologne at the heart of SPD-dominated North Rhine-Westphalia. The impact of this politicisation of individual stations is diluted by Federalism. Since political control varies between the Länder, however much political parties might control public broadcasting within an individual Land, it is very unlikely that any one political party could control the entire German public broadcasting system (Humphreys 1994: 321).

Federalism and German broadcasting

Federalism makes broadcasting policy and regulation more complicated and contentious in Germany, and more local, than in the other countries examined here. Under the German Constitution broadcasting and cultural policy are the responsibility of the Länder rather than the Federal Government, while telecommunications fall under federal jurisdiction. This division between the Länder and the Federal Government makes discussions over convergence particularly difficult and limits the amount of coherence that can be expected from German broadcasting policy. It also acts as a powerful constraint on German participation in EU discussions of broadcasting policy, which can frequently cut across the straight Land-Federal divide. In areas affecting the competence of the Länder over broadcasting, Germany will usually send two representatives to Council of Ministers' meetings, one as the representative of the Länder, the other from the Ministry of the Interior.[11] German insistence on Land competence in cultural matters runs counter to the arguments of those who suggest that globalisation requires media regulation to move to the highest possible level.

Commercial broadcasters are regulated by the fifteen separate Landesmedienanstalten (State media authorities – LMAs).[12] The Länder have made some moves to co-ordinate their media laws through an Interstate Treaty on Broadcasting, which covers issues such as media concentration, protection of minors, advertising regulations, the financing of public service broadcasters, and the Television Without Frontiers provisions on minimum European content. However, co-ordination only goes so far and the right of each Land to regulate broadcasting differently has been upheld by the Constitutional Court.[13] The organisation of the LMAs mirrors that of the public service broadcasters, with an executive body and a Director, supervised by an assembly which is made up of some direct political nominees together with representatives from a range of other social groups. Once again, while the aim of this corporatist structure is to promote pluralism, the results often fall short of those ambitions. In theory aspiring commercial broadcasters are totally dependent on the licensing and enforcement decisions of the State Media Authorities, and these are in turn *independent* of the State Governments. In practice the relationship is one of mutual interdependence.

The LMAs grant licences on a range of criteria, including the financial security of the applicants, and whether they will add to the diversity of programming available in the state – either because of their programming plans, their ownership structure, or the guarantees of journalistic independence that are offered (Hoffmann-Riem 1996: 128–9). LMAs also enforce rules on issues such as advertising, taste and decency, protection of minors, and the anti-concentration provisions of the Interstate Treaty. And while, with the exception of the Bavarian Media Authority, they cannot view programmes in advance, they can impose substantial fines for

violation of licence conditions or state media laws, and in extreme circumstances, withdraw or suspend a licence.

The single most potent weapon in the hands of most LMAs is the power
to control access to, and placing on, the cable networks within their Land.
Germany's thirty-channel analogue cable network is saturated, and, particularly in large centres of population such as those covered by the LMAs in
North Rhine-Westphalia, Hamburg, Bavaria or Berlin-Brandenburg, large
numbers of broadcasters are extremely keen to gain access to the network.[14] The LMAs are obliged to conduct investigations into the relative
merits of the different applicants, and can remove or downgrade an existing broadcaster if they feel that a new one would have a more beneficial
effect, either in terms of the overall diversity of the programming available,
or in meeting the demands of the local audience. The conference of
Directors of State Media Authorities (DLM) has agreed some guidelines
on the allocation of cable capacity, but individual LMAs still have a very
large degree of autonomy in this area. Broadcasters who are refused access
or removed from the cable network can seek judicial review of the LMA's
decision, but often the LMA prefers to seek a compromise, sometimes by
trying to get two channels to share a particular cable channel.[15]

Broadcasting policy as industrial policy

The ways in which LMAs exercise their licensing powers and allocate cable
capacity make for an extremely heterogeneous and complex system of regulation of commercial broadcasting. At one level this can cause problems
for commercial broadcasters but in other respects the very complexity of
the system can favour incumbents over new entrants.[16] Generally the level
of co-operation between regulators and broadcasters is far closer than
might at first appear, and the increasing preoccupation of State
Governments with the broadcasting sector as a motor for regional economic development has led to broadcasting policy becoming dominated
more by questions of industrial policy than by the constitutional requirements for pluralism and diversity.

All the major Länder, irrespective of their political affiliation, see broadcasting as a key element in their regional economic policies, and there is
intense competition between the sixteen states to attract broadcasters to
locate themselves there. Broadcasting is often seen as a way of replacing
old industrial jobs and of giving a modern go-ahead image to a state or a
city. Attempts at using broadcasting as part of regional economic development programmes have, however, eroded the supposed independence of
LMAs from their state governments, distorted licensing decisions, and
weakened the authority of the LMAs.

Discussions over the award of a broadcasting licence have been compared to an 'oriental bazaar' where prospective applicants try to outbid
each other in the number of jobs they claim they will create, while state

governments promise places on the cable system. These tendencies started early in the life of commercial broadcasting. A report from the Berlin LMA in 1989 remarked wryly that the 'extent to which the federal states have combined media law and location politics is a problematic development' (cited in Meyn 1992: 116, see also Hoffmann-Riem 1996: 144–5). More recently, in 1993, North Rhine-Westphalia produced a new state broad-casting law stating that companies locating in the Land would be given preferential access to the cable networks. Companies such as MTV and Eurosport argued successfully that the law violated Article 54 of the Eurpean Community Treaty guaranteeing the free movement of services, but although the law was amended it seems unlikely that aspirations of the North Rhine-Westphalia state government have changed, or that it is alone in having offered such deals.

Moves to attract inward investment can lead to what Humphreys has referred to as competitive deregulation, as Länder compete to offer the most liberal regulatory regime. Once companies are based in a Land, the LMA may come under pressure from the Land's Economics Ministry not to do anything which might act as a constraint on their business. Companies have been known to threaten that tough regulation will lead them to relocate to a State with a more understanding media authority and, while few have acted on such threats, if a sizeable number of jobs are at stake the LMA may be persuaded to seek a compromise. This may explain why the LMAs have not been more effective in the view of one commentator, either in 'ensuring diversity of opinion when issuing licences', or in 'making sure that there is journalistic variety in the pro-grammes actually broadcast', or in preventing substantial increases in media concentration over recent years (Lange, cited in Meyn 1994: 117).

The impact of cable TV on German regulation

Germany's programme of investment in cable construction started in 1982 as a direct political challenge to the status quo. Chancellor Kohl's Christian Democrats had arrived in Bonn that year. They were attracted by the idea of using their control of the Deutsche Bundespost to build a cable network which would open the way for the end of a politically unsympa-thetic public service monopoly, redress the balance of power between Land and Federal regulation, and help encourage growth in the media sec-tor. The cable programme – which unlike the French Plan Câble was based on old fashioned coaxial cable – was hugely successful on two out of the three counts, albeit at a considerable cost to the German taxpayer.[17]

In 1961 the attempt of the then Chancellor Konrad Adenauer to launch a Bonn regulated commercial TV channel had been frustrated by the deci-sion of the Constitutional Court to uphold the public service monopoly. But spectrum scarcity formed a key part of the Court's argument. With the advent of cable and satellite distribution the scarcity argument became much weaker and the Court changed its position. In three landmark judgements – one in 1981 and two in 1986 – it both authorised the creation of commercial broadcasting and laid down the conditions for its regulation. The 1981 judgement confirmed that commercial broadcasting was no longer contrary to the Constitution. It also created a two-tier approach to pluralism. Public service broadcasters were bound by internal pluralism, namely, the requirement for pluralistic programming within a single channel. In commercial broadcasting by contrast, external pluralism – where pluralism is assessed according to the balance of opinions broadcast across all the available channels rather than any one individual channel – was sufficient. The bases of this dual broadcasting system were spelt out further in a November 1986 judgement according to which the existence of public service broadcasters offering 'a basic service for all', concentrating on investigative, cultural, educational and minority programming, should be safeguarded by adequate financial, organisational and technical guarantees. In return, commercial channels should be left free to maximise ratings and not be expected to meet the same requirements of balance and range of programming expected from public service broadcasters (Dyson 1992: 87–8, Robillard 1995: 78). This distinction resurfaces on each occasion that public service broadcasters launch new channels or services, as commercial operators argue that they are exceeding their obligation to provide a 'basic service'.[18]

Once the technical and legal obstacles were removed, commercial broadcasting developed more rapidly in Germany than in either France or the UK. As commercial broadcasting expanded, so the original SPD opponents of liberalisation began to realise that commercial TV companies could bring welcome economic development to their areas. In both those respects the cable programme and liberalisation measures pursued by the Kohl Government were highly successful. But they were far less successful in accomplishing a long term change in the balance of power between the Länder and the Federal Government. Instead the Länder, through the agency of the LMAs, discovered that detailed regulation of the new, but overcrowded, cable networks gave them an additional battery of instruments with which to regulate the broadcasting industry. And, as the economic importance of the broadcast sector grew, so the Länder control of broadcasting became a greater source of potential frustration to the Federal Government. Länder control of cable networks meant that Chancellor Kohl was unable to secure nation-wide distribution for the digital channel DF1 launched by his friend Leo Kirch in 1996. Similarly, Länder competence in cultural matters constrained Bonn's ability to sign agreements on broadcasting with her EU partners. [19]

The United Kingdom

British broadcasting regulation in recent years has, by contrast, been characterised by tensions between the language of morality and that of the marketplace, tensions which were the hallmark of Thatcherism. The outcome has been a system marked by regulatory balkanisation (where a wide range of different regulators have overlapping and sometimes conflicting obligations), a preoccupation with sex, a neo-liberal system for the auctioning of broadcasting licences, and the creation of a regulatory haven from European Union quota controls which has made the UK the most important base for offshore broadcasting to Continental Europe.

Administrative structures

Britain is a centralised country, and broadcasting policy and regulation suffer from none of the territorial fragmentation that is inevitable in a country with a federal system such as Germany. There is, nevertheless, the traditional division between the two different government departments involved in telecommunications and broadcasting, the Department of Trade and Industry (DTI) and the Department of Culture, Media and Sport (DCMS), previously known as the Department of National Heritage (DNH). This is broadly reflected in the division between a regulator for telecommunications (OFTEL) and regulators for broadcasting (the Independent Television Commission (ITC), the Broadcasting Standards Commission (BSC), and the Radio Authority).

Several critics have commented on the way in which an unusually large number of regulators – at least fourteen statutory and self regulatory bodies – have proliferated in the UK through a process of 'historical accretion' with each claiming jurisdiction over one or other aspect of media and telecommunications (Goldberg and Verhulst 1996: 5, Collins and Murroni 1996: 173). In part this proliferation is the result of the separate regulatory structures for the BBC (regulated by the Board of Governors), commercial television (regulated by the ITC) and commercial radio (regulated by the Radio Authority), but it also reflects the way in which regulatory bodies and responsibilities have been created in response to new concerns.

One result is overlapping jurisdictions. Both the ITC and the Office of Fair Trading have responsibilities for ensuring fair competition in broadcasting. The ITC and the BSC are both involved in content regulation (although the first is limited to commercial TV whereas the BSC covers all broadcasters, both public and private). In the case of new digital technologies, OFTEL regulates the supply of conditional access services (officially in consultation with the ITC) while both the ITC and OFTEL are involved in regulating electronic programme guides.

This plurality of regulatory bodies, each operating with a fairly large degree of discretion, and a body of broadcasting law which 'traditionally has been minimalist and vague' combine to distinguish the UK system both from Germany, where as we have seen the law plays a very important role, and from France, where the tradition of independent regulatory authorities is far less well established (Tunstall 1992: 240). To a large extent the UK system operates according to a set of norms that have evolved amongst those regulating the industry. Those norms include an attachment to certain key principles such as programme quality (even if this is not always very clearly defined), political impartiality and independence, and the need for the broadcasting sector as a whole to serve minorities as well as seeking to maximise audiences. For many years there has been a widespread consensus about the continued existence of the BBC, and that the remit of public broadcasting should be interpreted broadly – to provide quality programmes for all tastes – rather than being restricted to the production of high culture, news and educational programmes for a minority audience.

While in practice it is the government which appoints the key regulators – the Chair of the ITC, the Chair of the BSC, the Director General of OFTEL, and the Chair and Governors of the BBC – those appointed have traditionally assimilated the culture of the organisations which they head rather than behaving as political placemen and women. The very existence of these various regulatory bodies tends to limit the extent to which any government can influence the day-to-day interpretation and implementation of media policy, but there is clearly regular contact between the relevant government departments and the regulators. Most recent changes in policy have been signalled in the Broadcasting Acts of 1984, 1990 and 1996 (together with the 1994 White Paper on the future of the BBC), and since, in each case, there were major commercial and political interests at stake, the Prime Minister's office was closely involved, along with the Department of National Heritage, in developing the legislation and helping to guide it through Parliament.

UK broadcasting policy: marketisation and its limits

UK broadcasting policy in recent years has been dominated on the one hand by a move to a more market-based approach to broadcasting, and on the other by an increased concern for the maintenance of programme standards, through stronger control of sex and violence, a preoccupation with political impartiality, and, after some initial hesitation, continued support for the BBC.[20]

Marketisation was first evident in the encouragement that the Thatcher Governments gave for the establishment of new media, through the establishment of a relatively light regulatory structure (but no public money) for the nascent cable sector, and then through the creation of a favoured category of non-domestic satellite licensees.[21] Companies such as BSkyB, which were based in the UK but were not using UK-allocated satellite frequencies, could obtain a non-domestic satellite licence from the ITC more or less on demand, and the DNH placed little pressure on them to comply with EU quota obligations on European content. The creation of this category of licensees seems to have been calculated to aid Rupert Murdoch's BSkyB – since non-domestic satellite licensees were exempted from the cross-ownership limits which, given his large stake in the UK newspaper industry, would otherwise have precluded him from operating a TV station, but it was also quickly seized on by other TV stations keen to beam their signals into neighbouring EU territories while escaping the tighter regulatory regime that was often applied to them in those states.[22]

The move towards a marketised broadcasting industry also lay behind the proposals in the 1990 Broadcasting Act for a system of franchise auctions for ITV (Channel 3) licences, and the requirement that broadcasters commission at least 25 per cent of certain categories of programmes from independent producers. Both had the effect of forcing terrestrial broadcasters to reduce their costs, often through challenging trade union power within the industry. In the case of the BBC, the pressures of a more competitive industry, combined with falling real revenues (itself a reflection of the Thatcherite hostility to public enterprises, and the BBC in particular) and the influence of new public management techniques, led to the introduction of an internal market system ('Producer Choice') which was also designed to reduce costs and make programme makers more cost conscious.

Increased government awareness of the economic importance of the audio-visual sector helped accelerate trends to marketisation. The relaxation of media ownership limits introduced in the 1996 Broadcasting Act was justified in terms of creating a UK broadcasting industry better able to compete internationally. Similarly, the BBC was encouraged to boost its commercial activities – by launching new channels and joint ventures with commercial partners such as Pearson – and to use its reputation and the quality of its programming to spearhead UK audio-visual exports to the rest of the world. The title of the 1994 White Paper on the future of the BBC – *Serving the Nation, Competing Worldwide* – gave a clear indication of the new path that the Government anticipated for the BBC.

And yet marketisation only went so far. Most politicians recognised that through a combination of regulation, accident and the talent of its programme makers, the UK had created a broadcasting ecology which was admired and emulated across the world. By 1990 the high tide of Thatcherite deregulation had passed, and many Conservative politicians were uneasy about the impact of a wholly deregulated broadcasting system on programme quality and standards.[23] Besides, the radical libertarian wing of the Conservative Party was far more influential when it came to weakening economic as opposed to social regulation. British politicians of all parties were agreed on the need for the UK to adopt more restrictive codes on sex and violence than applied in most other EU countries. The consequence was that at the same time as the ITC was licensing scores of foreign satellite broadcasters, the Government was acting to prevent satellite sex channels licensed elsewhere in the EU from marketing their wares in the UK.

The Thatcher wave of privatisations did not reach the broadcasting sector.[24] While in France one of the first moves of the incoming Government of Jacques Chirac in 1986 was to privatise the leading public service station, TF1, in the UK the BBC was spared such treatment, even if it was subjected to increased financial pressure. Similarly, the move to an auction system for the Channel 3 franchises was diluted by requirements introduced late in the day in the 1990 Act for the ITC to exercise a quality threshold in allocating licences, and by placing obligations on all Channel 3 licensees to meet specified minima for certain kinds of programmes. Moves to liberalise the rules governing media ownership in the 1996 Broadcasting Act involved a careful political calculation to ensure that neither of the two largest newspaper groups – News International and the Mirror Group – was allowed to increase their TV holdings, even as others saw their freedom of manoeuvre increase.

Finally, in the mid to late 1990s, there developed an increased awareness of the importance of adequate safeguards to maintain competition in the broadcasting sector. The debates on the 1996 Broadcasting Act laid great emphasis on the need for the continued universal availability of public service broadcasting in the digital age, for universal access to key broadcasting events to be protected, and for regulation to be introduced to ensure that BSkyB's dominant position in analogue pay TV – through its control of relevant satellite capacity and conditional access technology – should not extend into the digital market. Measures introduced to prevent designated 'listed events' from being shown exclusively on pay TV, and the introduction of a 'must carry' rule to ensure that public service channels were carried on digital cable networks, represented an explicit reversal of the liberalisation measures contained in the 1990 Act.[25] Finally, the vigour with which the Government decided to regulate digital conditional access systems, under the provisions of the European Advanced TV Standards Directive, demonstrated a more robust attitude towards BSkyB and News International, an increased awareness of the potential for monopoly abuse opened up by digital TV, and a retreat from any doctrinaire pursuit of deregulation in the broadcast sector.[26]

UK national policy and EU policy

The ambiguities of UK broadcasting policy in the 1980s and 1990s produced a somewhat ambivalent attitude towards EU policy initiatives. The liberalisation measures introduced by the 1989 Television Without Frontiers Directive were welcomed, so long as they brought broadcasters to Britain to beam their programmes abroad, rather than foreign broadcasters beaming 'unsuitable' programming to Britain. But EU attempts to introduce mandatory content quotas and to use subsidies to boost the EU programme industry were consistently resisted.

Generally, UK policy-makers saw broadcasting policy as a national preserve, and adopted a wary scepticism towards most EU initiatives. This position was not taken up for purely doctrinaire reasons. It also reflected the realities of the UK broadcasting market, which trades more with the US and Australia than with any single country in the EU. Language and geography also make the UK relatively immune to overspill from the terrestrial channels of neighbouring countries, in contrast say to Belgium or Austria. In addition, only a tiny number of programmes from continental Europe are ever aired on UK channels. The peculiarities of the UK broadcasting market and policy set the UK apart from her EU partners, limit the impact and appeal of EU initiatives, and have traditionally reinforced the UK view that broadcasting policy should be largely nationally determined.

Diverging approaches to analogue regulation

While the three countries compared here shared a common conviction of the need for broadcasting regulation, they each gave very different priorities to the purposes of that regulation. Given the cultural and political objectives of much broadcasting regulation and the very different national traditions and political and administrative cultures of Britain, France and Germany, as well as the differences between their national broadcasting industries, such variation is not surprising.

Table 2.1 identifies the main regulatory objectives and instruments that are common to the three countries. What is clear from the preceding account, however, is that whilst many of these features are common to the three countries the priorities given to the objectives, and the instruments used to achieve those objectives, varied considerably. Industrial policy objectives, for example, were a consideration in France, Germany and the UK, but Germany and France were readier to invest public money in infrastructure creation, via the cable networks, than was Mrs Thatcher's Britain, whilst Germany's Federal system meant that broadcasting's impact on *local* employment was consistently accorded more attention than in the UK and France.

Similarly, cultural regulation is reflected in all three countries by a variety of policies to encourage national (or regional) production, as well as the maintenance of public service broadcasters, but France's concern for her film industry led to a more rigorous system of investment obligations and quotas than existed elsewhere. While French preoccupations were often phrased in cultural terms, they were also driven by the greater economic importance of the French film industry, as well as a strong French sense of the cultural and economic threat posed by Hollywood. Political regulation to ensure impartiality is common to all three countries, although once again the ways in which it is enforced vary markedly. Limits on media ownership, specific programming obligations, and the structure and nomination process for the boards of public service broadcasters, all play their part. In addition, each country has established rules on taste and

Table 2.1 Broadcasting policy objectives and instruments

Policy objectives	Policy instruments
Industrial policy: e.g. promoting • national production • national media champions • new infrastructure	Subsidies/tax breaks for e.g. film industry Privileged treatment by national/local regulators State investment/regulatory privileges for infrastructure creation
Protecting and developing the national culture	Quotas for national and European production* Public service broadcasting
Preventing the emergence of undue commercial or political influence in the media	Controls on media ownership Competition law *
Political impartiality and pluralism	Positive content obligations: e.g. to broadcast a range of programme genres and provide impartial news coverage Licensing of broadcasters
Consumer protection	Advertising controls* Negative regulation of content, e.g. control of violence or pornographic material*

Note: While many of the policy instruments could be used to achieve a wide variety of the
objectives, for the sake of simplicity they have not been repeated each time.
*   indicates areas affected by EU as well as national policy.

decency, for controlling the amount of advertising, and for protecting viewers' privacy, which often go beyond those applied to the press.

The analogue model of regulation which has been described in this chapter is striking, not just for the diversity of national approaches, dictated largely by national political and administrative traditions, but also for the relatively limited impact of EU level broadcasting regulation. For the most part policy objectives and instruments were nationally determined, albeit within a European context. The following chapters look in more detail at the ways in which EU broadcasting policy developed.

3 European regulation of analogue broadcasting

Introduction

Advocates of a greater role for the EU in the regulation of analogue broadcasting had to overcome some substantial obstacles. The diverse nature and strong political and cultural roots of national broadcasting systems described in Chapter 2 represented the first major challenge. But the lack of any EU responsibility for this area was equally serious. Broadcasting was not even mentioned in the Treaty of Rome and the European Comunity acquired no cultural competence until the Maastricht Treaty came into force in 1993.[1] Community policy for the audio-visual sector only became possible after a series of judgements from the European Court of Justice(ECJ) in 1974 and 1980 defined broadcasting as a 'tradeable service' subject to the internal market provisions of the Treaty.[2] But the significance of broadcasting goes far beyond its impact on the internal market, and European intervention in broadcasting has usually been inspired by – if not always justified in terms of – those wider cultural, political and economic considerations.

Technological change and the prospect of a more international and more competitive industry are a recurring theme in calls for a more active policy role for the EU. The advent of commercial television and of new trans-frontier cable and satellite channels in the early 1980s created pressure for the 1989 Television Without Frontiers (TVWF) Directive, the first substantial legislative intervention in this area. A decade later it was the prospect of digital technology which dominated the discussions taking place between 1994 (with the publication of a Green Paper entitled *Strategy Options for the European Audio-visual Industry*) and 1997 over the renewal of the 1989 directive. It has, however, been easier to agree that changing technology may require new or revised policies, than to reach consensus on the goals of European audio-visual policy.

Arguments in favour of EU intervention have at various times focused on the economic case for a properly functioning internal market in TV programmes, the cultural and political importance of a successful European audio-visual industry, and the industrial and trade policy arguments for a European industry better able to hold its own in the face of American competition. These conflicting objectives have been translated, to varying degrees, into four main areas of EU intervention in the audio-visual industry. The first is the emphasis in the TVWF Directive on ensuring the free flow of programmes within the EU through the mutual recognition of national licensing regimes. Second, there is the support for the European programme industry, in terms of the European content quotas within TVWF and the MEDIA I and MEDIA II support programmes. Third are the various attempts at industrial policy in the audio-visual sector, initially through costly intervention to create a European High Definition TV Standard, and more recently through a far less interventionist approach to the setting of technical standards for digital television. Fourth and finally is the operation of community competition law, which is having an increasing impact on the structure and shape of the European audio-visual industry.

This chapter focuses on two EU initiatives in the regulation of analogue broadcasting – TVWF and recurrent attempts to establish EU rules on media ownership – with the aim of assessing the degree of coherence within these early initiatives, and the main sources of their support. The following chapters will look in more detail at the ways in which existing policies in standards setting, and competition policy and merger control, are evolving in response to digital television, and the impact they are likely to have on the future of digital regulation.

The contrasting goals of EU broadcasting policy

Coherence has never been the strongest aspect of EU audio-visual policy. Tensions between 'the economic aims of completing the single market (and) . . . the concern to protect cultural identity and a pluralist media' further complicate the more conventional EU conflicts between interventionists and liberalisers, and between integrationalist and intergovernmental approaches (Hitchens 1996: 71–2). Throughout the late 1980s and early 1990s the gulf between these differing motivations for an active European Community audio-visual policy often seemed unbridgeable. New commercial trans-frontier broadcasters and advertisers hoped that efforts to create a single audio-visual market would lead to the removal of many of the existing restrictions. But while many of the proponents of an active European Community broadcasting policy in the European Commission and the European Parliament (EP) wanted barriers to trans-frontier broadcasting to be lifted, their vision of the resulting 'European audio-visual space' was far more dominated by cultural, political and industrial policy goals than the vision of the broadcasters themselves, or indeed of the majority of Member States.

Conflicts between these two different approaches – what might loosely be termed the dirigiste and deregulatory visions, each with their particular supporters within the broadcasting industry, the European institutions, and among the Member States – have dominated European audio-visual policy for much of the last fifteen years (Collins 1994b). Deregulation was favoured by commercial broadcasters, advertisers, new entrants to the cable and satellite market, and, in time, a variety of publishing and multi-media companies entering the broadcasting and on-line markets. Political and administrative support usually came from the Internal Market Directorate (initially DG III and later DG XV), the Telecommunications and Information Society Directorate (DG XIII), and, on some issues at least, the Competition Directorate (DG IV), as well as from Germany, Luxembourg, the UK, and Denmark, although each of these states adopted this position for very different reasons.

Although the dirigistes shared a common desire for an active EU policy they were divided as to whether the primary importance of the audio-visual sector was economic or cultural. Among the cultural dirigistes there were further divisions between those who believed that the audio-visual sector could help create a united European cultural, and hence political, identity, and others who were content to support an audio-visual sector which both reflected and sustained the diversity of national cultures within Europe (Collins 1994a). Supporters of one or other versions of the dirigiste agenda usually included the Culture Committee of the EP, and DG X – the Audio-visual Directorate – within the European Commission. Industry support came from much of the film industry (particularly its French component), from new independent producers, and from some public service broadcasters (but not including the British). France was the Member State which most often adopted dirigiste positions in audio-visual discussions in the European Council but other countries, such as Italy, Belgium, and Spain, often joined in with support of dirigiste positions. Conflicts between France and the UK on audio-visual policy frequently polarised debate between the dirigiste and deregulatory positions (Collins 1997, Panos 1995).[3]

The 1989 Television Without Frontiers Directive

The 1989 TVWF directive was preceded by a seven-year period of debate and negotiation, and a stream of reports, recommendations and consultation exercises, each of which put a slightly different emphasis on the purposes of EU action.[4] Early documents situated audio-visual policy largely in terms of the EU's cultural and political goals. The 1982 Hahn Report from the EP stressed that 'Information is a decisive, perhaps the most decisive factor in European integration', and that European political integration was unlikely as long as 'the mass media is controlled at national level' (cited in Collins 1994b: 36–7). The 1984 Commission Green Paper echoed these sentiments, asserting that:

> European unification will only be achieved if Europeans want it.
> Europeans will only want it if there is such a thing as European iden-
> tity. A European identity will only develop if Europeans are adequately
> informed. At present, information via the mass media is (sic) con-
> trolled at national level.
>
> (Cited in Collins 1994a: 95)[5]

One Commission official closely involved in the Green Paper described its
significance in somewhat heroic terms, saying, 'A process got underway in
1984 that can be described as the discovery by the general public of the
European Community's cultural or civilising dimension' (Ivo Schwartz
cited by Verhulst and Goldberg 1997).

This early emphasis on the role of audio-visual policy in creating a
European identity did not last long. By the second half of the 1980s cultural dirigisme was more frequently phrased in terms of the maintenance
of national diversity than the creation of European unity (Collins 1994a).
Increasingly, cultural arguments were integrated with economic and industrial policy goals, both as a way of marshalling support and because of the
limitations of the Treaty of Rome. According to Jacques Delors in 1985:

> the culture industry will tomorrow be one of the biggest industries, a
> creator of wealth and jobs. Under the terms of the Treaty we do not
> have the resources to implement a cultural policy; but we are going to
> try to tackle it along economic lines. It is not simply a question of tele-
> vision programmes. We have to build a powerful European culture
> industry that will enable us to be in control of both the medium and
> its content, maintaining our standards of civilization, and encouraging
> the creative people among us.
>
> (cited in Collins 1994a: 90)

Four years later Delors reiterated this combination of cultural and mer-
cantilist arguments, telling the Parliament that European television policy
was required not just 'in the name of competitiveness, but also in the name
of cultural defence; the Community refuses to leave the monopoly of
audiovisual techniques to the Japanese and that of programmes to the
Americans' (cited in Grant 1994: 156).[6] In the French case, calls for vigorous European content quotas were motivated by more than purely cultural
concerns; the French film industry was, after all, the largest in the EU. (See
Chapter 2).

The 1989 Directive was prepared by the Commission's Internal Market
Directorate, and the concern to aid the circulation of programmes within
the Community's borders provided its dominant theme.[7] The Directive was
based on the principle of mutual recognition, that is, that a TV station
licensed in one Member State should be accepted in all other Member
States. But the price paid for agreement to the principle of this *mutual*

recognition of national rules, was the simultaneous adoption of minimum rules on matters such as advertising and sponsorship, the right of reply, and the protection of minors (de Witte 1995: 105). Generally, Member States were free to impose more stringent licensing conditions on their own broadcasters, but not to prevent the reception within their territory of broadcasters licensed elsewhere within the EU.[8] Violations of Article 22 – on the protection of minors – were the only exception to that rule, in which case a Member State could act unilaterally to prevent reception of a channel licensed elsewhere in the EU. But views varied greatly between Member States as to what, under Article 22 of the Directive, constituted 'programmes which might seriously impair the physical, mental or moral development of minors, [and] in particular those that involve pornography or gratuitous violence'. The UK was the country which used these provisions most frequently to ban reception of satellite services licensed elsewere in the EU.[9]

The Directive's most dirigiste and best known elements were contained in Article 4 which obliges 'broadcasters [to] reserve for European works . . . a majority proportion of their transmission time, excluding the time appointed to news, sports events, games, advertising and teletext services'. But the quota provisions were weakened by provisos specifying that Member States only need apply quotas 'where practicable and by appropriate means' and that quota performance was to be judged 'having regard to the broadcaster's informational, cultural and entertainment responsibilities to its viewing public' and 'achieved progressively, on the basis of suitable criteria'. These clauses were the price that liberal states such as the UK and Germany extracted for their agreement to the Directive, and were only very reluctantly accepted by the French.[10]

The requirement in Article 5 that 10 per cent of a broadcaster's programme budget or transmission time be devoted to works from independent producers was calculated to appeal both to liberalisers and the producers' lobby. The first were keen on measures they saw as challenging the production monopolies established by many public service broadcasters, while the independent producers hoped to profit from the production opportunities that would be created.[11] Fraser comments on how, while TVWF represented a victory for the European Community in imposing itself in an area previously outside its competence, it also offers '*un exemple, parfois caricatural, de l'extrême complexité, voire de l'inefficacité des mécanismes communautaires de décision. Etats, acteurs privés, et instances communautaires se livrent à un marchandage permanent, qui ne permet plus de distinguer le véritable lieu de décision*' (Fraser 1996b 18).[12]

Implementing the 1989 Directive

While implementation of directives is always the responsibility of Member States, in this case they rightly assumed that they had far more latitude than usual. The dirigistes' disappointment at the very loose wording of Article 4 was compounded by a statement to the EP by Commissioner Bangemann that 'where practicable' meant that 'attainment of the objectives can be overridden by technical constraints or economic imperatives' and that 'it was difficult to imagine specific cases of those Articles that could be the subject of a clear ruling by the Court of Justice' (cited in de Witte 1995: 114). The Spanish Government interpreted the requirement for 'progressive achievement' of the quotas as giving its broadcasters seven and a half years from the deadline for implementing the directive to achieve a 40 per cent proportion of European programmes. The Italians applied quotas just to cinema films shown on TV, while the UK's failure to impose any quota requirement on non-domestic satellite services meant that only the four terrestrial channels were subject to quotas. The result was that non-compliance was widespread.

The first monitoring report by the European Commission (EC) – for October 1991 to December 1993 – found that only seventy out of 105 TV channels surveyed had complied with the quota. The second report (for 1993-4) covered 148 channels of which ninety-one met the quota. This reduction in the proportion of channels complying – from 74 per cent to 61 per cent – was largely attributable to the increased number of satellite channels. Many of these held UK non-domestic satellite licences and they rarely complied with the quotas. The third monitoring report appeared in 1998, covering 1995 and 1996, with returns for 189 channels in 1995 and 214 channels in 1996. In 1996 142 out of the 214 channels had met the quota, a compliance rate of 66 per cent. The report found that while the compliance rate of broadcasters based in Denmark, France, Germany, Ireland, the Netherlands and Portugal was improving, the picture in Belgium, Greece, Luxembourg, and the UK was far more mixed, with some broadcasters improving their performance, while others declined. Once again the large number of cable and satellite broadcasters based in the UK meant that the UK's overall performance was below average (European Commission 1998m, *Agence Europe* 4 April 1998).

The true picture seems likely to have been worse than was reported, since in several countries governments made no attempt to check the figures submitted to them by broadcasters.[13] This failure to implement the quota requirements in anything approaching a uniform way had the paradoxical result that a directive designed to overcome obstacles to the creation of a single audio-visual market may itself have created further discrepancies in the regulatory framework operating in different EU countries. In 1994 *Le Monde* judged that the Directive had been far more successful in promoting the free circulation of American, as opposed to European, programmes (de Witte 1995: 123–4, 126; Commission Press Release 16 July 1996 IP/96/645; *Le Monde* 26 May 1994).

Renewing the 1989 Directive

The 1989 Directive included provisions for its revision after five years. Long before then there were calls for change, not least because of the apparent linkage between the growth of new TV channels and a deteriorating balance of trade. The number of TV channels in European OECD countries increased from sixty-two in 1980 to 131 in 1990 and then to 244 in 1995. Meanwhile, US programme sales increased from $330 million in 1984 to almost $6 billion in 1996 (OECD 1997c: 72). Digitalisation seemed to offer a mixed future. On the one hand, the 1993 Delors White Paper on *Growth, Competitiveness and Employment* predicted that audio-visual employment would rise from 1.8 million in 1993 to close on 4 million by the year 2000, and saw the industry as one where Europe 'was potentially less vulnerable to competition from low labour cost markets' than many others (EC1993a). On the other hand, if past trends were repeated, more channels would simply mean more imports.

The 1994 audio-visual Green Paper provided a key contribution to the review of the Directive. It looked into the question of how the EU might 'contribute to the development of a European film and television industry which is competitive on the world market, forward-looking and capable of radiating the influence of European culture and of creating jobs in Europe', a question phrased with a view to uniting all the possible sources of support for an active EU audio-visual policy. The European programme industry was diagnosed to be suffering from four ailments (EC1994b: 2, 8):

- its fragmentation into national markets, with a consequent threat to the survival of small producers
- the partitioning of national markets compounded by a low rate of cross-border programme distribution and circulation
- a chronic deficit spiral
- and an inability to attract European capital.

Most of these alleged shortcomings were derived from an analysis of the film industry. The European TV sector was, by contrast, reasonably profitable, generally based on national markets, attracted more investment by the year (as the wave of European mergers in the mid-1990s confirmed) and usually viewed cross-frontier trade in programmes as a useful boost to revenues rather than as something that was essential before a programme could be commissioned. The Green Paper distinguished between so-called 'stock' programmes such as drama and documentaries, and 'flow' programmes which had no shelf-life. The analysis was updated in terms of future digital challenges, but the proposed remedies were not that different from the solutions proposed by the Commission in the 1980s. They included measures to boost the production of 'stock' programmes by updating, reinforcing and targeting the 1989 'TVWF' Directive, adopting a new approach to financial incentives at the European level, and ensuring greater co-ordination between national support systems,

The Green Paper met with a cool response from those who had always opposed intervention. The UK Government argued that the Green Paper placed:

> undue emphasis . . . on pan-European solutions and underestimates the continuing importance of national markets. Given the number of languages used across the Community and the well-established structure of broadcasting, we consider these are characteristics which policy must take account of, not seek fundamentally to change. For example, the Commission has not demonstrated that productions specifically designed to have a European-wide appeal will have an important part to play in the future development of the market. Indeed, experience has already shown the dangers of producing 'Europuddings' which satisfy the appetite of no audience at all.[14]
>
> (House of Lords 1995: 33)

The French were far more enthusiastic about the Green Paper, and they held the Council Presidency during the first half of 1995 when the Commission was formulating its proposals for revision of the 1989 Directive. The French announced 'development of an ambitious audio-visual policy' and reform of the Directive as priorities for their Presidency, adding that the 'stakes for the European audio-visual industry, in particular its ability to offer an alternative to US products, make it indispensable to maintain a policy of support for the programme industry' (*La Lettre de Matignon*, Présidence Française de l'Union Européenne 1995: 11, 42).

Buoyed up by French support DG X's initial proposals reflected the Green Paper's analysis. They included plans to tighten up the European quota requirement by removing the phrase 'where practicable', to focus quotas on a narrower range of 'stock' programmes, dramas, documentaries, films, serials and series, thereby excluding game-shows, and studio based programmes as well as the news and sport that had been excluded from the 1989 Directive, to give Member States a choice of whether to apply quotas in terms of broadcast time or as a percentage of a channel's programme budget, and, finally, to remove ambiguities over which country had jurisdiction over satellite channels (with the aim of overcoming British claims that stations headquartered in the UK but whose signals were uplinked elsewhere were not subject to British jurisdiction).

When the Commission's draft Directive was published in March 1995 it was criticised on the one hand by many Members of the European Parliament (MEPs), who felt it had not gone far enough, and on the other by those Member States which were opposed to any reinforcement of quotas. In theory the co-decision process, under which the revision of TVWF would be decided, gave the EP a considerable influence over the outcome.

But since it was the EP which was most intent on change, and any failure to reach agreement between the Council of Ministers and the Parliament meant that the old Directive, with its ineffective quota provisions, would stand, the EP was in a weaker position than it might have seemed. Within the Council there was far less sympathy for the dirigiste approach than in the 1980s. Enlargement had brought in states (such as Sweden and Finland) which saw the EU in economic rather than cultural terms. There were worries about a repeat of the transatlantic battle over audio-visual services which had taken place in the 1994 GATT negotiations, and the existence of many new channels added to the number of industry voices that were opposed to dirigiste measures.

This shift in the political balance within the Council led to an early political agreement (in November 1995) to leave the existing Directive virtually unchanged. There then followed eighteen months of heated exchange between Council and Parliament as MEPs from the Culture Committee battled to achieve reinforced quotas and the inclusion of new audio-visual services in the directive (Goldberg and Verhulst: 13). These calls were rejected outright by the Council of Ministers in June 1996, but thereafter scope for a compromise did emerge.

First, the EP had initially voted that new televisions be fitted with a so-called V chip (which allowed parental control of access to programmes that had been rated according to an agreed system, depending on how much sex or violence they contained). Many Member States were aware of the practical and ethical issues involved in use of the V chip and sceptical as to its effectiveness, but equally they were wary of being seen to be unconcerned about violence on TV. A compromise was reached whereby calls for the compulsory fitting of V chips were abandoned in return for the promise of a Commission study into the subject within a year of the Directive coming into effect.[15] Second, Parliament had become increasingly exercised about access to sporting events and in May 1996 had adopted a resolution on the importance of ensuring that coverage of sporting events of general interest was available on free-to-air TV (EP, Resolution on the Broadcasting of Sports Events, B4-0326/96, 22 May 1996). This resolution was prompted by fears – which in the end proved unfounded – that the European rights for the summer and winter Olympics between 2000 and 2008 might be bought exclusively by a subscription broadcaster, rather than the public service broadcasters which had previously held them through the European Broadcasting Union (EBU). The Resolution was swiftly converted into an amendment to the Directive, approved unanimously by the EP in November 1996, which aimed at ensuring that viewers should have access to major (sports) events live on free-to-air television. After some negotiation the Council agreed to incorporate protection for sporting events.[16] Under the 1997 Directive Member States are free to draw up a list of events (either national events or others, such as the Olympic Games, the World Cup or the European

Football Championship) which have to be broadcast on free-to-air channels (reflecting the UK listed events provisions from the 1996 Broadcasting Act). It also ensured that channels based elsewhere in Europe could not circumvent these provisions by beaming subscription only broadcasts in by satellite. Third, the earlier Parliamentary support for the most controversial proposals – to extend the scope of the Directive to include video-on-demand, and to toughen up the quotas – was less solid than many had imagined. When Parliament voted in November 1996, neither proposal received the necessary majority of the MEPs entitled to vote.[17] The Council had compromised on those areas which neither required a more interventionist stand, nor gave more teeth to the Directive.[18]

Refocusing audio-visual policy

The signing of the 1997 revised TVWF Directive marked the end of the long-running debate over quotas. The political failure of those who advocated a system of strengthened quotas was complete. But even amongst their supporters, quotas were valued increasingly in terms of the symbolic rather than the real. Few believed that they could ever provide a powerful enough instrument to redress the trend towards increased imports. There were some purists in the Commission who argued for a reinforced system of quotas as a matter of principle, pointing out that adherence to Community Directives should be an obligation rather than a choice. But more frequently quotas had provided a rallying point for those who believed that audio-visual policy should not be left entirely to the market, that technological convergence did not make cultural objectives for broadcasting redundant, and that European policy towards the converging communications sector involved more than just liberalisation.

Even though the majority of Member States moved against quotas between 1989 and 1996–7, most members of the Culture Committee still believed that there was a role for some form of public intervention in broadcasting. There was a clear preference, however, for this to be decided at the national, rather than the Community level. This explains the willingness to see protection for key national sporting events underwritten by TVWF. It also explains the conclusions from a Culture Ministers meeting in Galway in September 1996, which expressed 'considerable and strong support' for the concept of public service broadcasting, and argued that public service broadcasters 'must continue to have access to major popular programmes comprising, in particular, sports events' and that funding of public service broadcasters should be 'adequate and guaranteed, and not subject to review under competition and state aid regime'. Some of these aspirations were later endorsed by the decision to append a protocol on Public Service Broadcasting to the Treaty of Amsterdam in June 1997.[19]

Traditionally quotas had been accompanied by a series of European support measures, designed to aid the European audio-visual industry to be better able to face US competition. The main support scheme was the MEDIA Programme which was allocated 200 million ECUs for a five-year period from 1991. The 1994 Green Paper suggested renewing and refocusing the programme, and the Commission proposed a MEDIA II programme, concentrated on three priority areas (training, development and distribution) with 400 million ECUs for 1996 to 2000. The Council of Ministers pared the budget back and MEDIA started in 1996 with a budget of 310 million ECUs.

Plans for a 200 million ECU European Guarantee Fund made less progress. As its name suggests, the Guarantee Fund was designed to facilitate commercial loans to the film sector by sharing the financial risks with commercial partners. The aim was to support the development of fiction works that the Commission judged had a chance of appealing to a cross-European or international audience. Opposition from Member States such as the UK and Germany meant that progress on the proposal moved very slowly. By mid-1998 the Commission had effectively given up hope of the Guarantee Fund being accepted, and was exploring the alternative idea of a 'securitisation' scheme where the Community would provide equity capital of, say, 25 million ECUs, with which a further 475 million ECUs could be leveraged from banks, for the production and distribution of films with an international appeal (EC 1998a, EC 1998d: 19).

All these financial measures were proposed under Article 130 of the Treaty and the required unanimity of Member States in the Council became increasingly difficult to achieve. That was, in part, the inevitable result of enlargement, but it also reflected the low esteem that European support schemes commanded in some quarters. Some criticised the schemes for inadequate funding, and others for ill-targeted and mismanaged funds. It could be argued that European funding was too small to make a substantial impact on the industry as a whole, while still being large enough to sustain a small group of producers who came to depend on 'playing the funding game'.

The added political dimension of many EU funding schemes, where Member States demanded equal shares, meant that the limited expenditure was dispersed so widely as to be less effective than might otherwise have been the case. Given the strategic importance it placed on the audio-visual sector, and the value of the European audio-visual market, the amounts of money involved in MEDIA 2 – less than 100 million ECUs per annum – were fairly puny compared to the 9.4 billion ECUs of licence fee income received by EU Public Service broadcasters in 1995, the 3.3 billion ECUs spent in EU cinemas in 1996, or the $6 billion trade deficit with the US (*Eurostat* 1998: 5,7). At just 0.06 per cent of the EU budget they amounted to only a third of the money spent on supporting EU tobacco growers. Generally EU expenditure on support for audio-visual content production was a mere fraction of that previously spent on the support of hardware initiatives, such as the MAC programme of the late 1980s and early 1990s (INA 1998: 9).

European regulation of media ownership

The beginnings of cross-frontier broadcasting, the passing of the 1989 TVWF, and a wave of mergers in the European media industry in the late 1980s and early 1990s led to demands that the EU should seek to regulate media ownership.[20] The Community's competition powers under Articles 85 and 86 of the Treaty of Rome already allowed it to intervene against anti-competitive agreements and restrictive practices in the media as in other sectors. After the Merger Regulation came into force in 1989 DG IV was able to vet all mergers with global sales over 5 billion ECUs, although, interestingly, 'plurality of the media' was one of the factors that Member States could cite if they wanted to dispute a Merger Task Force (MTF) finding.

In the first nine years of the MTF's existence it rejected ten mergers, five of which were in the broadcasting sector (Pons 1998b). But most Member States had their own specific media ownership regulations, and the advocates of a greater EU role in this area agreed that sector-specific action was required at the EU level too, rather than a simple reliance on the more vigorous application of competition policy. Agreement on the purposes of community action was, however, far harder. Once again the EP favoured action more for political and cultural than economic reasons, while the Commission argued purely in terms of the internal market.

The extreme political sensitivity of all media ownership rules meant that it proved far harder to build a coalition of Member States favouring Community action on media ownership than had been the case with TVWF. The result was that a proposed media ownership directive born of DG XV's desire to remove obstacles to the internal market, and of the Parliament's concern to safeguard pluralism, foundered. This was because of the difficulty of satisfying these diverse aims, and, more importantly, the opposition of the bulk of the European media industry and of key Member States such as Britain, France and Germany, which were opposed to any extension of Community competence into such a sensitive area.

Conflicting rationales for EU intervention

Seven years elapsed between the Commission's announcement that it was contemplating a media ownership 'Directive, whose aim would be to harmonise certain aspects of national legislation' and the discussion by the Commission of DG XV's proposals in March 1997 (EC 1990: 21).[21] In the intervening period the Commission produced a Green Paper, a Communication, and sent no less than three questionnaires to interested parties, soliciting views about whether any action was necessary, and if so, what form it should take.(EC 1992; EC 1994).

In addition a series of reports were commissioned and made available: on the economic aspects of media concentration, on the definition of the media controller, and on the feasibility of using audience share measures to assess the degree of concentration (e.g. European Institute for the Media 1994; GAH 1994). This long delay testified to the political sensitivity of the subject and the uncertain legal basis for action. The 1994 Green Paper on *Media Ownership* described its aims as being not just to conduct 'a formal consultation of interested parties but to launch a genuine process with an in-built momentum featuring a frank and open dialogue with operators', and commented on how the lengthy consultation 'process has led to the creation of a kind of network of persons and operators interested in the question of pluralism and media ownership' (EC 1994: 9). The largely technical areas on which the Commission's research papers focused – market definition and the measurement of influence – were similar to those where the Commission had previously succeeded in creating policy networks which helped inform and then promote its plans. But media ownership regulation was a far more political issue than others tackled under the internal market programme. And without agreement on the political, rather than the technical purposes of media ownership rules, it would be impossible to win support for European Community intervention.

From the first there was disagreement between the Community's institutions as to whether the primary purpose of Community action was the safeguarding of pluralism or the completion of a single European audiovisual market. The two different approaches were to have crucial implications for the legal basis and potential sources of support for any Community measure. Logically, if EU action was required to safeguard pluralism then its effect needed to be to create a more restrictive regime than that currently established by Member States. If, on the contrary, the aim was the completion of the single market in order to facilitate the operations of large EU-wide media companies, then any harmonisation was likely to involve the relaxation of existing national controls. This dispute reflected the wider ambiguity over the purposes of Community audiovisual policy referred to earlier.

The European Parliament launched the first calls for Community regulation of media ownership with a series of resolutions in the mid-1980s focused on the need to protect pluralism. Following the adoption of the TVWF Directive in 1989 the EP's calls for action became more strident (Harcourt 1996: 204). A resolution of February 1990 on media take-overs and mergers pointed out that 'restrictions on concentration are essential in the media sector, not only for economic reasons but also, *and above all*, as a means of guaranteeing a variety of sources of information and freedom of the press'. Parliament identified the 'dangers of media concentration for diversity of opinion and pluralism' together with their belief that 'national media legislation alone was no longer sufficient to safeguard diversity of opinion and pluralism in Europe' (emphasis added;

cited in EC 1992: 61). These views were reiterated in a later, 1994 resolution, which urged the Commission to adopt legislation without delay 'to enable the Community, where necessary, to take measures to limit media concentration on a European scale which threatens diversity of opinion and pluralism' and reminded the Commission that 'strengthening the overall competitiveness of European media must be accompanied by strengthening of economic and cultural pluralism in this sector' (*Official Journal* C 44:177–9, 14 Feb. 1994).

Initially the Commission appeared to share the EP's perspective. When, in 1990, it first stated that a media ownership Directive was under consideration, it explained that a priority for the Community's audio-visual policy was 'to ensure that the audio-visual sector is not developed at the expense of pluralism but, on the contrary, that it helps to strengthen it by encouraging, in particular, the diversity of programmes offered to the public', adding that Community competition law could not 'cover all the situations in which a threat to pluralism is posed' (EC 1990). But in the 1992 Green Paper, pluralism was downplayed. The Commission explained that 'Member States have the legal capacity to safeguard pluralism'; the 'objective of ensuring pluralism . . . does not as such create a need for Community intervention'; and that 'the . . . objective of safeguarding pluralism of the media . . . is neither a Community objective nor a matter coming within Community jurisdiction as laid down by the Treaty of Rome and the Treaty on European Union'. According to the Green Paper any Commuity action should 'have more to do with ensuring that the Internal Market functions properly than with maintaining pluralism as such'.

The problem that required Community action was the way in which differing national media ownership rules could act as 'an obstacle to the functioning of the single market' (EC 1992: 59, 99). Against this background the Green Paper's discussion of Community competition policy seemed slightly odd. Reliance on competition policy to ensure pluralism would be misplaced, it was argued, because effective 'competition is concerned with the economic behaviour of undertakings, while pluralism is concerned with the diversity of information' (EC 1992: 82–3). The point was well made but seemed out of place in a document which argued that the EC had no competence to protect pluralism. The central weakness of the Green Paper, however, was that whilst it identified many ways in which the internal market *might* be impeded by the status quo, it had to concede that, for the moment, these were only 'for the most part potential obstacles' (EC 1992: 99, 103). As a result the Green Paper proposed no action, seeking views instead on three alternative options: no action, a 'recommendation to enhance transparency' involving greater disclosure and exchange of information between Member States, or Community harmonisation of national media ownership possibly via a directive (EC 1992: 112–19).

In spite of the fact that a two-year-long consultation process produced more evidence of irritation with existing national rules than real enthusiasm for Community action, DG XV became more convinced of the need for a Directive. It argued that 'Community rules on media owner-ship' would:

> put an end to the disparities between national rules concerning the media and . . . make it possible in particular to do away with the two obstacles most often cited during the consultations, namely the lack of legal certainty, which restricts the freedom of establishment and the free movement of media services and which consequently discourages direct investment in the media, and the distortions of competition cre-ated by the differences in the levels of restriction.
>
> (EC 1994a: 32)

Both the 1994 Communication on Media Ownership and a draft text prepared for the Commission in September 1996 referred to the need to safeguard pluralism, whilst justifying action purely in terms of the internal market provisions of the Treaty.[22] This may have been designed to placate the EP but it also raised certain questions. As Harcourt puts it:

> why should pluralist objectives be reached with legislation designed to further the Single Market? The Directive would harmonise media con-centration laws with the objective of protecting the Single Market, whereas the national laws it sought to harmonise will have been initi-ated to protect pluralism. In the Council of Ministers the Directive would be approved by ministers for industry and not ministers for cul-ture. Principally, the basis for legislation, does not match the objective it attempts to reach.
>
> (Harcourt 1996: 206)

Winning support for a Directive

From the very first consultations on the Green Paper key Member States indicated their hostility to any EC media ownership directive. If the Commission was to have any chance of overcoming this resistance it needed to mobilise support from the media industry itself. Large media companies with Europe-wide ambitions had to be persuaded that Community intervention would speed up the liberalisation of existing national media ownership controls, thereby smoothing the way for their expansion at home and elsewhere in the EU. But this was difficult to rec-oncile with the calls for action on pluralism from the EP, which believed that national media ownership regulation was too often subverted by major media companies and that Community competence would put an end to politically inspired dispensations and ensure a more rigorous regime.

Since the Commission had concluded early on that the internal market would provide the primary rationale for action, Parliament's calls for a Directive focused on pluralism was both difficult to deliver and risked frightening off potential industry support. The Commission therefore had to conduct a delicate balancing act, trying to persuade industry that a media ownership Directive would serve their interests, whilst not antagonising the advocates of measures to protect pluralism.

The Report of the Bangemann High Level Group on *Europe and the Information Society* provided some much needed industry endorsement for Community action when it was published in May 1994. The group blamed national media ownership controls for impeding 'companies from taking advantage of the opportunities offered by the internal market, especially in multimedia, and could put them in jeopardy vis-à-vis non-European competitors' and called for 'urgent attention [to] . . . be given to the question of how we can avoid divergent national legislation on media ownership undermining the internal market' (EC 1994c). This approach reinforced the Commission's belief that the internal market case for action offered the best route forward.

DG XV's own consultations produced a far less ringing endorsement. The Commission placed an optimistic gloss on the responses to its 1992 Green Paper, summarising the majority industry view as being that:

> the current national rules on media ownership must change . . . to cope with globalisation and the impact of the new technologies. On the other hand, the question of the level – national or European – at which the change must occur is the subject of vague or divided positions.[23]

In reality, while several companies and federations used their responses to the Green Paper to complain about or call for the relaxation of existing national rules, few were enthusiastic about EU regulation of media ownership.[24] One of the few companies which had itself approached the Commission was ITV in 1992, but that was primarily because they felt themselves vulnerable to take-overs from EU media companies rather than from any desire they had to move into the European market.[25] In their responses to the Green Paper, Pearsons stressed the need 'to eliminate inequities in media investment opportunities in Member States which arise by virtue of diverse national rules' and for urgent action to ensure that 'emerging forms of broadcasting are not distorted in their infancy'. The Italian company Editoriale Espresso also argued for a European measure.[26] But the majority view from the industry was more closely reflected by groups such as the European Publishers Council which argued that 'it would be premature to initiate harmonising legislation at the European level', the Association of Commercial Television in Europe (ACT) which argued that the largely national basis of the European TV industry meant that EU action 'could appear premature', and major companies like News International and Fininvest which opposed any action.

The Commission tried to put a brave face on this outcome, arguing that those operators involved in cross-media activities and with European as opposed to purely national ambitions and a long term strategy, all tended to support Community action (EC 1994a: 14–15). But this did not explain why News International – which met at least two of these criteria – should be opposed to Community action. The Commission's other explanation for industry wariness, that some 'had the impression they were being asked to sign a "blank cheque"', seemed much closer to the mark (EC 1994a: 13).[27]

Faced with a lukewarm response from industry the Commission fell back on the impending 'Information Society' as a justification for action. It argued that while disparities in national rules might not pose an acute obstacle to the internal market at present, technological and market pressures would soon demand a rationalisation of media ownership rules, and if this were done purely at the national level new disparities in national laws, and hence obstacles to the internal market, would be created. Only European-level harmonisation of national laws could avert this new danger (EC 1994a: 20).[28]

Views differed within the Commission about the extent to which digitalisation, convergence and the proliferation of channels would remove the need for specific safeguards against media concentration. DG XV argued that there would always need to be some protection against all the new channels being controlled by a single operator. Some of the thinking encouraged by the Information Society Directorate, DG XIII, meanwhile, suggested that with more channels, pluralism might eventually be self fulfilling (EC 1994a: 34, KPMG 1996).[29]

The Commission's proposals

The measures that were proposed by DG XV to the Commission in September 1996 and then again in March 1997 were designed to attract industry support. TV companies were to be prevented from acquiring new licences or establishing or taking over new companies if their audience share in all or part of the areas in which they operated exceeded 30 per cent. The same limits were to be applied to radio companies. Cross-media companies involved either in TV and Radio, or broadcasting and daily newspapers, were to be limited to a 10 per cent audience share, where each medium made up one third of the total media market.

These proposals had already undergone considerable change from earlier Commission thinking. Previous plans to include public service broadcasters within the scope of the Directive – which had been well received by some commercial operators – were dropped by Commissioner Monti in the face of opposition from the public service broadcasters themselves and Member States. This seemed logical since public service broadcasters were not covered by the media ownership regulations of most Member States, and they were instead subjected to specific programme obligations, as well as a duty to respect pluralism and a diversity of views. Moreover, public service broadcasters were not available for sale or take-over, and their inclusion in a single market measure designed to harmonise the market for media control would have made little sense. Member States were given the freedom to exempt public service broadcasters meeting certain minimum criteria.

Another change introduced by Commissioner Monti between the Commission's first referral of the proposals in September 1996 and its reconsideration of the measure in March 1997 was for a flexibility clause, whereby during a ten-year period a Member State could allow a broadcaster to exceed the 30 per cent thresholds. Similar flexibility applied in cases where the application of the limits would involve a local broadcaster or newspaper disappearing without a replacement being set up. Member States could exclude a broadcaster as long as they were not simultaneously infringing the upper thresholds in more than one Member State and subject to other measures being used to secure pluralism. These measures might include establishing, within any organisation which breaches the limits, 'windows for independent programme suppliers' or a 'representative programming committee' (Doyle 1997b: 9).

The use of audience share as a measure of media influence was one constant in a changing set of proposals. It was open to many criticisms both as a concept and in its implementation. As a measure, audience share is fairly crude, since it draws no distinction between the influence exercised by ownership of the *Racing Post* as opposed to the *Financial Times*, or indeed between a Channel 3 ITV franchise and the pop music channel MTV. In designing their directive DG XV also made some contentious choices. Sunday newspapers were excluded from the scope of the draft. Radio and TV audiences and newspaper readers were all weighted equally.

Even more contentiously, in spite of years of preparatory work the Commission scored an own goal with its decision to apply the 30 per cent audience share limit *within any area where a station could be received*. This had the effect of hitting hardest the regional ITV stations in the UK which had been among the original supporters of a Community directive, since they would be prevented from expanding into new areas, or even establishing new channels. Barry Cox, the Director of the ITV Association, denounced the Commission's plans as 'very damaging', adding that 'If Commissioners agree them as currently drafted, they will pose a serious threat to the future of regional broadcasting in the UK and could stifle investment in digital terrestrial television' (*Agence Europe* 12 March 1997).

There was similar concern in Germany where a high degree of local cross-media concentration between local newspapers and radio stations is accepted practice, but would also fall foul of the Commission's proposals. This insensitivity to German local conditions – together no doubt with vigorous representations from Germany's major media companies – led Chancellor Kohl to write a well-publicised letter to President Santer in the Summer of 1997, warning him against introducing Community regulation of media ownership. The DG XV proposals were also opposed by the European Publishers Council, by the European Newspaper Publishers Association, and by the Luxembourg-based CLT (*Agence Europe* 5 March 1997; *Financial Times* 13 March 1997).[30]

Without the support of key cross-frontier media companies, arguments for a harmonisation measure to remove obstacles to the internal market rang rather hollow. Claims that such a measure was needed urgently to assure Europe's success in the Information Society looked similarly unconvincing, faced with the success of companies like CLT in establishing cross-border activities, with fourteen television channels in six countries and eighteen radio stations across eight countries. Besides, attempts to make the proposals more palatable by the introduction of flexibility clauses and a considerable degree of national discretion seemed to offer the worst of both worlds: neither the simplicity of straightforward harmonisation, nor the unfettered national control experienced under the status quo.

Even allowing for these flaws in the DG XV proposals, the chances of any measure receiving widespread endorsement had always been slight. In the end, most media companies preferred to negotiate with their national governments (or in the case of Germany the Länder Media Authorities and the Ownership Commission, the KEK) over questions of media ownership controls rather than place themselves in the hands of a potentially inflexible directive. Member States similarly felt that, as the UK Government put it, the 'need for Community-wide legislation has not been demonstrated by evidence that national laws are ineffective', the 'responsibility for safeguarding plurality within the media rests with Member States'. The 'argument that the number of different regulatory regimes is inhibiting the development of a European media industry ignores the point that broadcasting does not normally cross language and cultural barriers', and that therefore there were no 'grounds . . . for introducing harmonising legislation at the European level' (DNH, EC Questionnaire No III on Pluralism and Media Concentration in the Internal Market: United Kingdom Government Response, 1995: 4). The German Länder adopted a similar view, and in spite of the inconveniences of a Federal system of control of media ownership, most German media companies had learned to live with it.[31]

Several commentators have argued that it was precisely because of the power wielded by major media companies that a bold Community initiative was required to defend pluralism (Kaitatzi-Whitlock 1996; Doyle 1997b). But it is difficult to justify the use of the Community's essentially technocratic decision-making process to achieve political goals which are opposed by elected national governments. Aside from the questionable democratic basis for such action, it also ignores the limited competence that the EU has to intervene to defend pluralism, as well as the realities of Community politics. Action that fails to commands the support either of Member States or of a substantial combination of industrial players, seems likely to fail. Press reports in early 1998 that Commissioner Monti had decided to withdraw proposals for a directive, leaving the way open for the much weaker option of a code of conduct or set of guidelines, confirmed that media ownership regulation would remain a matter for Member States and European competition authorities, rather than sector specific Community regulation (*Johnstone* 1998).

The Commission's abortive attempts to develop a Media Ownership Directive represent a failure of politics and of policy. The political failure lay in the inability to mobilise support for what was, admittedly, a hugely ambitious directive. Member States saw a media ownership directive as touching on an area of high politics over which they wished to retain control, and where the Treaties gave them good grounds for doing so. Key Commissioners were never persuaded by the proposals.[32] Finally, the enthusiasm of the EP for a measure to safeguard pluralism could not compensate for the lack of support from the very industry that was supposed to benefit from the opening up of the internal market.[33]

Conclusion

Analysis of the 1989 and 1997 TVWF Directives, and the failed attempts to pass a directive regulating media ownership across the EU, reveal the difficulties faced by the Commission in pushing ahead with specific policies aimed at the broadcast sector. The lack of any agreement between (and frequently within) the European institutions on the key purposes of intervention has been a major problem. Once the key market-opening measures of the 1989 TVWF Directive had been implemented, the broadcasting industry showed a marked lack of enthusiasm for any further EU regulation in their sector. Measures that were justified in terms of promoting European competitiveness – whether in terms of support programmes or the proposed harmonisation of media ownership rules – failed to win the support of the very industry they were supposed to help. Instead, their proponents were forced to rely on the traditional advocates of a more dirigiste approach to European audio-visual policy, notably the French, the culture and film lobbies, and their supporters within the EP.

Yet the expansion of the audio-visual sector, and of the Community itself, meant that these forces were in a weaker position by the mid-1990s than they had been in the late 1980s. Commercial rather than public service broadcasters have come to dominate the European broadcasting industry, and tend to resist EU measures which use quotas to limit their freedom to broadcast what they want, or restrain their corporate strategies through media ownership regulation.[34] The majority of Member States preferred to retain control of the politically sensitive issue of media ownership regulation at the national, rather than the European, level. Given the absence of any industry clamour for European-wide rules in this area, and the subjective and ultimately nationally specific judgements involved in questions of pluralism, this made good sense. There was also, however, the purely political desire of the majority of large Member States (notably, Germany, France and the UK) to keep control of such an inherently political issue.[35] Finally, enlargement of the Community in 1995 – bringing in the Swedes, the Finns and the Austrians – moved the balance of opinion in the Council of Ministers away from support for the more dirigiste audio-visual policies.

By the mid-1990s it appeared that those involved in creating EU audio-visual policy had failed to adjust either to the change in the political balance of power within their sector, or the real impact of technological change. The 1994 audio-visual Green Paper offered mainly traditional cultural dirigiste policies, albeit dressed up in the language of the Information Society. By 1996–7 a consensus began to emerge supporting some forms of public intervention – through the support for public service broadcasters, regulation of access to key events such as televised sport, conditional access systems and of electronic programme guides – but few of these had featured prominently in the debates launched by the Commission in the run-up to the renewal of the TVWF Directive.

During the long period of consultation over a media ownership directive, the Commission often cited the developing Information Society as an additional reason for action but it appeared to lose sight of the way in which the technological changes that were under way in broadcasting were reducing the importance of ownership alone in conferring control in digital media. As Hitchens puts it:

> In planning for the information society and acknowledging the need for media ownership regulation, the Commission has not sought to move beyond the views already expressed in its Green Paper on media ownership regulation and the follow-up paper. . . . This is curious because . . . Asking 'who has control of a television licence' may no longer be the most significant question, particularly if the regulations only extend the scope of that question to other television interests along with radio and press. In the changing media climate, it may also be important to ask who has control of the access technology, the programme catalogues, the programme production companies, and the telephone networks.
>
> (Hitchens 1996: 63–4)

These are the issues that will be explored in the following chapters examining the shape of EU intervention in regulating digital broadcasting.

Part III

National and European responses to digital broadcasting

4 Regulating access to digital broadcasting
The Advanced Television Standards Directive

Introduction

The spread of conditional access systems will be one of the most dramatic changes accompanying the start of digital broadcasting. It will do much to change the viewers' experience of television. It also raises one of the most pressing issues about the regulatory framework for digital television. Since most digital broadcasts will be encrypted – either to facilitate charging or to protect the broadcaster from liability for rights payments outside the territory for which they have been purchased – viewers will require a conditional access decoder to receive those broadcasts. Those conditional access systems will operate as electronic turnstiles into the home, controlling which broadcasts and other services viewers can receive, and which viewers and customers broadcasters and other service providers can reach. Without adequate regulation, vertically integrated conditional access operators and broadcasters could discriminate against competitors and prevent viewers from accessing a full range of channels and other services. The incentives for such anti-competitive behaviour could, however, be substantial (Nolan 1997: 601).

Many of the key regulatory questions raised by conditional access – of common standards, of interconnection and interoperability between systems, and of measures to ensure fair access to the network – are all familiar from telecommunications. As in telecommunications, regulation of conditional access combines a mix of sector specific and competition regulation. In contrast to telecommunications and analogue broadcasting, however, because the widespread use of conditional access systems is a new phenomenon, European regulatory intervention has been relatively unconstrained by existing national arrangements. That intervention has taken two forms. The first is the key piece of European regulation specifically tailored to digital broadcasting, the 1995 Advanced TV Standards Directive, which is discussed in this chapter. The second is the operation of competition policy and the Merger Control Regulations which will be dealt with in the following chapter.

Although the 1995 Advanced TV Standards Directive (hereafter known as the Directive) is now best known for its attempts to regulate conditional access, it started life as part of the Commission's involvement in standards setting for High Definition TV through the so-called MAC Directives. The failure of that policy goes some way to explaining the more unusual approaches adopted towards the Directive. First, that as a piece of single market legislation, it was drafted in a way that did so little to facilitate the emergence of a single European digital pay TV market. Second, that at a time of increasing awareness of the importance of convergence between telecommunications, broadcasting and computing, the issue of interoperability in digital broadcasting was accorded so much less importance than in telecommunications. Third, that policy makers in Member States and the Commission were initially so reluctant to regulate for either common standards or access terms for Europe's future digital pay TV networks, preferring instead to defer to the decisions of the industry grouping: the Digital Video Broadcasting Project (DVB).

This chapter explores the reasons for this outcome. It starts by examining the main provisions and background to the Directive, together with the current state of the digital market. It moves on to study the role played by the DVB group and the EU's institutions in devising the Directive and then concludes with an assessment of the Directive's implementation, together with the prospects for a move towards common standards in digital TV.

Competing conditional access systems and a fragmenting European market

Many of the EU's interventions in the TV industry were justified in terms of the creation of a genuinely European audio-visual industry. But although the Directive's regulation of digital TV was founded on both the language and Treaty provisions of the internal market, it did little to encourage moves towards a single digital TV market.[1] While the Directive prescribes the use of agreed digital transmission standards it leaves operators free to use proprietary standards for conditional access and other gateway technologies, as long as they provide 'fair, reasonable and non-discriminatory' access for third parties to their conditional access systems. But the very existence of such proprietary systems increases the risks that their operators might abuse their positions as gatekeepers. Some of the ways in which this might occur have been identified by Martin Cave (Cave 1997: 587–8). They include:

- Denying access to services that might compete with the gatekeeper's own offerings.
- Pressuring new entrants to join their own package of channels.
- Deterring potential competitors by granting access on unfavourable terms.

- Forcing a new entrant to accept other services such as Subscriber Management Services (SMS) and conditional access services as a condition of obtaining access.
- Imposing contractual restrictions on flexibility thus preventing entrants from switching to rival packages (see also OFTEL 1998a).

The prevalence of proprietary conditional access systems also had implications for the development of an integrated European digital TV market. While an agreed transmission system means that satellite broadcasters can *transmit* their digital signals right across Europe, audience *access* is effectively limited to viewers equipped with the right kind of digital decoder. At the same time as increased digital satellite capacity and the removal of regulatory obstacles were appearing to improve the prospects for a single European television market, the limited scope of the Directive was entrenching the existing national segmentation of Europe's markets. According to Nolan, 'standardisation, compatibility, interoperability and application portability are essential pillars in the erection of a successful and competitive European digital television industry' (Nolan 1997: 610). But the start of digital satellite broadcasting in Europe was instead characterised by market fragmentation, with rival blocs of operators using incompatible decoder systems in different territories or, on occasions, within the same national or linguistic market.

Main features of the 1995 Directive

This fragmentation of the European market and the threats to competition were compounded by the limited scope of the Directive. It says nothing about the regulation of gateway technologies apart from conditional access. Vital technologies, such as the operating software (the applications programming interface – API) within the box, the verifier, or the way in which electronic programming guides interact with conditional access systems, can all be used either individually or jointly to prevent competitors entering the market, but are not mentioned in the Directive. Table 4.1 identifies the ways in which these technologies can be used anti-competitively.

The proliferation of proprietary conditional access systems and related technologies meant that the advent of digital TV increased the obstacles to the launch of truly pan-European satellite pay TV channels.[2] By early 1997, eighteen months after the Directive had been approved, the majority of the conditional access systems being used or planned were proprietary and mutually incompatible. In France, Canal Satellite Numérique and Télévision Par Satellite were using incompatible decoders, satellite orbital positions and application programming interfaces (APIs). In Germany, Premiere and Kirch's DF1 were each using different systems as they started digital TV. Similar hardware wars seemed possible in the UK – between

Table 4.1 Anti-competitive potential within the set-top box

Bottleneck	Purpose	Opportunities to limit competition
Verifier	Provides software checks to ensure integrity	Withhold necessary technical details
Electronic Programme Guide (EPG)	Provides schedule listings and links to on-line services	Programme exclusion
		Discrimination
		Cross-promotion
		Proprietary branding/ advertising
Application Programming Interface (API)	Provides link between low level operating system and user applications	Withhold necessary technical details
		Refusal to allow required integrated receiver/ decoder upgrades
		Software exclusion

Source: Cave and Cowie: 1998: 90

digital terrestrial TV (DTT) and digital satellite, and in Spain between the rival digital services of Via Digital and Canal Satélite Digital. (See Table 4.2.)

A variety of approaches could have been adopted towards digital standards in the 1995 Directive. Common standards for reception equipment and decoders would have reassured consumers that the equipment in which they invested would not become redundant. Failing that, an obligation for the early declaration and licensing of essential interfaces could have facilitated the interconnection of proprietary systems and networks. Alternatively, rigorous regulation of third party access to the network could have been proposed. There was, however, great reluctance amongst policy-makers at both the national and European level to pursue any of these options. The result was a measure which failed to achieve one of the key objectives listed in the Directive's preamble, namely, to ensure that 'all pay television providers can, in principle, provide all digital pay-television consumers in the European community with their programmes'.

Amongst the pro-competitive aspects of the Directive are its establishment of a common transmission standard, and the obligations for conditional access operators to keep separate financial accounts, publish unbundled tariffs, and offer fair, reasonable and non-discriminatory access to broadcasters. But these goals were compromised by the fact that there was:

- No standardisation of conditional access.
- No obligation to include a common interface to allow alternative conditional access modules to be plugged into a single set-top box.

Table 4.2 Digital access technologies in Western Europe*

Company	Country	Set-top technology API	Conditional access decoder
Via digital	Spain	Open TV	Echostar–Nokia
Canal Satélite Digital	Spain	Media Highway	Seca–Mediaguard
Premiere/DF1	Germany	Own embedded system (TeleOnline-Navigation Instrument T.O.N.I)	Irdeto—D-Box
British Digital Broadcasting (BDB)	UK	Media Highway	Seca–Mediaguard
BSkyB	UK	Open TV	Videocrypt
Telepiu	Italy	Open TV**	Seca–Mediaguard
Canal Satellite Numérique	France	Media Highway	Seca–Mediaguard
Télévision par satellite	France	Open TV	Viaccess
AB Sat	France	None	Viaccess

Source: Compiled from: *TV International* 15 December 1997, European Broadcasting Union 1998, Levy 1997: 663, Llorens-Maluquer 1998: 560

Notes
* Information based on published information available as at May 1998
** Following Canal+'s acquisition of Telepui, the new owners moved to replace the Open TV boxes with the Canal+ Media Highway system.

- No explicit reference to gateways within the set-top box – such as the API and the EPG – other than the conditional access system itself.[3]
- Imprecision in the requirements for 'fair, reasonable and non-discriminatory' access for broadcasters to conditional access systems.
- A requirement for a single transmission standard that is defined so narrowly as to leave it unclear whether all the key elements are included or not.

The background to the Directive

At first sight the limited scope of the Directive is surprising.[4] Discussion about the future regulation of digital TV and the two-year gestation period for the 1995 Directive coincided with the Commission's deliberations on how to approach the Information Society. While the Commission's approach to both issues reflected their concern to stay close to those identified as key industry players, the outcomes of each were very different.

'Interconnection of networks and interoperability of services and applications' were identified as 'primary Union objectives' in the 1994 report of the Bangemann High Level Group on the Information Society. But the group's message that 'open systems standards will play an essential role in building a European information infrastructure' seemed to carry little weight in the approach that was taken towards digital broadcasting (EC 1994c). In the case of the Directive fairly modest regulatory ambitions were agreed on at an early stage by the Commission and the Council of Ministers. Late in the day the European Parliament used its newly acquired power of co-decision radically to revise the Directive which – as originally proposed by the Commission – contained no mention at all of conditional access. The Commission's approach to digital regulation was coloured by three interrelated factors. The first was the desire to avoid any repeat of what were seen as past interventionist mistakes in the attempt to get analogue HDTV off the ground with the series of MAC directives. The second was a longer-term change in the approach to standards setting in general. And third, and partly as a result of the first two factors, there was the desire only to bring forward regulations that had the legitimacy of having received prior approval from the DVB, the industry-based consensus group.

The perceived failures of MAC weighed heavily on the Commission's mind as it approached the framing of the Advanced TV Standards Directive. According to Alan Cawson, the Commission's original decision to make the use of MAC technology mandatory for all high powered DBS services was motivated in part by a desire to 'prevent the Japanese from entering the European market with HDTV, and to protect the European IT firms in what was argued by the firms (and accepted by the Commission) as a "strategic" technology'. Both sides, DG XIII for the Commission, and the main European consumer electronics manufacturers, worked in what he describes as 'essentially a closed – corporatist – partnership between Commission actors and major firms, which produced proposals for validation by the Council of Ministers' (Cawson 1994: 73, 70).

When Martin Bangemann took over at DG XIII in December 1992 one of his first moves was to kill off the HD-MAC strategy, thereby recognising the inevitable given the proliferation of non-MAC satellite broadcasting via Astra by BSkyB and others.[5] The result was that the Commission approached the renewal of the MAC Directive in a new mood, chastened by past failures. The guiding principle of industrial and high technology policy was now to go with the grain of the market rather than to try to steer it too overtly, and this time, to avoid capture by the consumer electronics lobby. Indeed MAC and the whole HDTV saga had themselves represented a 'major exception to the policy of avoiding mandatory EC standards' (Thatcher 1996: 184). Increasingly the Commission conceived of its role as a facilitator, broker and legitimiser of industry consensus, rather than a regulator imposing decisions on a reluctant or divided industry.

This new role mirrored the move that the Commission had already made over the previous decade towards a new style of standard setting.

Early EC attempts at detailed harmonisation of technical standards in the mid-1980s had produced some notable failures: 'it took ten years to pass a single directive on gas containers made of unalloyed steel, while the average time for processing fifteen harmonising directives which were passed as a package in September 1984, was nine and a half years'. Meanwhile, 'private or semi-private standardization bodies in the Member States were producing thousands of technical standards each year' (Majone 1996: 24). Change was clearly necessary. With fast moving technologies, a ten-year wait for a harmonised standard made no sense.

With the adoption of *The New Approach to Technical Harmonisation and Standardisation* in 1985 the Commission retreated from previous attempts at detailed technical harmonisation. Community regulation was limited to health and safety issues, leaving non-binding technical standards to be drawn up by standardisation bodies such as CENELEC and CEN. These official standards institutions were urged to modernise their working methods, respond better to market needs and produce their results more rapidly. Improvements in the official standards procedures were accompanied by the proliferation of voluntary industry consortia operating by consensus procedures and drawing up specifications, whose timing and content were often closer to the needs of the market players than those standards produced by the official bodies (Farr 1996: 3).

The Commission's reform programme recognised that standardisation should remain 'a voluntary activity managed by private organizations' but also insisted on the need to ensure that 'this private activity effectively serves the public interest, in terms of its openness to all parties and its efficiency' (EC 1991: 28). Groups like the new European Telecommunications Standards Institute (ETSI), CEN and CENELEC were obliged to take account of a wide variety of interests as well as those of industry itself. But over the years concern grew as to whether they were in fact giving 'adequate representation to diffuse, ill-organised interests' (Majone 1996: 26). One account reflects this concern in describing ETSI's main input to EC telecoms policy as having been 'to offer powerful transnational economic actors a platform for difficult negotiations on establishing common standards – solely in their interest' (Esser and Noppe 1996: 558).

Consumer voices only gained belated recognition in the reformed official standards institutions, and there was simply no place for them in the many private standards consortia that developed in 'reaction to the limitations of formal standardization' (EC 1996d). The strength of such groups lay in their responsiveness to market needs. Their weakness lay in that they could be highly selective in their membership, have imperfect decision-making processes and by-pass some of the public interest safeguards within the formal processes. The growth of private standards consortia was accompanied by all the 'social risks inherent in [the] privatisation of a sphere of national and international co-operation for the provision of public goods' (David and Shurmer 1996: 803, 808).

The DVB Group and conditional access

The Digital Video Broadcasting Group (DVB) was part of this more general trend towards the establishment of voluntary industry-based standards setting bodies, and it received active support from national and European policy-makers. DVB played a valuable role in building consensus on several key specifications, but the way in which it was entrusted with the contentious issue of conditional access illustrates the weaknesses as well as the strengths of the new approach.

DVB was established in September 1993, on the initiative of Peter Kahl, an official of the German Telecommunications Ministry.[6] Membership was open to any organisation eligible to join the EBU or ETSI, and increased from eighty-three to 147 in DVB's first year. The main decision-making body, the Steering Board, reflected the breadth of membership, and consisted of broadcasters, operators, manufacturers and representatives of national governments plus one – non-voting – Commission representative. The DVB Technical Module worked to clear requirements – on issues such as price and functionality – specified by the Commercial Module. Cowie comments that this 'commercially led approach (was) in stark contrast to the more technologically led standard setting process pursued by those such as ETSI' (Cowie 1996: 475). While the DVB itself did not set standards, DVB approved specifications were often approved by the standards setting bodies such as ETSI.

DVB occupies a strange halfway house between the formal standards setting world and the plethora of private industry groups. Technically a private industry grouping it took a role which was much more than that might suggest. The fact that it had been established and was chaired by a highly placed German civil servant, and that it included European Union and national officials and consciously attempted to reach out to the entire European TV industry, did much to enhance its status. The desire of policy-makers for the DVB to take responsibility for digital standardisation also gave the group a particularly privileged role. DVB specifications usually made rapid progress through the formal standard setting procedures of bodies such as ETSI and CENELEC. On many occasions both the Council of Ministers and the European Commission delayed regulatory proposals in the hope that consensus agreements in the DVB might make them unnecessary.

In areas where there were no great vested interests at stake, DVB rapidly chalked up a series of standardisation successes. Agreements on a digital satellite transmission specification and a common scrambling algorithm were both reached by the end of 1993. But the limits of DVB's consensus decision-making were revealed particularly starkly in the area of conditional access, where the interests of existing analogue pay broadcasters in extending their control of proprietary conditional access systems to the digital market, pitted them against third party broadcasters who would need access to those systems. From the start of the DVB discussions existing pay TV operators sought to safeguard their right to place proprietary conditional access systems in the market and to ensure that no single standard for digital conditional access emerged and that the terms and conditions of third party access to their networks would escape external regulation.

The debate within the DVB focused around two alternative approaches to operating conditional access systems: Multicrypt and Simulcrypt. Multicrypt, favoured by the free-to-air broadcasters, would allow consumers to access different broadcasters' programmes through whichever conditional access system they possessed, by the insertion of a credit card sized standardised decoder card. The system required standardisation of the decoder socket or 'common interface' in order to receive the decoder card. Simulcrypt was proposed by the conditional access operators. The idea, whereby two or more streams of conditional access messages could be transmitted with a broadcast to allow its reception by multiple proprietary decoders, sounded simple. But it depended on broadcasters succeeding in negotiating with conditional access operators to ensure that their target subscribers could receive their programmes. Broadcasters feared that vertically integrated conditional access operators/pay broadcasters might use control of the network, and commercially sensitive information about the target market, to restrict the flow of programming from their competitors. Subsequent experience has shown that Simulcrypt is only likely to succeed where operators provide complementary rather than competing channels.

Attempts to resolve these conflicting positions dominated the proceedings of the DVB from December 1993 until the Autumn of 1994. The main conditional access providers – BSkyB, News Datacom, Canal Plus and Filmnet – tried to make the Simulcrypt option more palatable to third party broadcasters by offering a voluntary code of conduct on access to digital decoders. But the code was seriously undermined by its voluntary nature and by the fact that it neither guaranteed access to the conditional access network nor offered any enforcement or arbitration system or sanctions in the event of the code being violated. After months of negotiation DVB members were asked to vote in September 1994 on a code which had been substantially revised, but still fell short of guaranteeing access to third parties. The way in which the voting was conducted was also less than satisfactory, and whilst the DVB spoke of 'an industry-wide agreement', the non-pay broadcasters called for European regulation of access terms, rather than a voluntary arrangement (Levy 1997a: 668–9).

Negotiating the 1995 Directive

The EU Commission was closely involved in the DVB processes described above. Both the Commission and Council had a pronounced preference for resolving contentious issues over digital TV standards through the consensus processes of the DVB rather than through regulation. But as the prospects for such consensus faded, and conflict between the broadcasters and the operators intensified, paradoxically the Commission and Council seemed to place ever more faith in a DVB consensus solution. National and EU policy-makers were particularly sensitive to the arguments of those they expected to launch the first digital pay TV services and, on occasions, appeared to favour the interests of the operators over those of third party broadcasters or consumers.[7]

Initial Commission thinking, unveiled in November 1993 in a Communication on Digital Video Broadcasting, displayed a cautious but nevertheless more balanced approach than was to emerge in subsequent policy proposals. The Communication noted that 'the requirement to develop common European conditional access systems must be . . . resolved as early as possible' and identified 'the encouragement of appropriate standardization of digital television' and the 'protection of the public interest through ensuring free and fair competition and . . . consumer protection', as areas where Commission action was clearly required. Indeed, the Communication insisted that DVB recommendations would be just one of the many inputs that the Commission would have to examine, and urged the DVB to include consumer representatives in its discussions (EC 1993b: 23, 2, 25). But the Commission's draft directive, also published in November, set itself far more modest objectives than this suggested. Conditional access received no mention. The draft simply stated that 'completely digital television systems must use a transmission system which has been standardized by a European standardization body *but are otherwise not covered by this Directive*' (EC 1993c) (emphasis added).

From an early stage the European Parliament was far less willing to defer to the DVB than were other Community institutions. In March 1994 Gérard Caudron, the rapporteur for the main European Parliament committee, argued that: 'conditional access techniques must not be beyond Community intervention, standardization and/or regulation' and urged the Commission to prepare 'regulatory measures if the expected consensus [in the DVB] . . . is not achieved in good time and/or fair and open competition, consumer protection or other significant public interest so demand' (European Parliament Report 29 March 1994, A3–0198/94). Although the EP supported Caudron, Commissioner Bangemann rejected his demands, warning against repeating the top down approach taken to MAC analogue standards and the dangers of premature standardisation not accepted by industry, and suggesting that the Parliament should 'wait until the middle of May . . . when we have developed a common position with industry' (Debates of the European Parliament, 18 April 1994, no. 3–447: 11–16).

The delays within the DVB process led Telecoms ministers to defer discussing conditional access until the November 1994 Telecommunications Council. By then, although it was clear that the DVB had been unable to resolve its disagreements on conditional access, ministers were unwilling to intervene with regulation. Instead they endorsed a text which they explained 'reflects exactly what the market parties are prepared to support. The Council thought that any unilateral amendment of the content of this text could compromise the market parties' consensus and thereby call into question Europe's current role as leader in the digital television sector, which was dependent on that consensus' (see European Council 1994). The suggestion was that – uniquely – the launch of digital TV services would be jeopardised by any regulatory proposals which were not as devised by one side of the industry. It amounted to a peculiar form of privatisation of public policy.

Broadcasters and others who were unhappy, both about the DVB proposed Code of Conduct and the Council Common Position's reluctance to regulate conditional access, now turned their attention to the European Parliament. A vigorous lobbying campaign was launched as each side realised that the Parliament's new power of co-decision could force the Council to change its position.[8] Once again Gérard Caudron MEP played a key role, producing a report which was subsequently adopted by the European Parliament. Caudron proposed amending Article 4 of the Directive to ensure that broadcasters were granted 'fair, reasonable and non-discriminatory' access, that conditional access operators should keep separate accounts (which would help in the event of disputes as to whether charges for access were indeed fair), and that Member States should provide for an 'inexpensive . . . fair, timely and transparent' disputes procedure. The Caudron proposals were endorsed by all the main political groups and passed with the required majority, thereby amending the Council/Commission Common Position. A month later the Telecommunications Council reluctantly agreed the final, and much revised, Advanced Television Standards Directive.[9]

Implementing the Directive

The Directive that was finally passed represented an improvement on the proposals that had been discussed within the DVB, mainly because of the work of the EP in replacing the DVB's voluntary code of conduct with statutory access provisions. But the effectiveness of these requirements depended on how they were implemented at national level. Many aspects of the Directive were so vague as to leave national officials unclear as to what the provisions meant, and as to which of them really needed to be written into national law. The result was that national implementation varied hugely. The only degree of uniformity between Member States has been in the tardiness of implementation; none of the major European countries succeeded in implementing the Directive by the August 1996 deadline.

In the case of both France and Germany, the launch of digital satellite services preceded implementation. Germany included a very basic requirement for 'fair, reasonable and non-discriminatory access' to conditional access systems (and for electronic programme guides) in Article 53 of the revised Interstate Treaty on Broadcasting which came into force on 1 January 1997. In France, the key access requirements of Article 4 of the Directive were included in a Bill amending the 1986 Broadcasting Law, which was considered by the Assemblée Nationale in March 1997 but not implemented because of a change in government. It is now intended that the Directive's provisions will be implemented in three specialist pieces of legislation on digital telecommunications terminal equipment, digital satellite broadcasting, and digital cable television, as well as through a revised Broadcasting Law which is due to be introduced in Parliament during 1999 (Squires and Sanders, 1998, Annex 2: 177). (See Chapter 6.)

Initially neither French nor German legislators showed great concern about the prospect of competing and incompatible conditional access systems. There was no great enthusiasm either for rapid implementation of the Directive or for seeing how its provisions might be enforced most effectively. Conditional access barely surfaced in the French Parliamentary debates on the failed 1997 Broadcasting Bill, and the equal access provisions contained in the Bill itself were barely more precise than those of the Directive. The difficult task of ensuring fair and reasonable access was to fall first to the Broadcasting Regulator, the CSA, with the possibility that thereafter disputes could be referred on to the competition authority (Conseil de la Concurrence) should that prove necessary. Similarly in Germany, early discussions of conditional access were limited to the DLM, the Committee of Länder regulatory authorities. Whilst the DLM produced some guidelines, in practice each of the fifteen Land media authorities would have to decide how to interpret the Directive's access provisions for operators licensed within their area.

In Spain there was a more vigorous approach to implementation but this was largely because the issue was so highly politicised. In January 1997, one day before the launch of the first digital pay TV operation in Spain by Canal Satélite Digital (CSD), the Spanish Government announced that it would introduce a Decree Law to mandate the use of Multicrypt decoders, thereby rendering CSD's proprietary decoders illegal. The fact that this action was combined with an increase in VAT on pay TV services from 6 to 17 per cent and a proposal retrospectively to reduce the degree of exclusivity that CSD had on football contracts, was indicative of the Government's desire to mount a wide-ranging political attack on the Prisa group (part owners of CSD) which had been closely identified with the previous Socialist Government. The Government also hoped to favour the delayed launch of the rival state-sponsored Via Digital package whose investors included the newly privatised Telefonica and the Spanish public TV operator, and which was due to operate from the State-owned Hispasat Satellite (*New Media Markets*, 13 February 1997). The European Commission told the Spanish Government that the CSD decoders could not be declared illegal (the same decoder was already being used by Canal Plus in France), but the Government simply went ahead with a revised law on 3 May, which added to the problem by imposing the mandatory sharing of key football rights between pay per view operators. Since Canal Satélite had already purchased the key rights until 2003 and Via Digital had none, the law once again seemed targeted at helping Via Digital at CSD's expense.[10] The Commission took the very unusual step of opening infringement proceedings against the Spanish Government, arguing that the May law violated Treaty rules on the free movement of goods and the freedom to provide services, that there had been a failure to notify the Commission before the introduction of a technical rule of this kind, and that the law was incompatible with the Television Standards Directive (European Commission Press release IP/97/680, 23 July 1997). Finally, in September 1997, the Spanish Government backed down and revised the law to recognise the legality of the Canal Satélite decoder, and comply with the Directive. The Commission dropped their infringement proceedings against the Spanish but, given continuing concerns about the Spanish Government's intent, the Internal Market Commissioner Mario Monti warned that he was ready to revive the action if the Spanish Government did not comply (Llorens-Maluquer 1998: 579–84).[11] The best chance of these disputes ceasing came with the announcement in the Summer of 1998 of a planned merger between Via Digital and CSD.

The UK Government, for its part, was acutely aware of the politics that lay behind discussions of conditional access. The issue arose on many occasions during parliamentary debates on the 1996 Broadcasting Act and – largely because of the controversial role of News International in the UK media industry – took on a much higher political profile than in either Germany or France. This goes some way to explaining the paradox that it was in the UK, where implementation was carried out by a statutory instrument rather than by primary legislation, that the most thought was given to the questions raised by the Directive. Issues such as what would constitute non-discriminatory access, the appropriate charges for conditional access services, recovery of subsidies on set-top boxes, and whether the Directive should cover gateways other than conditional access, were all discussed in the consultative papers produced either by the DTI or OFTEL in the course of 1996 and 1997. The decision to regulate by issuing a class licence under the 1984 Telecommunications Act created a useful framework in which the competition issues raised by conditional access systems could be addressed. It also meant that the UK had a ready-made route – through the Telecoms regulator OFTEL – to deal with the requirement in Article 4e of the Directive for there to be an inexpensive 'fair, timely and transparent' disputes procedure. Equally though, the legislative route that was chosen for UK implementation was designed to depoliticise the discussions on conditional access and was initially used to justify a cautious approach towards implementation.[12]

These differences in implementation were, in part, the product of differing administrative cultures and political concerns, but they also reflected the extent to which a lack of precision in the Directive created considerable latitude for national variation. For those who wanted to see moves towards a single European TV market the risk was that the Directive would accelerate the fragmentation of the digital TV market. Technical fragmentation, through the use of rival and incompatible conditional access systems, seemed likely to be compounded by the regulatory fragmentation that would result from widely differing approaches to implementation and enforcement of the Directive across the EU.

Conditional access and the European policy process

The European Commission approached the regulation of Digital TV keen to avoid the mistakes of an overly interventionist strategy, and undue preoccupation with the needs of the European consumer electronics industry, which were seen to have characterised the approach to HD-MAC. With digital TV, in contrast, the favoured policy was one of minimal regulatory intervention, with some key decisions delegated to industry as represented through the DVB.

The DVB played an important role in facilitating agreement on some key standards, but as an industry body it could never be the proper vehicle for the devising of a regulatory strategy for digital TV. There were, however, occasions during the creation of the TV Standards Directive when public bodies delayed decisions and then deferred to the DVB in devising regulation. That was both questionable in itself and difficult in practice. The objection of principle was to the very idea that an industry grouping should, alone, be seen as providing the range of viewpoints that must be considered by policy-makers. The practical difficulty arose because the very breadth of the DVB, which was so important in boosting its claims to legitimacy, meant that members' interests inevitably diverged on many of the key regulatory issues. In a consensus-based organisation it was relatively easy for one sector – in this case the pay TV operators – to block any proposals that didn't suit them. The success of the pay TV operators in 1994–5 was to persuade Commission and national policy-makers that minimal regulation would maximise the chances for the successful launch of digital TV in Europe. When the Directive was passed in July 1995, pressure from the European Parliament ensured that it went further than either the Commission, the Council or the existing analogue pay TV operators wanted. By the late 1990s, however, policy-makers and the industry seemed less confident that minimal regulation had necessarily produced the best possible outcome.

Within a year of the Directive being approved by the Council of Ministers the Commission began to appreciate the dangers that might arise if digital TV was launched with a range of competing proprietary conditional access systems. Consumer demand might be dampened, the European market could become further fragmented, and the opportunities for anti-competitive behaviour would increase (see following chapter). These concerns were evident in June 1996 when Commissioner Bangemann called together a meeting of key pay TV operators in Paris to discuss whether a common approach to conditional access might be possible. At the time Kirch and Bertelsmann in Germany and Canal Plus and TPS in France were developing digital pay TV strategies based on proprietary conditional access systems. The Commissioner was reported as favouring a single set-top box and as being keen to see 'that the market is not fragmented'. Hints were dropped that if the industry could not itself develop a common approach to conditional access, then the Commission might choose to intervene.[13] The following month the Commission produced a Communication on Standardisation which included reference to the need for compatibility between set-top boxes, and that regulatory measures might be appropriate as 'the ultimate solution, in cases where no satisfactory consensus exists'. In contrast to its previous uncritical endorsement of the DVB process, here the Commission highlighted interoperability as an area where the industry-based standardisation process might be deficient:

> The public authorities have a responsibility with respect to public interests, such as ensuring sufficient interoperability between systems . . . If formal standardization is not capable of providing the appropriate solutions to meet such needs . . . then the European Union will be obliged to take administrative action.[14]
>
> (EC 1996d)

The Directive provided for the Commission to review national implementation and developments in the digital TV market by July 1997. This did not occur during 1997 but instead the Commission devoted a substantial section of the 1997 Green Paper on Convergence to a discussion of conditional access. Although the Directive was defended as combining requirements which 'are sufficiently light to encourage innovation and investment in a rapidly evolving technical and commercial environment, and sufficiently strong to protect fair competition and consumer welfare', the Commission asked for comments on whether 'the Television Standards Directive is adequate to cope with . . . technological change and its market consequences'. The technological features that the Commission had in mind were the Applications Programming Interface (API) and the electronic programme guide, neither of which were mentioned explicitly in the Directive, but which were covered in the implementing regulations in the UK:

> A new feature of the consumer's home terminal is the Application Programming Interface (API). The API is a set of software in the terminal, resembling the operating system of a PC. It is used to manage

interactive applications, including EPGs, carried by the terminal, and
to provide a specified interface for the development of applications by
third-parties. The PC industry owes its success in a large part to the
role of de facto standard APIs in facilitating the creation of a wide variety of third-party-developed applications software. At the time of
writing there are a number of different APIs used in set-top boxes in
Europe, risking fragmentation of the market and problems of inter-
operation. Furthermore the combined use of proprietary APIs
together with EPGs and conditional access leads to increased of risks
of abuse by operators controlling access to services.

(EC 1997d: 25)

These risks could be addressed through action by competition authorities to ensure fair access through the additional 'gateways' in the digital
set-top box, by explicit application of the access provisions of the Directive
to the entire range of gateway technologies including APIs, or by
Commission regulations or industry agreement on the standardisation of
key technologies such as the API. Interestingly, regulatory action seems far
more likely now than when the Directive was being discussed in 1994–5. In
France, Catherine Trautmann, the Minister for Culture and Communication, has indicated that she will give a higher priority than her
predecessors to ensuring the use of a single conditional access system
across the three French digital satellite services. In the UK OFTEL and the
broadcasting regulator, the ITC, have both recognised the problems posed
by incompatible APIs or the use of EPGs in an anti-competitive manner.[15]
And the competition authorities, both within Germany and in DG IV (see
following chapter) are increasingly pre-occupied by the ways that control
of proprietary technologies might be used to threaten competition within
the German digital pay TV market.

Perhaps the most interesting trend is the sign that within the industry
itself there is a greater desire than before to move towards common standards for the next generation of set-top boxes. The DVB reached
agreement in December 1997 to at least try to devise an open, harmonised
approach to the choice of API for the so-called Multi-media home
platform. The aim was that 'any digital content provider will be able to
address any advanced set-top box, TV set or multimedia PC' (DVB 1997).
A critical factor in this change within the DVB was that Canal Plus, which
had previously stood solidly alongside the proprietary approach of other
pay TV operators, decided to back an open standard for the API.[16] The
new approach by Canal Plus seems likely to have been related to changes
in the environment in which it was operating. The arrival of competition
in its home market reduced the advantages offered by a purely proprietary
approach to standards there, whilst its development as the largest and only
truly European pay TV company, with around nine million pay TV
subscribers in France, Benelux, Spain, Poland and Scandinavia, meant that

common standards could offer economies of scale in its pan-European operations.

Once a company as large as Canal Plus had shifted camp, other pay TV operators found it difficult to defend a proprietary approach to standards. Several were themselves facing competition in their home market. BSkyB in the UK for example was moving from being the sole supplier of analogue pay TV to operating in a digital market where DTT and digital cable offered alternative distribution systems which might well use different standards.

Digital TV companies had a powerful additional incentive to agree on common standards. As set-top boxes incorporated more and more processing power and memory, and many of the functions of the computer (including Internet access, interactivity, a return link to the broadcaster, and substantial storage on a hard disk), there was every chance that the standard which might prevail might be the scaled-down Windows CE operating system on offer from Microsoft, rather than one controlled by a broadcaster. The threat that the dominant proprietary standard in the set-top box could come from US computing rather than the European TV world played an important part in persuading some digital TV players to move towards common European standards. It is too soon to know whether the result will be the ending of the current competition between rival and incompatible proprietary conditional access systems.

Conclusion

Unlike more contentious areas such as Television Without Frontiers or media ownership control, Commission regulation of conditional access was inhibited more by a lack of will than a lack of power or legitimacy. True, the Commission's reticence to intervene reflected that of the Member States.[17] But it is also the case that if the Commission had been less constrained by past failures and had placed a higher premium on interoperability and common standards than on following industry consensus, it might have devised a regulatory framework to minimise the anti-competitive potential of early digital pay TV systems. In time, most policy-makers and many broadcasters were persuaded that benefits would flow either from a more vigorous approach to regulation or from common standards. The Commission's reluctance to follow either path in 1994–5 was indicative of a deeper trend in EU policy-making, where a technocratic approach to decision-making often placed undue emphasis on obtaining industry endorsement for key policy initiatives.

5 The impact of European competition policy on digital broadcasting

Introduction

The operation of European Community competition policy has already had more of an impact on Europe's broadcasting industry than any of the European regulation specifically targeted at the sector. Enforcement of the competition provisions of the Treaty of Rome already has – and will continue to have – a considerable influence on the behaviour of Europe's public service broadcasters, whilst preventing several commercial digital TV alliances and dictating the shape of others.[1] Competition policy is also playing an increasingly important part in deciding two of the key issues in digital TV: the way in which TV sports rights are sold and how access to conditional access systems is granted.

This chapter examines some of these areas of activity and argues that EU competition policy will continue to be the dominant mode of European-level intervention in the digital TV market for some time to come. This position is not based on any normative preference for competition policy.[2] Instead it reflects the realities of EU policy-making, where the difficulties in reaching political consensus over broadcasting regulation, and the wide discrepancies between the ways in which EU broadcasting directives have been implemented at national level, are to some extent counterbalanced by the quasi-judicial powers exercised by DG IV, the Competition Directorate.

The chapter examines four different areas of intervention by DG IV. In the first three such areas DG IV's decisions have been largely accepted by Member States and will have a lasting impact on the shape of the digital broadcasting market. They include: the increasing importance of the competition framework in deciding how key rights will be bought and sold in the EU audio-visual sector; the issue of access to conditional access systems and digital distribution networks and the development of the so-called 'essential facility principle'; and the decisions of the Merger Task Force on key digital alliances. The fourth area of intervention concerns DG IV's attempts in 1998 to arbitrate on disputes between commercial and public broadcasters and to develop guidelines for the funding of public service broadcasting, and is unusual for the degree of opposition it has aroused from the majority of Member States. Uniquely perhaps, this is an area where a narrow reliance on the competition powers of the Treaty would have the effective of simultaneously reducing the freedom of manoeuvre of all EU Member States.

Access to broadcast rights

Community competition policy has aimed, in the broadcasting sector as in others, to 'keep markets open and prevent barriers to market entry'. In the late 1980s, as the broadcasting sectors of several countries started to evolve from monopoly to competition, it was perhaps inevitable that it was the previous monopolists, the public service broadcasters, who found themselves the focus of many of the complaints to the Commission.

Conflicts often focused around access to broadcast rights as new entrants tried to acquire attractive content with which to fill their schedules. DG IV was keen that the new broadcasters should 'have appropriate access to attractive programmes', and acted to prevent 'programme material being withdrawn from the market as a result of collective long-term agreements' (EC 1990: 20). The agreement between the German public broadcaster ARD and MGM/United Artists, whereby ARD acquired German rights to 1,350 films for an average of fifteen years, was one of the first rights deals to be challenged by the Commission. In a 1989 decision the Commission obliged ARD to alter its agreement with MGM/United Artists, so that other broadcasters could acquire sub-licences which allowed them to show the same films during the period of the contract. A similar case arose when Screensport, a satellite TV sports channel, complained that the EBU's collective purchase of sports rights disadvantaged any non-EBU members who were attempting to launch TV sports channels. DG IV backed the Screensport challenge, but in the end approved the EBU agreement subject to a sub-licensing agreement whereby non-EBU members could have access to delayed highlights of the EBU purchased rights (Pons 1996, Collins 1994b: 147–9).[3]

Some have seen these cases as evidence that in the late 1980s and early 1990s DG IV was engaged in an 'implacable pursuit of European public service broadcasters', and that its liberalising and deregulatory instincts underestimated the contribution that vigorous and independent public service broadcasters could make to providing pluralistic sources of information (Collins 1994b: 155–6).[4] It is true that the way in which the Treaty of Rome is drafted is not particularly sympathetic to public enterprises, including public service broadcasters, and while the Protocol on Public Service Broadcasting adopted at Amsterdam in 1997 goes some way towards redressing this situation, its interpretation is still open to question.[5] Even in the 1980s however, the challenge from DG IV was not unremitting. In the Screensport case, the Commission indicated to EBU members that sub-licensing offered one way around the problem and the

EBU won an exemption on that basis, at least in part, because of the recognition by DG IV that the universal availability offered by public service broadcasters was in the public interest.[6]

Since his arrival as Competition Commissioner in 1992, van Miert has gone out of his way to emphasise the wider context of competition policy:

> Let me make one thing clear straight away: the application of competition principles is not an end in itself. Competition policy is a tool which can be used to help achieve the fundamental aims of the Community. The Commission's competition policy does not operate in a vacuum. It has to take account of its repercussions in other areas of Commission policy, such as industrial policy, regional policy, social policy and the environment.
>
> (van Miert 1995)

This approach created a more favourable environment for public intervention generally, and led van Miert to endorse the role played by public broadcasters in preserving media pluralism.[7] This change in personnel and priorities in the competition sphere coincided with a new phase in the development of the European TV market. By the mid-1990s commercial TV was well and truly established right across Europe. The most serious barriers to entry were those posed by the first movers in digital TV who, by their collective purchase of rights and attempts at monopoly control of conditional access systems and other gateways, appeared to be effectively foreclosing on the digital pay TV market in respect of future competitors. DG IV's concerns moved away from the rights purchasing practices of public service broadcasters towards the policies of pay broadcasters and, increasingly, the selling arrangements of the sporting bodies themselves. Van Miert reflected this new approach in noting that:

> television markets in the EU are marked by two phenomena. Firstly, an increasing concentration of market power in the hands of a limited number of nationally very powerful private companies. Secondly, increasing consolidation between market players in both national and European ventures. The challenge is to avoid the creation of de facto private monopolists.
>
> (Ibid.)

Among the problems he identified were access to conditional access systems, and the way in which programme rights were controlled in the digital pay TV market:

> Consumers are willing to pay to view recently released quality films and to see their favourite sports. The prices paid by pay-television broadcasters for these rights reflect this. Demand for these services is proven

and will, at least in the short term, be the driver for all other forms of more innovative digital services . That is why we will continue to take a close interest in contracts between film studios and sports bodies on the one hand, and pay-television broadcasters on the other. No one operator can be allowed to control the broadcasting of first-release films and sports for an excessive period of time. We will examine the scope and length of exclusivity granted in these contracts. Our aim is not only to ensure competition in the pay-television market, but also to ensure competition in the emerging digital services market.

(van Miert 1997a)

Sport, as one of the key drivers of digital pay television, has taken up a more prominent position in Commission thinking on audio-visual policy in recent years. The 1997 revisions to Television Without Frontiers, which authorised and granted mutual recognition to national lists of protected events, were passed partly in response to fears that only pay broadcasters would be able to buy the key live TV sports rights, with the consequence that the majority of the population would no longer see them. Sporting bodies were increasingly the beneficiaries of a much more competitive market for their TV rights. Table 5.1 shows how the estimated prices paid for football rights in Europe's major countries rose by up to 229 per cent between 1995 and 1998. The prices paid by European broadcasters for coverage of the Olympics rose by 900 per cent over an eight year period, whilst that paid by UK broadcasters for Premier League football increased by more than 1,000 per cent between 1991 and 1996 (BBC 1996, 1998). As TV rights prices rose, players were paid more, and sports clubs and sporting bodies became large and highly profitable businesses, with some football clubs even being floated on the stock exchange. The Commission then began to turn its attention to the question of who owned the rights to games, whether it was the teams themselves or the relevant league or association. The collective selling of sports rights was challenged, along with the length and terms of sporting rights contracts, by the Commission and, in the UK, by the Office of Fair Trading (OFT) who referred the BSkyB/BBC/Premier League contract to the Restrictive Trades Practices Court, as well as by courts in the Netherlands and Germany.

In the space of a few weeks between December 1997 and January 1998, DG IV issued a formal complaint to FIFA, world soccer's governing body, that its licensing system for football agents was unacceptable, challenged FIFA's right to demand that home games be played at the 'home' club, started an investigation into the allegedly monopolistic way in which the Federation Internationale de l'Automobile (FIA) had granted an exclusive twenty-five year contract to Bernie Ecclestone's Formula One Holdings, and warned the German Football Federation that plans by the German Government to exempt football from German competition rules would be unacceptable (*Financial Times*, 23 January 1998).[8] All these interventions

Table 5.1 Estimated value of football rights per season, 1994–5 and 1997–8 (in $ million)

	1994–95	*1997–98*	*% increase*
France	76	223	193
Germany	130	428	229
Italy	152	315	107
Spain	97	291	200
UK	234	385	76

Source: Murroni and Irvine 1998 23, based on Screen Digest, September 1997

by the Commission were highly political, and had the potential to have a more rapid and dramatic effect on the digital pay TV market within Member States than most regulatory measures devised in Brussels. The apparent willingness of DG IV to challenge the length and exclusivity of contracts, as well as the rationale for collective purchasing of rights, had far-reaching implications. As digital TV develops and the pressures for control of valuable sports rights increases, there is every indication that DG IV will take an even stronger interest in the ways in which sports rights are bought, sold and televised (Pons 1998a, Wachtmeister 1998, Schaub 1998).[9]

Access to digital networks, 'bottlenecks', and the essential facility doctrine

At the same time as the Commission was involved in regulating access to conditional access systems, through the Advanced Television Standards Directive, DG IV was also considering the potential offered by the new digital networks to limit competition:

> the post-monopoly and future multimedia environment is likely to be characterised by situations where firms singly or jointly control facilities – such as networks, conditional access systems or critical software interfaces – which may provide an essential route to customers. Access and interconnection agreements may . . . generate substantial collusive behaviour and market foreclosure, as well as abuse of dominant positions. The non-discriminatory access to essential facilities on reasonable terms is of central importance in this context.
>
> (EC 1996f: 22–3)

The reference to access to 'essential facilities' was highly significant. The Commission had first applied the 'essential facilities' doctrine in the 1980s in some key decisions applying the provisions of Article 86, regarding abuse of a dominant position, to resolve a series of cases where ferry companies were denied equal access to ports owned by rival ferry operators. The most celebrated such case centred around Holyhead where Sealink was both the owner of Holyhead port and B and I's only competitor on the Holyhead to Dublin route. Since B and I's berth was in the mouth of the harbour, each time a Sealink vessel passed the B and I ship had to stop loading or unloading and lift the ramp connecting the ship to the dock. Sealink then altered its sailings so that B and I's loading was interrupted even more frequently. The Commission decided that Sealink could not discriminate in this way in favour of its own car-ferry activities. Defining an essential facility as 'a facility or infrastructure without access to which competitors cannot provide services to their customers', it ruled that a dominant company which both owned or controlled and itself used such a facility 'and which refuses its competitors access to that facility, or grants access to competitors only on terms less favourable than those which it gives to its own services, thereby placing competitors at a competitive disadvantage, infringes Article 86'. According to John Temple Lang the duty to provide access to a facility may arise where a competitor can show that:

- A refusal of access would have serious effects on competition.
- That the competitor cannot obtain the goods or the services elsewhere and cannot be expected to build or invent them itself.
- And that the dominant company has no legitimate business justification – such as limited capacity – for the refusal (Temple Lang 1994: 262, 283–4, 286).[10]

One of the key questions in the communications sector relates to how the 'essential facilities' doctrine can be applied to the terms on which access is granted to conditional access decoders, and to digital networks.[11] Commission officials have alluded to this question, but without resolving it conclusively in advance of any specific complaint about denial of access (Ungerer 1995, Temple Lang 1996a, 1996b and 1997).[12] The outcome of any such challenge will depend on the detailed circumstances surrounding the case. According to Temple Lang, the factors that might weigh in any decision could include: whether or not the conditional access system includes a common interface; whether alternative competing conditional access systems on, for example, cable networks had been successfully established; and whether a 'normal reasonably efficient competitor following an appropriate strategy could be expected to provide an alternative facility or system itself' (Temple Lang 1997: 70).

The Commission's adoption of a Notice on the Application of the Competition Rules to Access Agreements in the Telecommunications Sector on 31 March 1998 marked a dramatic move forwards in developing an essential facilities doctrine which can be applied 'in a consistent way across the sectors involved in the provision of new services, and in particular to access issues and gateways'. Whilst the guidelines were framed with the telecoms sector in mind there is a clear intention to apply them to areas such as digital broadcasting where comparable access problems arise (EC 1998e and press release IP/98/309, Ungerer 1998a and 1998b).[13]

The 'essential facilities' doctrine can provide valuable support for parties who are refused access, or access on reasonable terms, to conditional access systems. But the importance of the telecommunications access guidelines is that they have the potential to reduce the defect of all EU competition law, which is that decisions can take years, and by the time they are received the aggrieved party may already have gone out of business.[14] Adequate regulation – along the lines of the DTI and OFTEL implementation of the Advanced TV Standards Directive in the UK – has the advantage of deterring anti-competitive behaviour in advance, rather than leaving aggrieved parties to seek retrospective redress from a potentially powerful, but generally slow EU competition policy framework. The telecommunications access notice, together with subsequent reflections by DG IV officials on the regulation of a range of digital 'bottlenecks' that might threaten competition without necessarily meeting all the requirements to be defined as 'essential facilities', suggests that DG IV is looking for a much closer connection than before between the roles played by competition policy and sector specific regulation (Coates 1998, Ungerer 1998a and 1998b).[15]

One alternative route that DG IV could pursue in ensuring access through these key gateways would be to require structural separation of vertically integrated content suppliers and network operators. This radical step would reduce the incentives for anti-competitive behaviour by integrated broadcasters/network operators, and remove the need for much of the detailed and intrusive regulation of prices and access terms currently used to ensure fair, reasonable and non-discriminatory access. Interestingly, DG IV has already proposed structural separation in cases where dominant telecommunications operators also own the dominant cable infrastructure. Cable networks were cross-owned by the incumbent telecommunications operator in more than half of the EU's Member States in 1997 and DG IV argued that for these situations the existing 'accounting separation . . . [required by the Cable Directive] . . . has been shown to be insufficient to facilitate pro-competitive development in the multi-media sector' (Ungerer 1998b, EC 1998f). Whilst these Commission proposals for structural separation focus on the telecoms sector, a similar approach could also be used if vertically integrated broadcasters/network operators were ever deemed to exercise the degree of control over digital television that some dominant telecoms operators currently hold over the cable sector in their countries (see Table 5.2).

Merger control

One of the most dramatic ways in which EU competition policy has intervened in the audio-visual field is through its vetting, and occasional vetoing

Table 5.2 Telecommunications companies and cable networks

Country	Operator*	Subscribers**
Italy	Stream	100%
Portugal	TV Cabo	97%
Germany	Deutsche Telekom	93%
Denmark	Tele Danmark Kabel	75%
Sweden	Telia Kabel-TV	61%
Switzerland	Cablecom	47%
Norway	Telenor Avidi	34%
France	France Telecom Cable	21%
Netherlands	NV Casema	20%
Finland	Telecom Finland Cable	16%
UK	BT Cable Services	1%

Source: Wall Street Journal, 9 December 1997
* Cable operator owned by dominant phone company
** Percentage of national cable subscribers connected to its network.

of mergers. Unlike the rest of EU competition policy, which has offered retrospective remedies, under the Merger Regulations the Commission can veto proposed mergers before they go ahead. Since the move to digital broadcasting has been accompanied by a wave of mergers and strategic alliances among the major companies in the European media and communications industries, it is hardly surprising that an increasing number of media mergers have been referred to the Merger Task Force (MTF). As noted above, five of the ten negative decisions taken by the MTF since 1989 have concerned the audio-visual sector (Pons 1998a: 8). Not all of their decisions were welcomed by the Member State, or States, in which the companies were based.

The German MSG Media Services joint venture between Bertelsmann, Kirch and Deutsche Telekom for the provision of technical services for pay TV was rejected in 1994.[16] In 1995, two other mergers, Nordic Satellite Distribution and the alliance between Holland Media Group/RTL/Veronica and Endemol, were also rejected.[17] A proposed joint venture – between the Spanish State Telephone operator Telefonica and Sogecable (Canal Plus Spain) to create Cablevision – was initially approved by the Spanish authorities, who decided that the merger did not require notification to DG IV. DG IV disagreed and in November 1996, after Cablevision had been trading for several months, the Commission rejected the merger on the grounds that it would lead to the strengthening or creation of positions of dominance for Telefonica and Canal Plus Spain. Three days later Telefonica and Sogecable abandoned their venture and Cablevision was left under the control of Sogecable. Other mergers, such as that between Bertelsmann's broadcast arm UFA and CLT, and the revised

Holland Media Group/RTL venture, were given permission to go ahead (Pons 1996: 6, EC 1997a: 50–1). More recently a major German digital venture has been vetoed, and far reaching conditions imposed on two UK-based digital alliances.

Many of these cases were acutely politically sensitive, because they often involved either state run companies, national champions or companies with very close relations to their national governments. Karel van Miert identified a common theme:

> The original versions of the Media Services Group (MSG) in Germany, and Nordic Satellite Distribution (NSD) agreement in the Nordic market had to be blocked because they involved, amongst other things, network operators, enjoying essentially gatekeeper functions extending dominance into related broadcasting and content markets. With the same basic concerns in mind we launched investigations into the plans of national telecom operators in countries like Spain and Italy to venture into the cable-TV market. And we will carefully examine the new venture between BT and BSkyB in the UK . . . [i.e. BIB, see below] The issue is the control of the gates between the components of the future systems.
>
> (van Miert 1997a)

Often cases focused primarily on national rather than Community markets. Only with Nordic Satellite was the cross-frontier dimension clearly to the fore.

MSG

In the MSG case in 1994, Bertelsmann, Taurus of the Kirch Group, and Deutsche Telekom proposed the creation of a joint venture called MSG Media Services GmbH (MSG) which would handle technical, business and administrative requirements, including conditional access and subscriber management systems for pay TV in Germany. The Commission's rejection of the joint venture (only the second ever such rejection since the merger regulations had come into force in 1989) was based on the view that MSG would have a dominant position in three key markets. First – because of the large programme catalogue which Kirch controlled – it would dominate the market for pay TV. Second, it would create a 'durable dominant position' in the provision of administrative and technical services for pay TV, such as conditional access and Subscriber Management Systems. This was because of the existing subscriber base that Bertelsmann and Kirch controlled through their joint investment in Germany's only pay TV company, Premiere, and the likelihood that, once MSG had established an extensive network of rented conditional access systems, others would find it difficult to enter the market. And third, DT's near total dominance of

German cable would be protected and strengthened by MSG. The Commission's view was that if the merger went ahead it was 'scarcely conceivable' that competing companies would be able to enter the pay TV market in Germany. The first-mover advantage that the MSG venture would acquire – through the establishment of a conditional access standard for digital television by a company also involved in supplying programmes – was judged to be substantial since households were only likely to want to acquire a single decoder. Undertakings offered by the parties to the Commission were insufficient to allay fears that the alliance would act as an obstacle to others entering the market and thus each partner to it would eliminate the risk of competition from the others (Temple Lang 1996a: 20–2).

While the arguments being developed within the Commission for EU-wide media ownership controls were linked to the supposedly increased trans-frontier nature of European broadcasting, the Commission's MSG ruling was striking because of its focus on the impact the merger would have *within* the German national pay TV market. The Commission recognised that European television operated primarily within national markets, and that the factors which both caused and reinforced that situation, namely 'language barriers and regulatory differences in particular will continue to exist'.[18] Intervention was justified as much because of the inadequacy of national regulation as it was by application of the more conventional test of the cross-frontier nature of the activity. As one Commission official commented, the MSG 'case demonstrates that new media cases ... tend to escape the traditional national legislation designed to control the media and assure pluralism, thus giving Community competition policy, as an inherently Europe-wide mechanism, a central role' (Ungerer 1995: 58).

Scandinavian and Dutch alliances

Nordic Satellite Distribution (NSD) was the first case after MSG to be vetoed by DG IV. NSD brought together three major companies in the Scandinavian market to transmit satellite TV programmes, either for direct-to-home reception or for reception via a cable network. The Commission vetoed NSD on the grounds that it would have created or strengthened dominant positions in each of three different markets: in the supply of satellite capacity to Scandinavia, in the operation of cable TV networks in Denmark, and in the market for the distribution of pay TV and other encrypted channels to satellite TV subscribers. The effect would be that 'both the downstream market positions (cable TV operations and pay TV), and those upstream (satellite transponders, provision of programmes) would have been mutually reinforcing. The parties would have achieved such strong positions that they would have been able to foreclose on the Nordic satellite television market for competitors. Essentially, NSD would have obtained a 'gatekeeper' function for the Nordic market for satellite television broadcasting (Ungerer

1995: 59, EC 1996f: 49). NSD proposed a compromise that would have given competitors improved access to the satellite transponders they controlled, but failed to persuade the Commission that the deal should go ahead.

The third important case in which a merger was prohibited was the Holland Media Group (HMG) case involving the three companies, RTL, Veronica, and Endemol. This case was unusual, first, in centring on the control of programme content, and on competition in the TV broadcasting and advertising markets, rather than on the control of access technologies and delivery systems, and second, because it was the Dutch Government which requested a Commission investigation, on the grounds that the merger would affect trade between Member States. Under the joint venture, RTL transferred its two Dutch channels to HMG, Veronica provided a third commercial channel, and Endemol, the largest independent producer of TV programmes in the Netherlands, would supply programmes to HMG.

The Commission concluded that HMG would have at least 40 per cent of the market for free-to-air television in the Netherlands, and over 60 per cent of advertising revenues. Endemol's position in the production market would be reinforced, and its participation could prevent other programme producers selling to what would be the largest broadcaster in the Netherlands (EC 1996f: 49–50). Although the venture was primarily concerned with analogue broadcasting, the Commission asked 'why the parties need such a strong position in the Dutch TV market to the detriment of other Dutch broadcasters', going on to point out that: 'given the combined strength of the parties, HMG could become the only major player in the future digital TV. This could even be counterproductive to the development of digital TV in the Netherlands' (*Official Journal* no. L 134: 32ff., 5 June 1996, paragraph 110).

In 1996 the Commission approved a revised HMG alliance, where Endemol had withdrawn and where the proposed transformation of RTL 5 from a general entertainment channel into a news channel would leave HMG in control of only two general entertainment channels and 50 per cent of the advertising market. In the Commission's view these changes 'removed the competition problems in both the TV production market and the TV advertising market' (EC 1997a: 50).

UK digital TV – British Digital Broadcasting (BDB) and British Interactive Broadcasting (BIB)

In 1997 two alliances for the launch of digital TV in the UK came under Commission scrutiny.[19] The case of BDB arose after the UK regulator (the ITC) had advertised for applicants for the first digital terrestrial multiplexes in the UK. Two consortia had applied, and the ITC decided to award the franchise to BDB, an alliance of two ITV companies, Carlton and Granada, together with BSkyB. Before awarding the franchise the ITC asked for the advice of the European Commission. This was a rare case where 'a national non-competition authority . . . formally sought the advice of the Commission under Community antitrust law, [and] the Commission's advice has determined the outcome'. The Commission view was that BSkyB's participation might strengthen and extend the dominant position of BSkyB in pay TV (a view shared by the UK telecommunications regulator, OFTEL), and the ITC awarded the licence to BDB on condition that BSkyB's equity participation in BDB ceased (Temple Lang 1997: 32). This was not too punishing for BSkyB since the remaining partners were then obliged to buy out their share in the joint venture (for a reported £75 million) and BSkyB was still guaranteed a five-year programme supply agreement with BDB. A complaint to the Commission by the only other applicant to the ITC was rejected by DG IV, but only after the ITC had imposed additional conditions on BDB's licence. Programme supply agreements were to be limited to five years; BDB was obliged to support the use of open technical standards on integrated TV sets; and conditions were imposed to ensure that, given Granada's 11 per cent equity stake in BSkyB, BDB should not be prevented from competing with BSkyB.[20]

British Interactive Broadcasting (BIB), a joint venture for the launch of digital satellite TV and interactive services, was also submitted to DG IV in 1997. BIB is the first of a new brand of digital alliances which extend way beyond the traditional media sector. BSkyB and British Telecom each own 32.5 per cent of BIB, while HSBC/Midland Bank owns 20 per cent and Matsushita – the consumer electronics company – owns 15 per cent. The combination of a dominant telecommunications operator with the UK's dominant pay TV operator, and the use of a heavily subsidised proprietary standard set-top box for delivery of a wide range of interactive services, means that BIB might reasonably raise more competition concerns than in the case of BDB (Marsden 1997: 21). On the other hand, unlike the pro- posed German alliance which would have dominated all digital delivery systems in Germany, BIB will face competition in the UK digital pay TV market from digital terrestrial and cable services. This may have guided the thinking behind DG IV's preliminary approval for BIB in May 1998, which was made conditional on guarantees that other companies would be granted access to BIB's set-top boxes and related software, that BT sever their links with the cable industry through the sale of their franchises in Westminster and Milton Keynes, and that BIB create a separate subsidiary for the business of box subsidy from the subsidiary engaged in the supply of interactive services (EC 1998g, Commission Press Release 23 October 1998, and *Wall Street Journal* 21 May 1998). These were far-reaching condi- tions and the provisions on timely access to specifications for the BIB set-top box and related software, in particular, went far beyond the provi- sions of the 1995 Advanced TV Standards Directive. Whether or not these conditions achieve the Commission's aims of preventing any strengthening of BSkyB's position in the pay TV market, and of ensuring that the creation of BIB does not eliminate competition in the supply of interactive services, is too soon to say. One of the requirements imposed on BIB by the

Commission, namely that digital satellite TV customers could buy a sub-sidised BIB set-top box for £200, without being under any obligation to take any of BSkyB's pay TV channels, could ironically place BIB at an advantage over its terrestrial competitor, BDB (now trading as On Digital), since DTT consumers are still obliged to commit to purchasing DTT pay services or otherwise pay the full, £400 cost of a DTT set-top box.

MSG II

In January 1998 the Commission opened an in-depth investigation into its most controversial case since that of MSG in 1994. Once again the pro-posed alliance involved Bertelsmann, Kirch, Premiere and Deutsche Telekom and many dubbed this new case MSG II. After the Commission's vetoing of MSG there had been a period of turmoil with a series of alliances being formed and then abandoned. Kirch entered an alliance with BSkyB and tried to launch its own digital TV package, DF1. But the high cost of the Kirch set-top box (the D-Box retailed for between £400–500), regulatory objections from the majority of Länder regulators to granting DF1 cable distribution, the large choice of free-to-air channels available in the German market, and a rival analogue pay TV service offered by Premiere, all led to disappointing results.[21] Having been the first digital pay TV venture to launch in Germany, by July 1997 after one year of opera-tion DF1 only had 30,000 subscribers as against forecasts of 200,000. Kirch had committed itself to spending up to ten billion DM on acquiring long term rights to Hollywood film rights, and by the end of 1997 it was facing pre-dicted losses of over one billion DM. BSkyB pulled out from the venture, and speculation was rife that digital TV might bankrupt Kirch.

'MSG II' seemed to offer a way through these problems. Kirch would dissolve its DF1 digital package and merge it, along with its specialist sports channel DSF, with the new Premiere Digital service, thus granting Kirch potential access to about 1.5 million Premiere analogue subscribers, and Premiere access to the rights held by Kirch. Premiere would use the Kirch conditional access system, the D-Box, thereby removing the threat of a hardware war between two rival systems. DT's involvement guaranteed dis-tribution on the German cable network, as well as a single set-top box for digital cable and satellite. All three companies were to share control of the Kirch owned technical services company, Beta Research, which provided conditional access and subscriber management.

If MSG II had been allowed, it would have created the single most pow-erful digital TV player in any single national market, with control of key rights, access to the all-important German cable network, and a single pro-prietary conditional access system across all the available digital delivery systems. Hence the deep suspicion with which DG IV viewed the venture. In December 1997 Commissioner van Miert warned that: 'These three companies are trying to create a pay-TV monopoly' (*Wall Street Journal*

19–20 December 1997). Even before their full investigation started, the Commission banned Premiere/DF1 from selling the D-Box set-top box to any new customers, on the grounds that the marketing campaign which promoted the D-Box as the new German standard effectively pre-empted any Commission decision (Commission Press release IP/98/77 23 January 1998).

The Commission's decision to prohibit the deal (in May 1998) was prompted by two main concerns. First it decided that the merger between Bertelsmann, Kirch and Premiere would have an adverse impact on the market for pay TV. The merger would replace the competing services of DF1 and Premiere with a single Premiere pay TV service, with a dominant position in the market for pay TV in Germany and the German language market. The very attractiveness of the deal for the participants – that it allowed the combination of Premiere's subscription base with the programme libraries of Bertelsmann, and above all Kirch – was seen by the Commission as preventing the development of an alternative pay TV broadcaster in Germany. Worse, Premiere 'would permanently become the only pay-TV and marketing platform in Germany which could be in a position to determine the conditions under which other broadcasters could enter the pay-TV market'.

Second, Beta Digital would dominate the market for technical services to pay TV (essentially conditional access systems). One of the strengths of the joint venture – that all cable and satellite delivered pay TV would use the proprietary conditional access technology of Beta Digital – put the participants in a very strong position. In addition the proprietary nature of the Beta Digital system – the D-Box – meant that other operators could only enter the market through a licence granted by Beta Digital. The joint control of Beta Digital by the three parties allowed them to control who received licences in Germany to use the conditional access system, and to control the future development of that system. This was a serious impediment to competition in the pay TV market generally. The Commission was particularly concerned that in the cable sector it placed DT in a position to control entry by other independent cable operators (Commission Press release IP/98/477 27 May 1998, *Financial Times* 28 May 1997).

The Commission veto only occurred after weeks of negotiations with the parties. The Commission had been seeking some way in which the chances of other operators entering the German market might be increased. Under pressure, the parties had agreed to bring third party shareholders into Beta Research, and that 25 per cent of the pay TV film rights held by Kirch should be made available to other broadcasters. But while Kirch accepted the Commission's insistence that independent cable companies should be allowed to sell their own PPV packages either alongside or including those of Premiere, Bertelsmann refused this concession, leading to the Commission decision to veto the deal (*Financial Times* 28 May 1998). Bertelsmann was the stronger of the two TV partners, and had less reason to make concessions than Kirch.

The impact of EU merger policy on the broadcasting sector

Four conclusions can be drawn from DG IV's application of the merger regulations to the emerging digital broadcasting sector.

First, DG IV's recognition of the largely national nature of European TV markets has not proved an obstacle to intervention through competition policy. In the HMG case intervention in a national market was justified on the grounds that although:

> the relevant geographic market was the Netherlands . . . the [merger] . . . affected trade between Member States because it would influence conditions for new entrants on the Dutch TV broadcasting market and would have an impact on the acquisition of foreign-language programmes and because the joint venture itself is based in Luxembourg, where two of its channels are 'licensed' by the Grand Duchy of Luxembourg.
>
> (EC 1996f: 50)

The first two arguments are particularly interesting, since they could justify Community intervention in almost *any* case of substantial media mergers within a national market, even if they did not meet the merger regulation threshold. It will be interesting to see whether the HMG case sets a trend for increased intervention in the future.

Second, the way in which the merger regulations have been applied reveals the application of increasingly sophisticated market analysis. In its 1990 Communication on Audio-visual Policy the Commission identified three distinct markets within the audio-visual sector where competition problems had arisen, namely: the production and distribution of cinema and television films, the market for TV broadcasts, and the market for satellite broadcasting services (EC 1990). Since then, market definitions under the merger regulations have tended to multiply, and hence narrow. The Commission has now identified a wide range of markets including free-to-air television, pay TV, technical and administrative services for pay TV, access to satellite capacity, cable television, and satellite broadcasting. Within the overall free television market, Commission decisions have also distinguished between general entertainment channels and thematic channels, and focused particularly on sports channels. This increasingly sophisticated approach has already allowed DG IV to identify problems of dominance that would not previously have been caught up in the application of competition policy.

Third, the treatment of merger cases has shown a particularly keen awareness of the ways in which vertically integrated companies controlling access to content, access to distribution, and access to the customer through conditional access and subscription management systems can foreclose competition in the emerging digital market. Even where the parties involved have offered various behavioural guarantees, as happened with the MSG and NSD cases, the Commission has been unwilling to allow the mergers to go ahead, in part at least because of the difficulty in policing such guarantees and the limited resources available to the Commission to do so. The Commission's concerns have been well expressed by Commissioner van Miert:

> We must move towards multi-media without creating new communications super monopolies . . . we must be careful that multi-media will not mean new super monopolies. We need many multi-media companies not only one. We need more horizontal competition, in order to be able to allow more upstream and downstream vertical integration and convergence. This is the way in which we can reap the benefits of digital technologies.
>
> (van Miert 1997a)[22]

Finally, these cases, and in particular the 1998 MSG II decision, confirmed the intensity of the politics surrounding digital TV mergers, and the unique ability of DG IV under Karel van Miert – among all the other national and EU decision-making processes – to withstand such pressure. Chancellor Kohl's office left Jacques Santer and Karel van Miert in no doubt that they expected a green light for MSG II. Karel van Miert also faced pressure from several Commissioners (notably Edith Cresson, Martin Bangemann, and Marcelino Oreja) to give the go-ahead (*Les Echos* 28 May 1998). It was only Bertelsmann's refusal to accept compromise solutions proposed by Kirch that persuaded the Commission to give its unanimous support to van Miert's veto, but that still left him having to face charges of putting back the progress of digital TV in Germany, and of possibly forcing one of Chancellor Kohl's closest friends, Leo Kirch, into at best a precarious financial position, and at worst bankruptcy. Had the joint venture been subject only to German law it seems certain that domestic political pressures would have led to its approval. Similarly, had the power to decide on the merger rested with the Council of Ministers it is likely that Chancellor Kohl would have mobilised sufficient support from other EU Heads of Government to ensure it went ahead. Uniquely, the combination of the EU Merger Regulations and a strong minded Competition Commissioner – who was not seeking a renewal of his term of office – had led to a decision about a largely domestic matter which flew in the face of the preferences of the most powerful politician in Europe.

Funding of public broadcasting

DG IV's involvement in disputes between commercial and public service broadcasters marked a rather more reluctant and even more controversial form of intervention.

The origins of DG IV's involvement go back to 1992 and 1993 when

Spanish, French and Portuguese (SIC) commercial broadcasters complained to the Commission about the public service broadcasters in their countries, each of which received a mix of advertising and public funding. Several of the commercial broadcasters alleged that this dual funding represented unfair competition for advertising revenues, that the public service obligations on the PSBs were inadequate, and that their receipt of licence fee revenues might constitute an illegal state aid. DG IV responded by commissioning a report on whether the public obligations of public service broadcasters could be costed, and producing a first draft of guidelines on public funding in the cultural area. These were discussed at an informal meeting of Member State representatives in 1995. The conclusion drawn from the consultants' report, however, was that any detailed costing of public service obligations was probably not possible, whilst the meeting with Member States' representatives produced no firm agreement on the way forward. Faced with this intellectually and politically difficult territory, DG IV delayed resolving the complaints, other than that against the Portugese broadcaster. This was relatively easily resolved, since the Portugese state only granted public funds to Portugese Television for very specific, narrowly defined, and tightly costed public service tasks.

During 1997 and 1998 two different developments occurred which made it clear that further delay would not be acceptable. First, the launch of new digital services by PSBs attracted the hostility of commercial companies. In Germany the Kinderkanal and Phoenix digital channels of ARD/ZDF attracted a complaint to DG IV from the German Association of Commercial Broadcasters (VPRT). In the UK, BSkyB complained to DG IV that the UK Government's approval of a new licence-fee funded BBC 'News 24' channel, initially distributed on analogue cable but intended for digital distribution later in 1998, represented an illegal use of state aid. And in Italy, a 1994 complaint from the Berlusconi-owned company Fininvest about the Italian Government's underwriting of the debts of the Italian public service broadcaster, RAI, was lodged again in 1998. Second, the Court of First Instance ruled in September 1998, that the length of DG IV's delay in resolving the complaints against the Spanish public broadcaster RTVE, was unacceptable, and that, after five years, a decision from DG IV was required urgently.[23]

By the autumn of 1998 DG IV needed to find a way of dealing with the growing file of complaints against PSBs and the increasingly tense atmosphere between public and commercial broadcasters over the launch of digital services meant that more complaints seemed inevitable. At the same time, it seemed clear that the Amsterdam Protocol on public service broadcasting had created some doubt over the extent to which competition policy could be brought into play in complaints against public service broadcasters.

It was perhaps with the aim of resolving these issues that officials from DG IV's State Aids Unit produced a completely new set of draft guidelines on the funding of public broadcasters. These were discussed at a meeting with Member State representatives in October 1998. Although these draft guidelines appeared to recognise the right of Member States under the Amsterdam Protocol to decide on the funding and remit of their PSBs, in fact they challenged this principle with the assertion that PSBs in receipt of advertising and licence-fee funding could not justify the showing of films, entertainment programmes or most sports coverage as part of their public service remit. Karel van Miert distanced himself from the draft guidelines, and when they were discussed with national representatives in October 1998 the majority view appeared to be that complaints against PSBs should be handled by the Commission on a case by case basis, rather than through the production of guidelines (*Financial Times* 21 October 1998).[24]

The wariness of Member States about any DG IV encroachment on the ways in which they chose to fund and organise public broadcasting was confirmed in November 1998. Culture and Audiovisual Ministers meeting in Vienna agreed a resolution on PSB. This was highly significant for its reaffirmation of the Amsterdam Protocol, together with its emphasis on the need for PSBs to offer a wide range of programming and reach a wide audience, and for PSBs to develop and diversify their activities in the digital age (Council of Ministers 1998). It seems likely that over the coming years DG IV will increasingly be called upon to arbitrate between the complaints of private broadcasters about the 'market distortion' caused by the existence of PSBs, and the belief of most Member States that public service broadcasting remains an essential part of their policies for the communications sector. This is the area where there is perhaps the greatest potential for conflict between the policies adopted by national governments and the way in which DG IV might interpret the competition provisions of the EC treaties.

Competition policy and sector-specific regulation

The observation at the beginning of this chapter – that EU competition policy has had a greater impact on the European digital TV market than any attempts at sector-specific regulation – is surprising but true. For example, DG IV's interest in whether the conditional access systems used in digital joint ventures included a common interface and its decision to ban further sales and marketing of the proprietary D-Box conditional access system in Germany whilst the Kirch/Bertelsmann joint venture was examined, went far beyond any action that would have been allowed under the Advanced TV Standards Directive.[25] The same was true of the conditions imposed on BIB by the Commission, and of those imposed by the ITC on the BDB licence, after 'consultation' with DG IV. In each case these went further than anything prescribed by the national or EU regulations in force. Generally, DG IV's interventions across the range of broadcasting issues have (with the exception of attempts to rule on the legitimacy of public funding for public broadcasting) been more readily accepted by Member States, than most attempts at sector-specific regulation.

The comparison between proposed European media ownership regulations and the application of the merger regulations offers the most striking contrast. Among the justifications for Community action on media ownership given in the 1992 Green Paper on Pluralism were that the use of Community competition policy to ensure pluralism would be both inappropriate and ineffective. The Green Paper accepted that keeping 'markets open to new entrants is good for pluralism' and that there was some convergence between competition policy and pluralism, but argued that at root they were 'fundamentally different things [since] effective competition is concerned with the economic behaviour of undertakings, while pluralism is concerned with the diversity of information' (EC 1992: 82–3). The distinction was undoubtedly true, but in practice the measures taken by DG IV to protect competition in the market, prevented a variety of threats to pluralism that would not have been picked up under any of the proposals for a European media ownership directive. Simple measures of audience share, or the number of channels held, of the kind favoured by media ownership regulation, whether at the national or the EU levels, would have had little if any impact on the merger regulation cases examined here. Whilst proposals to harmonise media ownership regulations across Europe depended on identifying occasionally tenuous barriers to cross-frontier trade, the competition authorities were instead more able to recognise the reality – that broadcasting markets were predominantly national or linguistic – without denying themselves the right to intervene to control potential threats to fair competition (and often pluralism as well). At the same time as DG XV was arguing that a media ownership harmonisation measure was needed because of EU competition law's inability to deal with pluralism issues, competition policy was itself evolving and paying more attention to some of the key issues of media control that would dominate the digital age.

The ways in which the application of competition policy evolved in the mid to late 1990s were significant for the digital TV market. Attempts to develop sector-specific regulation – whether through the ATVS Directive or the hapless Directive on Pluralism and Media Ownership – rarely found their mark as well as the operation of competition policy. EU attempts at regulation were more susceptible to being diluted after pressure – whether from industry or Member States – both when making their way through the Community's legislative processes or being implemented at the national level.[26] On occasions, proposals for directives affecting broadcasting were stopped in their tracks, as happened with the Pluralism Directive. In other cases, the drafting of directives such as those on Television Without Frontiers and Advanced Television Standards was sufficiently vague for the way in which they were implemented to be almost entirely dependent on the political will and the circumstances prevailing within each Member State.

The contrast between the efficacy of EU competition policy and sector-specific intervention should not be taken as indicating that competition policy offers the best possible way of regulating the media sector at EU level. There are many respects in which EU competition policy is either uncertain, untested in the media field (as with the essential facilities doctrine) or so slow as to be ineffective. On the other hand, there are areas where DG IV's intervention through, for example, the operation of the merger regulations or structural separation, can have a decisive impact on a sector. In part this reflects the quasi-judicial powers accorded to DG IV under the competition provisions of the Treaties. But it also reveals a political difference between the ways in which sector-specific regulation and competition policy are viewed. In an area as sensitive as broadcasting policy, Member States will tend to offer a strong defence of subsidiarity. For many Member States, EU intervention which is couched in terms of the economic goals of ensuring fair competition will usually be seen as more legitimate than regulation specifically targeted at the broadcasting sector.[27] EU sector-specific regulation of the broadcasting industry will, at best, be seen as constraining the autonomy of action of Member States in a politically sensitive area. At other times it will be seen as intervening in areas of such significance to national (or in the case of Germany, Länder) cultural, social, political and industrial policy concerns that most Member States will demand far greater evidence of the need for community action than in non-media-related sectors.

6 National approaches to digital regulation

The mid-1990s were marked by an unprecedented wave of reform of broadcasting and media policy in Europe's major Member States. France, Britain, Germany, Italy and Spain all made substantial changes to their broadcasting legislation. 1996 saw Britain's first new Broadcasting Act for six years, a major revision to Germany's Interstate Treaty on Broadcasting, and a Law on Information Superhighways in France which created a framework for pilot digital broadcasts. In 1997 Germany approved two new pieces of legislation on the regulation of new media services (one at the Federal level and one at the level of the Länder), while the UK's Telecoms Regulator, OFTEL, created Europe's most detailed regulatory framework for conditional access systems, and (together with the broadcasting regulator, the ITC) what was at the time the only set of guidelines anywhere in Europe on the operation of electronic programme guides. In France, after the initial reform proposals of Alain Juppé's government were abandoned because of electoral defeat, the socialist Government of Lionel Jospin went on to develop its own plans for broadcasting reform during the course of 1998–9.

This chapter provides an overview of the main regulatory reforms in Britain, France and Germany, and assesses the degree to which they led to a narrowing of differences between national regulatory approaches, or to a similar convergence between telecommunications and broadcasting regulation within each country.

National agendas for digital regulation

Politicians regularly cited technological change and digitalisation as necessitating reform of national media regulation. Yet whilst to a large extent the technology deployed across the three countries was similar, each responded in its own particular way. In practice the policy solutions adopted for digital television in France, Germany and the UK were dictated more by the unique political and market structures which prevailed in each country than by a common response to a single digital technology. Even in Britain and France, where there were changes in government while the regulatory framework was being devised or implemented, the approaches taken by opposing political parties within each individual country were generally closer than those between parties of the same political hue across different countries. Generally, politicians shared a common concern to maintain or reassert regulatory authority over a technology that threatened to escape their control, but the ways in which they attempted to do this reflected each country's particular traditions and circumstances, and the differing political sensitivities within that country.

France

France's approaches to digital regulation were coloured by her long-standing view of communications policy as a form of modern-day Maginot line, a vital defensive instrument in a war where France was threatened on both the industrial and cultural fronts. With cable and satellite TV penetration at only 10 per cent of Germany's, only half as many Internet users as the UK or Germany, and a position near the bottom of the European league table for mobile telephones France perceived herself as technologically backward and as ideologically isolated in international organisations such as the World Trade Organization (and increasingly on audio-visual matters within the EU as well), as well as culturally threatened by the popularity of American programming (Commissariat général du plan 1996: 35). For some time French policy had been directed at building strong national media companies and promoting modernisation of the country's infrastructure whilst keeping Hollywood at the greatest possible distance from French TV and cinema screens. With the advent of digital broadcasting traditional preoccupations were retained, but increased emphasis was placed on the industrial and economic – rather than purely cultural – aspects of broadcasting policy.

The first step in regulating for digital broadcasting was the Law on Information Superhighways (1996), designed with trial digital terrestrial television (DTT) and video-on-demand (VOD) services in mind (La Lettre du Conseil Supérieur de Audiovisuel, 74, November 1995). The new law exempted VOD services from complying with the normally rigorous transmission quotas for French and European content. VOD operators were, however, still obliged to meet quotas for investment in French and European production; to keep a certain proportion of French and European works in their catalogue; not to make films available before the video version was released; and not to interrupt films with advertising breaks. The consequence was that this 'liberalisation' measure left French VOD services subject to a more onerous regulatory regime than that of any other major European country, largely because of the way in which concern for the film industry had, once again, dictated the shape of French broadcasting legislation (See French Senate, Compte rendu des Débats, 19 February 1997).

Attempts at more far-reaching reform have had great difficulty in mobilising sufficient political support. The first such attempt was made in 1997 by the then Minister of Culture, Philippe Douste-Blazy. His 1997 Bill aimed to extend CSA control over programme content, and for the first time obliged satellite stations headquartered in France to comply with CSA licensing requirements. It also included provisions to implement the conditional access clauses of the EU TV Standards Directive, and to amend media ownership restrictions for satellite channels. Later, Catherine Trautmann, his Socialist successor as Minister of Culture, unveiled a far-reaching set of reform proposals at the beginning of 1998, which by the end of the year had proved sufficiently controversial to be cut in two, with a new bill dealing primarily with the public service channels. Initially scheduled for introduction to the National Assembly in December 1998, this was then postponed until 1999 (*Le Monde* 4 December 1998).

Media ownership

The 1994 Carignon Law had raised the ownership limit from 25 per cent of any terrestrial TV station to 49 per cent of the capital of one channel plus a maximum of 15 per cent of a second channel and up to 5 per cent of a third channel. Under the 1997 Bill the Conservative Government proposed to bring satellite channels within the media ownership rules for the first time, but with a much more liberal limit of 50 per cent of all the satellite channels receivable in France. The government argued that the 'international aspect of satellite broadcasting and the ease with which an operator can move abroad if the French regulations are too strong' called for a relaxed approach. But the bill would have allowed a single operator to own *all* the thirty-two French-language satellite channels and still have scope to own a further 30 per cent of the total of 153 satellite channels receivable in France. Pressure from its own supporters led the government to apply the 50 per cent limit solely to the French-language satellite channels (Levy 1997b: 32).

Socialists attacked the 1997 Bill for not introducing more restrictive media ownership controls. Several sought a return to the pre-1994 rules and some proposed a 10 per cent limit or the prohibition of all cross-ownership between companies dependent on public contracts and media firms. Either change would have transformed the French media landscape. The building and cable company Bouygues would have had to reduce their 39 per cent share in TF1, and the water and cable companies Lyonnaise des Eaux and Compagnie Générale des Eaux would have had to reduce their major share-holdings in M6 (34 per cent) and Canal Plus respectively (*Le Monde*, 5 and 10 June 1997, 17 December 1997, *Les Echos*, 10 June 1997).

When the Socialists came to power in May 1997 there was some fairly successful lobbying to persuade the new Minister for Culture and Communication, Catherine Trautmann, that targeting successful French companies might simply undermine the competitiveness of the French media industry (*Le Monde* 27 February 1998). In presenting her first attempt at a new broadcasting bill in January 1998 she appeared to have taken concerns about over-zealous controls on media ownership to heart, arguing that reducing ownership thresholds served little purpose, and that where there was a controlling shareholder it mattered little whether the share that was held was 25 per cent or 39 per cent. Similarly, according to Mme Trautmann, whilst the cross-ownership between utility and media companies was regrettable, action to reverse this trend would simply destabilise the French media sector, and weaken its ability to compete with English, German and American firms.

Instead she proposed a series of alternative safeguards for pluralism. Companies would have to create separate holding companies with their own board of management for their media interests. Directors of media companies would be prohibited from sitting on the board of the parent company, and the CSA was to be given a much more active supervisory role so far as media ownership was concerned (*Le Monde* 11 March 1998). The CSA would have to draw up an annual list of all companies controlling more than 25 per cent of any media market, while any proposed media take-over or increase in shareholding was to be subject to prior approval by the CSA. Media companies would also have to inform the CSA of any changes in their ownership structure, or of any links with companies involved in public contracts. Satellite operators would also have to reserve some capacity on their programme package for channels in which they had no ownership interest. Together these measures would have been significant but there were those – not least the CSA itself – who had doubts as to how easy it would be to implement them.

The immediate effect of these measures was to leave major companies freer than before to increase their media holdings. Shortly after the plans were announced the Compagnie Générale des Eaux took complete control of Havas, which in turn owned a 34 per cent share in Canal Plus (*New Media Markets* 5 February 1998). Yet major media companies continued their lobbying against what they regarded as excessive controls while some Socialists criticised the government for being too timid. The result was that no media ownership proposals were included in the bill that Mme Trautmann planned to introduce in December 1998, but which was then postponed until 1999 (*Le Monde* 11 November 1998, 22 April 1999).

Protecting competition rather than promoting culture: a new emphasis in French regulation?

Other elements of the initial Trautmann proposals focused on ensuring fair competition in France's highly successful digital satellite market.[1] The previous government had sought to end Canal Plus's monopoly of pay TV not only by persuading France Telecom and France Television to launch a digital satellite service – TPS – which could rival Canal Plus, but also by limiting the availability of France Television's digital services to TPS alone.

The Socialists, however, took a more consumer-focused view of competition, deciding that France Television's services should be available on all digital platforms, and announcing that satellite operators would be encouraged to make their decoders compatible, even if there was some uncertainty as to what specific action the government had in mind. Similarly, action was also promised over exclusive control of programme rights. In accordance with the new Article 3a of the Television Without Frontiers Directive, access to major – mainly sporting – events on free-to-air television was to be guaranteed under the law.[2] The Socialists' January 1998 plans also proposed limits on the acquisition of other exclusive programme rights – e.g. for PPV use – in order to encourage the development of a secondary market for films and other programmes. This measure seems to have been targeted at what some saw as Canal Plus's excessive control of the programme rights market in France, an issue that the CSA had drawn attention to in a 1997 report (CSA 1997).

Generally these initial proposals from the Socialists would, if implemented, mark a change in the emphasis of French broadcasting regulation. Cultural concerns were still regarded as important, but Mme Trautmann made it clear that she wanted to look beyond them as well, noting that: 'the cultural exception which has been hard won and remains under threat is not enough to ensure the development of our programme industry'. Great emphasis was placed on the economic importance of the audio-visual industry to France. When Mme Trautmann announced her reform proposals, her first observations were about the value of the sector in terms both of turnover (about 90 billion francs) and the 60,000 jobs it accounted for (Trautmann 1998). Under her January 1998 proposals the focus of the CSA's work was to move beyond detailed policing of production quotas and to work together with the Competition Authority, taking into account economic issues such as relations between independent producers and broadcasters, and the compatibility of, and terms of access to, conditional access systems.

The CSA's increased ability to intervene in the operation of the audio-visual market was offset, however, by a reduction in its traditional licensing powers. Henceforth only terrestrial broadcasters were to require detailed licences from the CSA while satellite and cable operators were to be granted licences in response to a simple declaration made to the CSA. If implemented, this change would amount to a very fundamental liberalisation in the French system, and would bring French procedures more closely into line with those operating in the UK where non-domestic satellite licences were issued by the ITC, more or less on demand.

The proposed change amounted to an admission that France's previous policies of operating much tougher cable and satellite licensing requirements than her neighbours were, for two reasons, no longer sustainable. First, this was because French-based operators had become increasingly tempted to consider relocating outside France in order to avoid French transmission and investment quotas. And second, because the European Commission had notified France that her refusal to issue cable retransmission licences to services already licensed elsewhere in the EU (such as Time Warner's London based channels TNT and Cartoon Network) was in contravention of the Television Without Frontiers Directive. The CSA's initial reaction – of removing licence requirements for foreign-based channels – was criticised by French operators as placing them at a disadvantage (*New Media Markets* 27 November 1997). Rather than retain tough licensing conditions which could only be applied to French-based channels, the Socialists decided to relax the licensing conditions altogether.[3] The trend towards 'competitive deregulation' had begun to impact on the country which – in the media field at least – had long been seen as one of the most resilient to its advances.[4]

The difficulties the Socialists faced during 1998 in deciding on the content of any major reform of commercial broadcasting reflected their increased awareness of the economic and political costs they might incur from pursuing their traditional approaches to broadcasting regulation. This was evident in their reluctance to impose media ownership limits, and even in their approach to the limited reform they proposed at the end of 1998 for France's public service broadcasters. At one level, the government's proposal to reduce the amount of advertising on France Television – from twelve to five minutes per hour – could be seen as an attempt to ensure that the public service broadcaster pursued 'purer' public service goals. (This proposal was later diluted to a phased reduction from twelve minutes to eight minutes per hour by 2001.) But the government must have been aware as well that any such measure would also have a beneficial impact on existing commercial broadcasters, primarily TF1 and M6. A change in the programming policies of France Television could in the medium to long term be expected to help their competitors' audience share. More immediately, a sudden reduction in the advertising time available on France Television would leave them in a position to raise the prices of their advertising space as advertisers switched from France TV to them. It appeared that the main focus of French regulatory responses to digital broadcasting was on relaxing existing regulatory constraints and rebalancing their impact, rather than introducing regulatory measures specifically designed with the new technology in mind.

UK reform

The UK's approach to digital broadcasting was characterised by more enthusiasm about the opportunities on offer, a greater emphasis on the role of public service broadcasters, and more time being devoted to establishing regulations tailored to digital broadcasting rather than simply blocking off the loopholes that had emerged in previous legislation. However, it too laid considerable emphasis on the maintenance of government control in the face of technological change. Government policy – whether under the Conservatives prior to May 1997 or the Labour Party thereafter – was underpinned by the belief that:

> for some time to come broadcasting, and in particular public service broadcasting provided by the familiar terrestrial network, is likely to continue to have a distinctly influential position in national life [and that] there is an important central role for public service broadcasting for the foreseeable future as technology develops.
>
> (DNH 1997; see also DCMS 1998d)

Aside from media ownership, re-regulation rather than deregulation was the hallmark of measures which imposed tough regulations on digital conditional access systems and a 'must carry' regime for public service channels on digital cable networks, provided protection against key sporting events only being shown on pay channels, and promoted the launch of DTT.[5] The arrival of Labour in power saw a change of tone rather than substance; the consensus on the broad direction of UK broadcasting policy remained pretty well intact.

Two of the most distinctive features of UK broadcasting digital policy were the emphasis given to Digital Terrestrial TV – and the accompanying preoccupation with analogue switch-off – and to the regulation of conditional access. Both reflected a similar preoccupation to ensure that digital TV developed on different lines from those which had characterised the growth of analogue pay TV in the UK.

Digital terrestrial broadcasting

The Conservative Government's efforts to promote DTT not only placed the UK at odds with its neighbours, who were much more cautious about DTT, but also looked like a surprising attempt at industrial policy by a party which normally shunned such efforts. From the government's perspective DTT had the advantages of:

- Providing a national digital transmission system with guaranteed coverage for the existing free-to-air public service terrestrial channels.
- Offering a nationwide distribution system under UK Government control. Digital satellite transmission via the Astra satellites used by BSkyB also reached the bulk of the nation but had the disadvantage of being controlled (and partly owned) from Luxembourg rather than London.
- Opening up the possibility – if it succeeded – of an eventual switch-off of analogue transmission and consequent auction of the spectrum which had been released. DTT's unique feature among digital broadcasting systems in being receivable with a simple set-top aerial (rather

than requiring connection to a cable system or a satellite dish) was thought vital for increasing the acceptability of any future plans for switch off.

- Finally, and perhaps most importantly, creating a rival digital system to BSkyB's digital satellite services. This aim was rarely articulated by a government which was wary of being seen openly to challenge Rupert Murdoch's broadcasting interests. On the other hand there would have been concern if BSkyB had been able to establish the same hold over digital TV that it already had in the analogue pay TV market.

Initially most broadcasters viewed DTT as an expensive method of achieving nation-wide coverage for a mere twenty to thirty channels as against the 200 plus channels that digital satellite could offer. There were doubts whether consumers would buy DTT set-top decoders if they were not compatible with those used for BSkyB's digital satellite services. The government's licensing framework for DTT was designed to overcome these fears. Existing terrestrial broadcasters (BBC, ITV, Channels 4 and 5 and S4C in Wales) were all given guaranteed access to digital frequencies for their existing services, and applications were invited for three other DTT multiplexes which were to be offered for a renewable twelve-year licensing period. Applicants were, uniquely, not required to make any cash bid or pay an annual fee.[6] Together, these factors amounted to a huge incentive for companies to commit to DTT. Despite their initial scepticism all the terrestrial broadcasters took up their reserved DTT capacity and there was a contest between two applicants, DTN and BDB. BDB was finally awarded the licence after BSkyB had withdrawn from the consortium. But OFTEL criticised the ITC decision, and further consultation was needed between the ITC and DG IV before the licence could be issued.[7]

The ITC became involved again in early 1998 when BDB chose the Canal Plus conditional access system rather than that used by BSkyB. BSkyB threatened legal action, arguing that this would reduce the degree of interoperability between digital satellite and digital terrestrial, a strange argument from a company that had argued for some years that it was possible to operate via two different conditional access systems, using simulcrypt technology (see Chapter 4). The ITC retaliated by issuing a consultation document ('Interoperability and Open Access') aimed at promoting common standards which would allow viewers to switch between transmission methods – DTT, Dsat and Dcable – without problems. The ITC document warned that the Commission 'would be concerned if any of its licensees were to raise unreasonable barriers to interoperability and open access which might prejudice fair and effective competition' (ITC 1998b). The hope was that BSkyB would take steps to make its system interoperable with that of BDB. But the ITC's initial proposals were diluted after they met with a frosty reception from the UK Government, and BSkyB (IT 1998c). Questions were raised as to whether the ITC had the powers to impose a single technical solution on all UK digital TV providers, or indeed whether such a measure would be appropriate. By the end of 1998 there was very little prospect of purchasers of the first UK DTT set-top boxes being able to use them to receive Digital satellite programmes, or vice versa.

Analogue switch-off

The economic argument for DTT lay in the value of the analogue spectrum that might be released once digital TV was widely available. National transmission of a single analogue TV channel is extremely costly in terms of spectrum. Initially digital terrestrial transmission involves the use of more, rather than less, spectrum, because of the need to broadcast analogue and digital signals in parallel (simulcasting). UK thinking in this area was influenced by US moves towards auctioning off spectrum, and the setting of a date – 2006 – for the switch-off of analogue broadcasts. In May 1996 the Conservative Government issued a White Paper on management of the radio spectrum which outlined plans to use spectrum pricing to help prevent undue congestion, and this idea was taken forward in the Labour Government's 1997 Wireless Telegraphy Bill.

Plans for the early switch-off of analogue transmissions brought into conflict the rival needs of maintaining broadcasting as a universal service, and of extracting the greatest possible economic benefit from the spectrum. The 1996 Broadcasting Act had provided for a review of the date for analogue switch-off, either after five years had elapsed from the start of DTT, or when 50 per cent of the population were using one or other form of digital TV. In September 1997 Chris Smith, the new Labour Secretary for Culture, Media and Sport (the Department changed its name after the election) identified speeding up the transition from analogue to digital TV for viewers as one of the government's priorities, 'not least because of the national resource which the freed radio spectrum currently occupied by analogue terrestrial broadcasting represents' (DCMS press release 49/97, Cambridge RTS Speech of 18 September 1997; see also Smith 1998).

A consultants' report produced for DCMS in February 1998 recommended that analogue transmissions should be switched off within ten to fifteen years. But the government distanced itself from this politically controversial path, saying that it would not switch analogue transmissions off before 'digital receivers are as universally installed in households as analogue ones are now' (*Financial Times* 13 February 1998). This set a very high threshold – 99.4 per cent of households – for digital penetration. It was assumed that government would either have to switch off analogue transmissions more rapidly than its commitment to universality suggested, or take steps to accelerate the switch to digital, possibly either by publicising the timetable for switch-off as an incentive to consumers to replace existing TVs with digital ones, or by providing subsidised set-top boxes for the last 10 per cent or so of households who would otherwise not switch to digital (DCMS 1998a, NERA/Smith 1998).[8]

Conditional access, electronic programme guides and gateway issues

Much of the very detailed regulation in the 1996 Broadcasting Act did not concern digital broadcasting as such, but rather just digital terrestrial broadcasting. And yet many of the key issues in digital broadcasting – on access to digital gateways and electronic programme guides – went beyond DTT, and affected all digital distribution systems. A comprehensive framework started to develop in parallel as the Broadcasting Bill was being debated in Parliament in 1996, and was then built on in regulations emerging from OFTEL and the ITC in the following years.

The UK debate on conditional access regulation focused on Rupert Murdoch's BSkyB, whose control of key programming, dominance of the existing analogue pay TV market, large installed base of subscribers, and exclusive rights over a major encryption technology, meant that it seemed likely to become dominant in digital TV and could, in the absence of adequate regulation, restrict competition. (At the same time as the Broadcasting Bill was under discussion the Competition Authority – the Office of Fair Trading – was undertaking a Review of BSkyB's position in the wholesale pay TV market, largely in response to complaints from cable operators about the terms on which BSkyB supplied them with programming (Office of Fair Trading 1996).) In the UK therefore, implementation of the EU Directive on conditional access took on an unusual degree of political and economic salience. The Department of Trade and Industry consulted three times on proposed implementation measures, with each successive draft going further to patch up possible loopholes in the Directive itself (DTI 1996a, 1996b).

The conditional access guidelines produced by the telecommunications regulator, OFTEL, were unique for addressing issues such as the ways in which control of proprietary technology, the pricing of conditional access services, attempts to recoup subsidies for set-top boxes, and the operation of EPG technologies could all be used to undermine the Directive's non-discrimination requirements (OFTEL 1997). OFTEL went further than any other European regulator in its regulations on pricing of conditional access services and the treatment of set-top box subsidies. In contrast to other EU regulators it also explicitly included several of the new gateways (such as the electronic programming guide and the API or the software in the box) within the category of technical services related to conditional access services which might be covered by the access and non-discrimination provisions applying to conditional access itself. In addition, OFTEL's requirement for the network operators to co-operate with broadcasters before services started, was very important in ensuring that third parties could get fair access in practice.

In 1997 a further innovation emerged from OFTEL in the form of the proposed 'Access Control Licence'. This would extend the conditional access regime to cover interactive services as well as digital TV. The ITC, meanwhile, also moved during 1997 to produce a wide-ranging code of conduct for EPGs (ITC 1997b). The code builds on the power granted to the ITC under the 1990 Act, to ensure fair and effective competition in the TV industry. Under the code operators of EPGs require a licence from the ITC, viewers should have easy access to free-to-air services, and there are restrictions on the extent to which EPGs can be branded by any broadcaster. One of the main aims of the code is to ensure fair, reasonable and non-dis-criminatory access for third party broadcasters to present their channels on EPGs run by operators who are themselves broadcasters, a principle which was effectively adapted from the conditional access regulations. Indeed OFTEL and the ITC both had jurisdiction over EPGs, OFTEL because of the way in which EPGs were technically linked with the provision of conditional access services, and the ITC in terms of the way in which channel information was presented. This joint OFTEL/ITC regulatory regime for EPGs was followed up in May 1998 by an ITC/OFT/OFTEL statement which announced their intention to co-operate more closely on all issues that crossed their regulatory boundaries, together with the creation of a Standing Committee on Competition in Communication. This would bring together officials from the Office of Fair Trading, OFTEL, the ITC, the DTI and DCMS) (ITC press release 54/98, 21 May 1998).

Media ownership

Reform of media ownership rules took up a major part of the UK 1996 Broadcasting Act. Publication of the Bill had been preceded by a pro-tracted media ownership review during which:

> newspaper companies argued the case for their control of broadcast-ers; terrestrial broadcasters wanted access to satellite channels; and radio companies wanted simplification of the rules governing their sector. Consumer groups, advertisers, academics and trade unions emphasised the need to protect diversity.
>
> (DNH 1995: 11, 17)[9]

In spite of its neo-liberal philosophy the UK Conservative Government rejected the most radical proposals for deregulation, arguing that com-petition law on its own would be insufficient since: 'special media ownership rules, which exist in all major media markets, are needed . . . to provide the safeguards necessary to maintain diversity and plurality' and that the 25 per cent market share threshold used in UK competition pol-icy might lead to the dominance of 'a handful of very powerful companies' (DNH 1995: 3). Many of the old limits on the number of independent TV franchises that could be held were replaced with a simple rule prohibiting any company from owning TV licences (of whatever kind) which together commanded more than 15 per cent of the national TV audience. For the first time national newspapers with less than 20 per cent market share were free to own TV licensees outright, subject only to the 15 per cent limit of the TV market and a public interest test administered by the broadcasting regulator, the ITC. The key political significance of the change was that the choice of a 20 per cent threshold for cross-ownership between newspapers and TV had been carefully calibrated to prevent both the Mirror Group and Rupert Murdoch's News International from taking over any existing terrestrial TV franchise. When Labour came into power, they showed no sign of wanting to reawaken these politically charged debates about the role of media owners – primarily Rupert Murdoch – within the UK communications sector, preferring to leave media ownership rules unchanged.

Sports rights

Access to live coverage of televised sporting events became a controversial issue in the 1996 Broadcasting Bill debates. BSkyB's badly timed experiment with their first pay per view boxing match in the spring of 1996 occurred just as the issue of televised sport was moving up the UK political agenda. That, combined with the News Corporation bid to buy rights to the Olympics until 2008 for $2 billion, fuelled concern among politicians across Europe that, without regulation, key national and international sporting events might no longer be available on TV to the majority of the population who were without Pay TV.[10] In February that year, the House of Lords inflicted a surprising defeat on the Conservative Government. This extended the protection for the existing list of eight sporting events to ensure that live coverage of them could not be shown exclusively on any form of pay TV, as opposed to just on pay per view TV as had previously been the case. The government had opposed the change, but the majority of politicians feared the consequences if key sporting events such as the FA Cup Final, or the Olympics should only be available on pay TV.

When the Labour Party came to power Chris Smith established a review body to re-examine the list of protected events, and to see whether for some other events shown live on pay TV there might also be an obligation for highlights to be available to free-to-air channels. In June 1998, just as the World Cup (itself a listed event) was attracting record TV audiences, DCMS announced the outcome of the review. Test cricket was removed from the list of protected events, although overall their number was increased. In addition a new B list of events was created, where highlights would have to be made available to free-to-air broadcasters if the live coverage was carried on pay channels.

Germany

German approaches to the regulation of new digital services contrasted considerably with those adopted in Britain and France and often seemed somewhat perverse. In other countries discussions were driven by technological change. In Germany federalism and constitutionalism predominated. Discussions during 1996–7 on the impact of digital technology focused, not on the field of broadcasting where digital services had already been launched, but rather on questions such as the treatment of video-on-demand, a service that would not be available on any extensive scale for several years.

Definitions of new services

If constitutional rather than technological considerations appeared to drive the German convergence debate, this was primarily because of the way in which new multimedia services appeared to challenge the existing separation between Federal jurisdiction over telecommunications and the Länder's responsibility for broadcasting. Months of negotiations between Federal Ministers and the Minister Presidents of the Länder focused on the borderline between broadcasting and telecommunications – an issue that in other countries barely surfaced on to the political agenda. The compromise that resulted saw two pieces of multimedia regulation, an Interstate Treaty on New Media Services, and a Federal Information and Communication Services Act (IukDG), operating alongside a revised Interstate Treaty on Broadcasting. All three came into force during 1997 (See Koenig and Roeder 1998, Braun and Schaal 1998).

The IukDG regulated 'teleservices', defined as services for *individual* communication (e.g. home banking, data exchange), those providing access to the Internet or other networks, and services offered for information or communication with *no editorial role or potential impact on public opinion*.[11] Teleservices covers 'individually and interactively designed on-demand services' along with other services such as on-line catalogues and games (German Government 1997). The Interstate Treaty on Media Services, meanwhile, applied to 'all information and communication services (media services) in form of text, audio or video that *are directed at the general public*' (author's italics); the assumption is that their features will make them closer to broadcasting than interactive teleservices'.

The Interstate Treaty on Media Services gave examples of the services that it was intended to cover, ranging from online news, teleshopping, VOD and NVOD, but some services could straddle the two pieces of legislation, with jurisdiction determined according to whether or not they had any editorial input or impact. This could lead to some surprising results. Thus video-on-demand services involving entertainment programmes or content 'which is intended to contribute to the forming of opinion' are to be regulated by the Länder, whereas other video-on-demand services which did not meet these criteria will be regulated under the Federal law. One commentator has remarked how: 'from a legal perspective, such a political compromise on a constitutional question is more than questionable, and it will probably only be a question of time until the allocation of competences will be challenged in court' (Chrocziel and Dieselhorst 1996: 196).

One of the most debated aspects of these laws concerned the responsibility of service providers for the content on their networks. The IukDG law drew a threefold distinction between the different levels of responsibility. At the two extremes were, first, the service providers who offered their own content on the Internet who were to be held responsible for that content (this would apply to the content provided by Compuserve or AOL) and, second, those operators who were merely Internet access providers (as is the case, say, for BT Internet in the UK) who would not be held responsible for the content that their customers accessed.

The most controversial category fell between these two. Service providers who themselves provided access to third party content (through for example hosting newsgroups on their server) could be held responsible for illegal third party content in cases where they knew about the existence of such content, and it was both technically feasible and practical to block such content. (IukDG 'Brief outline' as above) The IukDG's intention can be summarised as only wanting to hold service providers responsible for the intentional, or at least conscious, dissemination of illegal content (Squires, Sanders and Dempsey and Analysys 1998).

One innovative aspect of both pieces of legislation was their recognition that prior licences should not be required for either 'teleservices' or 'media services'. The German approach had the virtue of attempting to identify the purpose or nature of the service that was to be regulated, rather than relying entirely on the delivery system that was used. On the other hand, since the categories were the result of a constitutional compromise over the competence of the Länder and the Federal Government, there was little chance of these categories being applied in a flexible way. The Länder drew up their Media Services Treaty precisely because they feared that the IukDG was aimed at pre-empting their right to act in an area that they saw as clearly falling within their responsibility. Attempts to update the lists of services under each piece of legislation seem likely to lead to new controversies.

Limited focus on digital broadcasting

The relative constitutional simplicity of broadcasting – it was clearly the responsibility of the Länder – meant that the Interstate Treaty on Broadcasting devoted very little attention to what in other countries was regarded as the burning question of how broadcasting regulation should adapt to the advent of digital TV. As a result, Kirch was able to start

Germany's first digital TV service, DF1, in 1996, before there was any proper licensing regime for digital broadcasting. The fact that it operated on a so-called trial or experimental licence, led to several legal challenges to DF1's right to be distributed outside its home territory of Bavaria. The only sense in which the Treaty acknowledged digital broadcasting was by the inclusion of a single article (53) implementing the provisions of the TV Standards Directive, specifying that operators of conditional access services should grant fair, reasonable and non-discriminatory access to third parties. The interpretation of these terms was left entirely up to the Land Media Authorities and the German Competition Authority. While the Interstate Treaty went beyond the Directive in applying the non-discrimination principle to the operation of electronic programme guides as well to conditional access systems, a lack of clear guidance from the Land Media Authorities weakened the impact of this provision. In addition, since Kirch's DF1 platform was launched before the Treaty came into force, it was not initially subject to any regulation in this area (Grimme 1997: 147).

Media ownership

For most commercial operators the real significance of the 1996 Interstate Treaty on Broadcasting lay in its moves to liberalise the media ownership regime. Under the 1991 Interstate Broadcasting Treaty companies were prevented from controlling more than two nationwide TV stations and two radio stations, and no single company could own more than 50 per cent of one general entertainment channel together with 25 per cent of any additional channel. These limits prompted similar complaints to those heard in the UK, namely that they placed constraints on nationally based companies which did not apply to foreigners. It was true that by 1996 more than 56 per cent of the shares in German TV stations were controlled by foreign investors, with the influence of the Luxembourg company CLT in the German market and Rupert Murdoch's 49 per cent share in VOX among the best known examples. But it was also the case, as in Britain, that companies had resorted to ever more ingenious devices to get round the law. The tough intentions of the 1991 rules were further complicated by the way in which individual Länder used their autonomy in media matters either to apply different rules or to interpret the Interstate Treaty in different ways. By 1996 companies had become accustomed to the idea of 'forum shopping', of basing themselves in the Land which applied media ownership rules in the most beneficial manner.[12]

The 1996 Broadcasting Treaty focused on the liberalisation and rationalisation of the old rules. The previous channel-based system of limits was replaced by an audience share rule where companies were allowed to control up to 30 per cent of the TV audience, irrespective of the number of channels they owned. This amounted to the most significant liberalising move in Europe. Its impact was increased by the way in which audience share figures were calculated. Shareholdings of under 25 per cent of a TV channel were disregarded in assessing a company's total audience share (Humphreys 1998: 543). Since public service broadcasters, who accounted for 42 per cent of the national audience, were included in the audience share figures, the new 30 per cent limit per company simply recognised the duopoly whereby the two major companies, Kirch and Bertelsmann, shared the balance of the audience between them. It was the product of a political compromise designed to favour the CDU-aligned Kirch and the SPD-supported Bertelsmann both equally.

The change in the law gave both companies increased scope for manoeuvre. Bertelsmann was freed to launch a bid to merge its broadcasting arm, UFA, with the Luxembourg-owned CLT, a merger which would give the new company control of 'four private TV channels in Germany amounting to 25 per cent of Europe's largest TV market (and half of Germany's commercial TV market) as well as a number of TV channels operating under the RTL emblem in several other European countries' (Humphreys 1997: 6).[13] Kirch, meanwhile, seized the opportunity of the new rules to increase its holdings in the commercial channel Sat 1 (Ridder 1996: 24–6). One of the few counterweights to these liberalisation moves lay in the creation of a new national media ownership commission, the KEK, which was established both to monitor market shares and ensure greater coherence in how the different Länder applied the media ownership limits. In theory the KEK could ensure putting a stop to the more obvious examples of rules being bent by the LMAs to favour 'their' companies, although the Treaty still left quite a lot of scope for local 'interpretation' of the media ownership provisions.

Adjusting to digital broadcasting

The 1996 Broadcasting Treaty represented the high-water mark of the liberalising trend in German broadcasting regulation. But its preoccupation with the very familiar areas of media ownership rules was accompanied by a relative neglect of the issues raised specifically by digital broadcasting. Conditional access and electronic programme guides were only dealt with in the most cursory way; no licensing regime was established for digital TV, and no thought was given to how digitalisation of the German cable system might proceed.

One of the quid pro quos for a relaxation of media ownership rules was an increase in the licence fee for Germany's public service broadcasters, thereby ensuring their ability to launch new digital channels. But as long as Deutsche Telekom (DT) refused to upgrade its cable network from analogue to digital, commercial operators were understandably wary of new public service channels, since their 'must carry' status would inevitably force some commercial channels off the cable networks. From this conflict stemmed a protracted period of hostilities between the commercial TV channels, represented by their trade association, the VPRT, and the public service channels, ARD and ZDF, with the VPRT arguing against the very idea that public service broadcasting could extend beyond a 'basic service' and launch thematic channels, such as the children's channel and documentary channel offered by ARD and ZDF in their digital package.

The limitations of Germany's analogue cable system, and the failure of DT to upgrade it to digital, underpinned several of the problems within German broadcasting. The vigorous conflict between public and private broadcasters was a symptom of the difficulties in launching digital TV in Germany. Even before the advent of digital, the market had suffered from a surfeit of players. Only two German commercial TV stations ran at a profit. Deutsche Telekom's cable operations also ran at a loss despite running Europe's biggest cable network and enjoying the privileged position of being able to demand that channels paid it for carriage, rather than the other way round, as happens, for example, in the UK and France. With thirty free-to-air channels available on cable, the launch of digital pay TV would always be more difficult than in countries with a more limited choice of free channels. When Kirch and Bertelsmann competed to launch digital TV, each with incompatible proprietary decoders, they simply compounded the problem, and undermined consumer confidence in the interoperability of digital decoders, leaving Kirch's DF1 with lots of content but inadequate distribution, and Premiere with access to distribution, but no major Hollywood film rights. Yet while co-operation of the kind proposed by Bertelsmann, Kirch and Deutsche Telekom, using a single conditional access system, the Kirch D-Box, improved the prospects of digital TV succeeding, it also posed very serious threats to competition in the German digital market (see Chapter 5 above).

European competition authorities were more advanced than German regulators in recognising the risks posed by the way that German digital TV was developing. During the first half of 1998 DG IV looked in detail at the implications of the adoption of the Kirch D-Box – and at Kirch's control of key rights – for competition in the German market, at a time when these matters were not the subject of any sectoral regulation at all in Germany. The conference of the directors of the regulatory authorities of the Länder decided at a meeting in 1997 that a new treaty was necessary, and 'reached an agreement on ten criteria for the introduction of digital broadcasting including equal access to broadcasting, non-discrimination in the provision of services for operators, open access for users and uniform standards for digitalisation' (Squires, Sanders and Dempsey and Analysys 1998).

In a similarly belated move, it was only after Television Without Frontiers provisions allowed Member States to draw up lists of protected sporting events that Germany started to consider such action. It was partly in response to Kirch's purchase of rights to the World Cup for 2002 and 2006 that the Minister Presidents of the Länder agreed at a meeting in early 1998 to create a list of events which could not be screened exclusively on pay TV.[14] Previous lobbying by Kirch had led the government to oppose increased regulation at the European level, and had prevented any listed events-type regulation being included in the revised 1996 Interstate Treaty on Broadcasting. Popular concern about football coverage, however, had meant that it proved impossible for Kirch to win this argument.

Comparing national regulatory responses to convergence

After this brief survey of the differing ways in which France, the UK and Germany changed their regulatory structures in the mid-1990s, it is worth considering two questions. First, there is the question of the extent to which these changes in national legislation demonstrated a shared set of concerns and responses to digital Television. Second, even though the countries may have adopted differing policies, whether digitalisation had an impact on their regulatory structures by forcing countries with differing traditions to move towards establishing converged national regulatory frameworks.

Comparing policy responses

There were several similarities between the policy agendas in these three different countries. They all considered revised media ownership rules; all three proposed greater protection for televised sporting events; and they all made some moves to implement the EU TV Standards Directive regulating conditional access. But in each case the ways in which these issues were approached revealed as much about the differences between the three countries as about any similarities between the issues that they were addressing.

Conditional access regulation was in some respects the area where one might have expected the greatest similarity between the three countries, since they were all implementing the same EU Directive. But even here the political salience of the issue varied greatly between the three countries, with substantial impacts on the way in which the Directive was implemented. In the UK, the highly technical subject of conditional access attracted considerable political attention, and rigorous regulation, largely because of the high political profile of Rupert Murdoch, who owned 40 per cent of BSkyB. Whereas in France and Germany the Directive was not implemented until months after digital services had been launched, thereby making vigorous regulation unlikely, in the UK BSkyB delayed even placing orders for its set-top boxes until the details of the regulatory regime were clear. Minimal, or at best belated, implementation was the order of the day in France and Germany, whereas in the UK the approach was rather more rigorous.

The contrast between the approaches of France and Britain is particularly striking. In Britain concern centred on the risk of inadequate competition in digital TV, while the fear in France was rather of an excess of competition as three rival and incompatible digital satellite systems each tried to tempt consumers with their wares.[15] None of the French digital TV companies attracted the political controversy that surrounded Rupert Murdoch's media empire, even if there was some disquiet about the potential impact of their parent companies' dependence on public construction and utility contracts. Finally, while in Britain ITV and the BBC were vociferous in urging tough regulation, for fear that without it they might be unable to gain fair access to digital viewers, the decision of two major French free-to-air broadcasters, TF1 and France Télévision, to work with Télévision par Satellite (TPS) which used its own proprietary conditional access system, initially neutralised two powerful advocates of a more vigorous approach to conditional access regulation.

In the case of media ownership each of the countries reformed and liberalised its own system, but the extent and form of that liberalisation varied greatly. Germany went furthest along the path to liberalisation, with Britain and France trailing behind. But in each country the choice of systems and thresholds for cross-ownership was heavily influenced by domestic political concerns and lobbying by local media companies. Although an increased sense of interdependence led to moves to harmonise media ownership rules across Germany (through the creation of the KEK), none of the three countries was prepared to go one further and endorse any shift of responsibility for such a contentious area from national capitals to Brussels (see Chapter 5). The most noticeable impact of EU proposals for media ownership reform was not so much in persuading countries to endorse a role for EU regulation, as in the adoption of the EU approach in measuring influence in terms of audience share rather than the number of licences held or limitation of the percentage holding in any particular company.

Politicians and policy-makers in each of the three countries were concerned that digital broadcasting and the growth of pay TV should not limit the universal access that people had become accustomed to in the television field. These concerns were reflected in the measures taken in every country to prevent key sporting events only being exclusively available on pay TV. They were also reflected in the continued funding of public service broadcasting. The commitment to public service broadcasting seemed greatest in the UK, where it was shared by both the Conservative and the Labour Parties. The role of public service broadcasting was more controversial in Germany, while in France the case was not helped by the high-profile resignation in 1996 of Jean Pierre Elkabach, Director General of France Television, amidst a scandal over inflated fees paid to several well-known figures from the entertainment world.

Nevertheless, all three countries agreed on increases in licence fees between 1996 and 1997 and endorsed the launching of new digital services by their public service broadcasters.

Reforming regulatory structures

Not one of the three countries achieved a far-reaching reform of its regulatory structure, or even came close to endorsing the ideas of regulatory convergence outlined in the Commission's 1997 Green Paper. There was no shortage of advocates for such a change, but national governments were reluctant to bring it about.

Often the most strident calls for change came from telecoms regulators and Ministries of Industry. Each expected that they would emerge from any moves towards regulatory convergence in a stronger position. In the UK OFTEL argued from as early as 1995 that as:

> the traditional scarcity of broadcasting channels becomes an issue of the past, and as traditional telecommunications systems begin to offer video-based services, broadcast services will become increasingly difficult to distinguish from other services [and] the traditional regulatory distinctions between broadcasting and telecommunications will be difficult to sustain.
>
> (OFTEL 1995: 4)

In Germany the Federal Government's Council for Research, Technology and Innovation launched a thinly veiled attack on the Federal States' responsibility for broadcasting arguing that: 'to permit the free unfolding of market forces in the new multimedia services and to avoid putting German suppliers at a disadvantage in international competition, a *uniform national regulatory framework for the media should be introduced*' (author's italics) with regulation 'restricted to the absolute minimum' (Council for Research, 1996: 24). Even in France a report from the Commissariat général du Plan offered qualified endorsement for the idea that there should be greater convergence between broadcasting legislation and telecommunications regulation, noting:

> *Il est donc apparu essentiel . . . que, sans ignorer leur finalité distincte, législation sur l'audiovisuel et réglementation des télécommunications puissent évoluer dans le sens d'une plus grande convergence. L'entrée dans la société de l'information suppose, à terme, que l'ensemble des nouveaux services multimédias puissent relever d'une réglementation unifiée qui garantisse notamment la neutralité juridique en ce qui concerne les supports.*
>
> (Commissariat général du Plan, 1996: 37–8)

In spite of the apparently logical case that was made for regulatory convergence, and the weight of support it attracted in international fora and among the telecommunications and multimedia policy communities, few of Europe's governments were prepared to move very far in that direction. The treatment of video-on-demand, viewed as one litmus test of how the boundaries between broadcasting and telecommunications regulation would be drawn, was left firmly in the hands of broadcasting regulators in Britain, France and Germany. Similarly, demands for the creation of a converged regulatory framework at national level made very limited headway in the three countries.

In Germany the Federal structure made regulatory convergence a constitutional impossibility, whatever the preferences might be of individual actors. The result was not one that anyone viewed as entirely satisfactory: fifteen separate Land Media Authorities made little sense for an industry where the audiences were largely national, even if the location decisions of major media companies had a major impact on local employment. One observer criticised Germany's multi-layered approach to broadcasting, telecommunications, teleservices and media services, as 'chaotic' and inefficient, lacking transparency and not cost effective (Holznagel 1998: 3).

In France, while – as already noted – economic imperatives were accorded greater consideration than before, there was no attempt to alter sectoral definitions or move towards a converged regulatory framework at the national level. The Conservative Minister, Philippe Douste-Blazy, had specifically rejected the idea of a converged regulator in the debates on his 1997 Bill, noting that:

> If in apparent contrast to the convergence between telecoms and audio-visual, the Bill maintains a distinction between the two regulatory authorities in these sectors – the CSA and the ART [the new Telecoms regulatory authority] – it is because the concerns about programmes and content, which have a cultural dimension, are clearly very different from the concerns relative to the regulation of telecommunications which have a technical dimension . . . Like the whole Parliament I am an ardent defender of the cultural exception, that's why it seems to me indispensable to keep a regulatory authority which is based on the Audio-visual sector – the CSA – and even indeed to reinforce its tasks.
>
> (*Journal Officiel*, 19 February 1997: 875)[16]

While his Socialist successor, Catherine Trautmann, gave a less ringing endorsement of the cultural exception, she still spoke of increasing the role of the CSA, and of improving co-operation between the CSA and the ART rather than creating a single communications regulator. Similarly, there was no attempt to alter the rather far-reaching French definition of broadcasting, which under the 1986 Broadcasting Law extends to all forms of 'the transmission for the public (or for certain categories of the public), by telecommunications transmission means, of any signs, signals, text, images, sounds or information of any nature which do not constitute private correspondence'. Since private correspondence was defined in a 1988 Prime Ministerial order as existing only when 'the message is expressly designed for reception by one or several determined and identifiable, either physical or legal, persons', services such as VOD, which might be seen as borderline cases elsewhere in the EU, are very clearly broadcasting in France. It appears that instead of seeking to restrict or change these definitions, French Governments have preferred to request a degree of flexibility from broadcasting regulators as to how they treat such services.

UK approaches to regulatory convergence are less clear. The previous Conservative Government gave OFTEL, the telecommunications regulator, lead responsibility for conditional access, but this was done for political and administrative convenience rather than as part of any plan to reform the structures of communication regulation. In opposition the Labour Party had proposed an 'OFCOM' which would carry out essentially economic regulation across both the telecommunications and broadcasting sectors, whilst retaining a role for specific content regulation through a reformed ITC (Labour Party 1995: 8–9).

Since it came to office the Labour Government appears to have moved against the idea of a single OFCOM. Early on the new Secretary of State said: 'our proposals do not mean a . . . monolithic regulator for the media, or even for television. They are, however, likely to mean that the regulatory structure will not in future be defined exclusively by the particular medium concerned' (DCMS 1997 press release 49/97, 18 September 1997). When a Green Paper on the future of regulation was published in July 1998 it was far less radical than earlier opposition thinking had suggested. Dismissing the 'false choice between tearing up our regulatory structures or sticking to the status quo' the government declared that it would 'follow an evolutionary path'. Regulators in the first instance were encouraged to co-operate on managing overlaps and anomalies rather than to be subjected to any radical overhaul. A small standing group of the relevant regulators and competition authorities (OFTEL, the ITC, OFT, DCMS and DTI) was set up to fulfil this task, and the government promised to try and create greater consistency of regulation for similar material delivered on different transmission systems (see page 110).

The Green Paper expressed a desire to avoid regulating for a 'future which may not be as we expect', and to combine care to ensure that 'regulation does not hold back the development of new services' with a continuing concern to 'ensure that public interest objectives are protected' (DCMS 1998c). It confirmed the government's desire for regulatory stability, the avoidance of a Broadcasting Bill before the turn of the century, and that there should be no radical restructuring of Government Departments to produce a single, merged DTI and DCMS.

This contrasted with the wishes of the House of Commons Select Committee on Culture, Media and Sport. Their report had recommended the creation of a new Government Department of Communications, which would take over the broadcasting and media responsibilities of the existing Department of Culture, Media and Sport, and the telecoms and Internet responsibilities of the Department of Trade and Industry. It had also proposed the establishment of a single Communications Regulation Commission, which would absorb all existing media regulatory bodies, and also regulate the BBC (House of Commons 1998, DCMS 1998d). The government's response not only disagreed with the regulatory arrangements proposed by the Select Committee but also took issue with the Committee's very optimistic predictions about the rate of penetration of the new technologies (DCMS 1998b).

Conclusion

The dominant theme that emerges from this brief study of the broadcasting reforms of three major EU Member States during the mid-1990s is one of very limited moves towards policy convergence despite a shared need to respond to digital broadcasting. Even when policy agendas converged, as was the case in questions of media ownership control or the implementation of a European directive on conditional access, policy outcomes diverged considerably in response to differing political circumstances and preoccupations. In each of the three countries examined, broadcasting policy emerged from the interplay between a web of institutions – of politicians at national and Land level, of regulators, the courts (in the German case), officials and the broadcasters themselves – that were both specific to each country and which made Rose's observation that 'new programs cannot be constructed on green field sites . . . they must be introduced into an environment dense with past commitments' particularly pertinent (Rose, cited in Dolowitz 1996: 353). Technological change tended more often to lead to minor reforms of existing institutional structures (which were themselves the product of hard-fought political, commercial and bureaucratic battles) than to be used as an opportunity for a radical overhaul of either these institutions or hitherto shared policy objectives.

7 From the European Information Society to convergence

Co-ordinating or transcending national responses to digital broadcasting?

Introduction

Previous chapters have revealed how analogue broadcasting occupied a relatively minor role in European policy. While there were occasions when broadcasting policy was put higher up the EU agenda – as with the quota provisions of the Television Without Frontiers Directive or the discussions on a cultural exception for broadcasting during the 1993 GATT negotiations – for the most part analogue broadcasting policy was left to national governments only operating on the sidelines of EU policy-making. The European competition and internal market provisions impacted on broadcasters, but broadcasting policy as such rarely commanded the lasting attention of European policy-makers. In that respect the treatment of broadcasting stood in marked contrast to that of telecommunications policy which by 'the early 1990s . . . had come to account for most of the regulatory policy emerging from' the European Commission (Cram 1997: 78).

The development of the EU's various Information Society (IS) initiatives after 1994 led to attempts to apply many of the approaches used during telecoms liberalisation to the wider communications sector, and meant that broadcasting – and in particular digital broadcasting – began to be viewed as far more central to Commission concerns. This change in approach was consolidated after 1996 as increased awareness of the Internet fuelled interest in the regulatory implications of convergence within the European Commission and in wider international fora such as the OECD. Convergence was seized on by some policy makers as justifying the liberalisation of the entire communications sector, and the replacement of national broadcasting regulation with a new light-touch converged regulatory framework operating at the EU or international level. This chapter focuses on the origins and key elements of the convergence debate within the EU, and the extent to which convergence removed existing obstacles to the EU playing a greater part in the regulation of the broadcasting sector, while the subsequent chapter proposes a regulatory framework for the converging communications sector.

Broadcasting, the Information Society and convergence

Telecommunications liberalisation and the Information Society

From the publication of the Delors White Paper on *Growth, Competitiveness, Employment* in December 1993, the information industries were identified as a key area for growth and employment within the EU.[1] A high level industry group was convened under the chairmanship of Commissioner Bangemann. Its report – on *Europe and the Global Information Society* (hereafter referred to as the Bangemann Report) – was endorsed by the June 1994 European Council meeting in Corfu, and many of its recommendations were included in an Information Society Action Plan produced by the Commission in July. Since then large areas of activity have been included within the Action Plan, with timetables set and progress monitored through regular updates and reports issued by the Commission.

This new-found enthusiasm for the Information Society (IS) meant that broadcasting changed from being viewed as a purely cultural or, at best, a relatively minor economic part of Commission concerns, to become a key provider of the 'content' which it is recognised will drive the development of IS networks and services. In spite of this increased interest in content, the regulatory paradigm for the IS was far more influenced by telecommunications interests and policy-makers than by those of broadcasting. The consequence was that whilst the IS was to have a huge impact on EU policy-making for broadcasting, the world of broadcasting had a relatively limited influence on the policy options that were adopted, or on the processes that gave birth to them. Indeed, while the IS perspective increased the amount of attention given to broadcasting within the EU, it also changed the balance between the key Commission DGs involved in agenda setting, brought new interest groups into the policy process, and had a considerable impact on policy outcomes.

A cynic might observe that the extent of support for the EU's IS programme has been directly linked to the ill-focused and all-embracing nature of its objectives. The EU used the 'Information Society' as a portmanteau term to lend coherence to an extremely wide range of policies, both existing and new; to act as a mobilising slogan rather as the 1992 programme did before it; and to suggest dynamism and a preoccupation with modernisation and competitiveness. The breadth of the vision has allowed policies ranging from highly technical issues of standardisation and telecommunications numbering to education and research plans, regional policy, social policy and consumer affairs issues, all to be included and justified in terms of the 'Information Society'. At the core of the IS programmes, however, lay a more prosaic agenda focused on the completion of existing EU telecommunications liberalisation policies, their extension to take account of the new communications networks, and the belief that Europe's future growth and employment depended on creating a competitive communications sector (Campbell and Konert 1998: 45).

The Bangemann Report established much of the tone and agenda for the EU's IS programmes. It was prefaced with strong free-market rhetoric, warning against 'more public money, financial assistance, subsidies, dirigisme, or protection' being used for the IS, and advocating instead the need to foster 'an entrepreneurial mentality to enable the emergence of new dynamic sectors of the economy'. This deregulatory tone was reflected in the group's approach to the audio-visual sector which was singled out as being financially and organisationally weak (which was also the analysis of the 1994 Audio-Visual Green Paper; see Chapter 3 above), and 'burdened with regulations', some of which, it was predicted 'will soon be rendered obsolete by the development of new technologies', all themes that would re-emerge over the succeeding years in discussions about convergence (EC 1994c: 11).[2] But this may have reflected the fact that only two out of the twenty members were broadcasters. Indeed, in other areas many of the report's recommendations (namely, to speed up the pace of telecommunications liberalisation, update the regulatory framework for the information industries, improve European standards setting procedures, ensure universal service, and to instigate EU legislation covering media ownership, intellectual property, and privacy) amounted to a call for increased regulatory intervention by the EU to fill the void left by deregulation at the national level. This aspiration was made explicit in the call for the creation of a single European Telecommunications Authority.[3]

The Commission's approach to the Information Society was strongly influenced by the pattern of intervention already established in telecommunications. There EU action had been necessary at least in part because, as the Commission explained, 'a strong public service monopoly tradition' together with an industrial policy of creating 'national champions' had 'created a strong national orientation for the sector, and consequently the loss of potential opportunities for a European-wide market' (EC 1998h). Policies to end national monopolies, liberalise access to infrastructure and networks, and introduce a more relaxed system of class rather than individual specific licences, all followed, largely as a result of Commission activism. Many of these actions, and in particular, the introduction of telecoms class licences, had a significant impact on the degree of autonomy exercised by national authorities.[4] Even the traditional 'social' arguments for monopoly provision and national regulation – namely, the need to ensure equal geographical access to telecommunications services in uneconomic areas – were weakened by Commission guidelines on universal service. These had the aim of defining what constituted access to a basic level of telephone service and ensuring that widely differing approaches to such social obligations did not have the effect of fragmenting the internal market or of advantaging incumbent providers.[5]

Some of the regulatory questions raised by digital broadcasting regulation could quite legitimately draw on the lessons learnt from EU telecommunications policy. Digital broadcasting would increasingly be delivered through switched networks – either by telecommunications, cable or satellite – and the EU's measures to ensure access for third parties to telecommunications networks, and interconnection and interoperability between networks, had a direct relevance to the new broadcasting environment. Neither of these issues was covered by any of the EU's broadcasting regulations, and without regulation 'borrowed' from the telecommunications and ICT sectors competition in digital broadcasting would have been an even more remote possibility.

In other areas EU telecoms policy-makers were inclined to portray differences between broadcasting and telecommunications policy as reflecting the 'backwardness' rather than the distinctiveness of broadcasting. Broadcasting's fragmentation into national markets and the diversity of national regulatory frameworks were seen as outdated obstacles to be overcome, rather than as a reflection of the regulatory traditions within each Member State and the quite natural differences in the cultural and other policy objectives pursued. Similarly, the system of individual channel licences, common in broadcasting regulation even after telecommunications had moved towards class licensing, was not seen as reflecting the inevitable complexity of content regulation – where for example judgements of quality are inevitably more subtle and subjective than in telecoms – but as an anachronistic hangover from an age of channel scarcity, and evidence of a lack of transparency and political independence within broadcasting regulation.[6]

The Internet

During the course of 1996 the EU's IS agenda became increasingly preoccupied with the Internet. The minimal regulatory framework and trans-frontier nature of the Internet appeared to confirm key IS themes about the need for deregulation, and for regulation to move to the EU or international level. Similarly, the multi-functional nature of the Internet and World Wide Web, where users could move swiftly between private communication and a publishing or broadcasting model, appeared to reinforce the case for reducing regulatory distinctions between broadcasting and telecoms. However other aspects of the Internet called into question some of the assumptions underpinning the IS approach. The Internet offered the prospect of a world where *existing* infrastructure might bring multimedia services to the home in a way that it had previously been assumed could only happen through the creation of new, universal, broadband fibre optic networks (KPMG 1995: iii).

More seriously, there was increased public concern about how the Internet was being used for the exchange of child pornography and other illegal activities. The arrest of the paedophile killer Marc Dutrou in Belgium in August 1996 fuelled widespread press and public comment about the uncontrollable nature of the Internet. Policy-makers in the EU and within national capitals had to find a balance between offering reassurance to the press and the public that the Internet was not a law-free zone, whilst calming fears that over-regulation of new services in Europe would further disadvantage the domestic IT sector as against its US rivals.

For a time it was unclear which course European governments would choose. Some Home Affairs and Interior Ministers wanted tougher limits on the uses to which the Internet could be put, and control of encryption technologies so that the security services could intercept e-mails with the same ease as a transatlantic telephone call. There were those in the cultural and broadcast industries who feared that, without controls, new Internet technologies such as video-streaming could be used to bypass EU and national TV regulation and expose Europe to the risk of Disney-on-demand. Most Telecoms and Industry Ministers, meanwhile, felt that without minimal regulation Europe would continue to lag behind the US, both in terms of the degree of Internet penetration, and in what was predicted to be a burgeoning market for electronic commerce.[7]

The solution to this dilemma emerged over the course of 1996–98 in a series of Commission initiatives.[8] These went half-way to meeting the industry's desire for limited regulatory intervention on behalf of the Internet by recommending the establishment of hot lines and greater international co-operation to deal with illegal content on-line, whilst promoting the development and use of content classification schemes and self regulation to deal with content that might be harmful to minors.

The key principles underpinning the EU's approach to Internet regulation were established at the July 1997 Bonn Conference jointly organised by the German Federal Government and the European Commission, bringing together ministers and industry representatives. The industry representatives in Bonn used the occasion to establish their desire for a more 'horizontal' approach to all communications regulation, requesting that 'regulation should be as light-handed and flexible as possible' and arguing that convergence meant that 'divisions between telecommunications, broadcasting, publishing and information technology [would no longer] make sense'. Regulators were asked to 'reappraise the basis of existing regulatory regimes because of the convergence of technologies', to create a 'future legal framework . . . based on general principles of law, not on sector-specific legislation', and to ensure that 'self regulation and technical solutions, such as voluntary content filtering and rating, should play a central role in content control'.[9]

The Ministerial Declaration was not as categorical, but many of its key themes, for example, on the need for greater reliance on content classification, filtering software and self regulation, chimed with those of industry. Ministers also went further in stressing that 'the rules on responsibility for content should be based on a set of common principles so as to ensure a level playing field' and that 'intermediaries like network operators and access providers should, in general, not be responsible for content. Due account should be taken of whether such intermediaries had reasonable grounds to know and reasonable possibility to control content'. This was an important point at a time when some on-line service providers, such as Compuserve in Germany, were being prosecuted for material posted on news groups hosted on their servers, over which they argued that they exercised no editorial responsibility.

Convergence

EU discussions of the impact of convergence emerged from these preoccupations first with the IS and then with the Internet. When the Convergence Green Paper was published in December 1997 it singled out the Internet as the 'symbolic and prime driver of convergence' (EC 1997d). The Green Paper explained this in terms of the ease with which the Internet substituted for previously dedicated networks, for example voice telephony or broadcasting, and because of its user-driven – as opposed to supplier-driven – nature. In addition the decentralised character of the Internet, its exponential growth, and its constant shifts between the publishing and private communication modes as users move between viewing a web page (akin to publishing), ordering a video (akin to video-on-demand) and then e-mailing individuals, or interacting with on-line providers, were all cited in support of this case. For the authors of the Green Paper it symbolised how minimal regulation could facilitate technical innovation and commercial success. The assumption was that if the rest of the communications sector followed suit and freed itself from outdated regulatory rules it too might realise its full potential.

At the core of the Green Paper on Convergence lay three arguments, each of which had been developed over the year to eighteen months preceding production of the Green Paper itself. The first argument was that technological convergence challenged existing regulatory categories and boundaries, primarily those between telecommunications and broadcasting. The second was that the move from a scarcity to a multitude of outlets and channels meant that regulation needed to be relaxed; it was no longer possible or appropriate to regulate the digital world to the same extent as the analogue one. Increasingly the Internet model – of a lighter touch regulation, or indeed only the constraints of civil law together with self regulation – was presented as the model for the converged communications industry. And third, there was the argument that as the communications industry became more international, so attempts at national regulation would be ineffective, inhibit innovation, and increasingly act as a source of regulatory fragmentation within the European internal market. The solution, it was argued, lay in moving to regulation at a higher level, in fact at either the EU or even the global level.

The foundations for the 1997 Convergence Green Paper were laid in a series of Commission publications following on from the 1994 Bangemann

Report, which argued that technological convergence demanded greater convergence between telecommunications and broadcasting regulation. A 1994 Green Paper on liberalisation of telecommunications infrastructure and cable TV networks complained that: 'differences within Member States between the treatment of broadcasting and telecommunications threaten to impede the development and distribution of advanced information/ communications services' (EC 1994d). The Commission later sought to offer reassurance that 'the aim is not to extend telecommunications regulation to the broadcasting or other sectors', whilst at the same time offering a 'number of basic principles . . . which may assist in the formulation of a coherent regulatory approach to the future debate on regulating for convergence'.[10] Among these were the propositions that regulation should be 'technology neutral', that there should be a 'coherent regulatory structure' for IS services, and that 'artificial regulatory barriers' be lifted, all of which were later to surface in the 1997 Green Paper on Convergence. Similar propositions were contained in the recommendations of an industry group established by Commissioner Bangemann, which reported in early 1997.

During the same period a series of consultants were commissioned by DG XIII to produce reports on convergence which would help establish the key principles for the Convergence Green Paper.[11] The most influential of these reports was that produced by KPMG and Ashhurst Morris Crisp, on the 'Public Policy Issues arising from telecommunications and audio-visual convergence' (KPMG 1996). Its launch at a major conference in Brussels added to the sense that its recommendations were not all that far removed from DG XIII thinking. KPMG focused on the differences between national regulatory frameworks – and the more general failure to adapt regulation to the new circumstances – as constituting one of the most serious threats to the successful development of the new converged services.[12]

Having made the case for changes in regulation, the report went on to argue that as convergence reduced the impact of spectrum scarcity and entry costs were reduced and the choice of channels increased, so many of the arguments for specific broadcasting regulation would be removed, and the lighter touch content regulation applied to publishing became more appropriate. KPMG distinguished between economic and public interest regulation, arguing that whilst economic regulation – for fair competition and access to the new digital networks – required reinforcing, many of the public interest aspects of regulation could be relaxed. KPMG suggested that policies designed to promote culture, quality, diversity and pluralism should be relaxed over time, since many of these objectives would be 'self-fulfilling' under convergence (KPMG 1996 Summary Report: 19–20). For those Governments which still felt the need to intervene in the provision of content, KPMG recommended that they might move away from funding public service broadcasters to the public library model, where the desired material was commissioned and purchased from outsiders, and then made available through virtual libraries.[13]

From DG XIII's perspective the value of the KPMG report was substantial. It offered a more far-ranging discussion of the regulatory implications of convergence than anything previously produced. What is more, its radicalism was useful in providing external legitimation for many of the ideas that DG XIII had itself been developing on the regulatory implications of convergence and bringing to the surface potential sources of opposition to any plans that the Commission itself might develop.

Many of the issues raised by KPMG appeared in a DG XIII draft Convergence Green Paper circulated to the Commission services for consultation in September 1997. It prompted a vigorous response from DG X questioning the draft Green Paper's analysis of the market, most of its conclusions and recommendations, and even the competence of DG XIII to touch on areas dealing with audio-visual policy in a Green Paper on regulatory structures. The result was a substantial rewriting of the Green Paper, and revisions continued as Commissioners' Cabinet staff met to negotiate its contents through the month of November. The Green Paper that was finally adopted by the Commission on 3 December bore the marks of this intense political battle, and was far less prescriptive and more open-ended than the original DG XIII draft. In a passage that almost directly reflected the contrasting positions of DG XIII and DG X the Green Paper reflected on the two views on the future of regulation:

> One view is that the development of new products and services is being held back by regulatory uncertainty – that existing rules were defined for a national, analogue and mono-media environment, but that services increasingly cut across different traditional sectors and geographical boundaries, and that they may be provided over a variety of platforms. This calls into question the underlying rationale beneath regulatory approaches in the different sectors affected by convergence. Proponents of this view would argue that such regulatory uncertainty holds back investment and damages the prospects for the implementation of the Information Society.
>
> An alternative view would hold that the specific characteristics of the existing separate sectors will limit the scope for service convergence. It further would contend that the role of the media industry as the bearer of social, cultural and ethical values within our society is independent of the technology relied upon to reach the consumer. This would mean that regulation of economic conditions and that of the provision of information services should be separated to ensure efficiency and quality.
>
> (EC 1997d: iii)

The Green Paper was peppered with such attempts at balancing contradictory positions. Thus national licensing regimes were presented positively 'as a key regulatory tool through which public authorities can exercise control over their national markets, particularly in relation to the provision of telecommunications and broadcasting networks and services'. However, they were implicitly criticised a couple of paragraphs later where it was pointed out that:

> The global dimension of the Internet and other communications and broadcast services will also impact on approaches to the enforcement of licensing, and call into question the relevance of national licensing of activities carried out either within a Member State or delivered by regional platforms, for example, by satellite.
>
> (EC 1997d: 22)[14]

The Green Paper offered an analysis of the regulatory obstacles to convergence. Among the potential barriers identified were the uncertainty caused by differing approaches to the classification of new services; the multiplicity of regulatory bodies that operators might have to deal with as well as the very varied ways in which they carried out their tasks; the differing licensing regimes that prevailed in different countries; and the contrasting approaches adopted to spectrum allocation in telecommunications and broadcasting. Other obstacles mentioned were the problems of access to conditional access systems, to networks and to premium content, and the lack of agreed standards supporting interoperability and interconnection of the converging networks.

Several proposals were advanced to deal with these 'potential obstacles'. Among the suggestions were the relaxation of existing licensing procedures and greater reliance on self regulation, as on the Internet; the possibility that broadcast channels might be licensed in groups (i.e. for a whole satellite package or all the four to six services on a terrestrial multiplex service – as happens under the UK's DTT licensing regime) rather than individually; and a common set of principles for licensing authorities. The Green Paper also proposed extending the existing requirements for fair, reasonable and non-discriminatory access to conditional access services, to take in electronic programme guides and the software within the set-top boxes.[15]

One of the most contentious areas of the Green Paper was its discussion of the future role of public interest objectives – and therefore of content regulation and of public broadcasting – in the converging communications industries. Initial proposals suggesting that 'must carry' requirements for public broadcasters be reviewed or dropped, and that the market would meet many of the requirements for pluralism and cultural diversity in the converging market, were removed from the final Green Paper. On the other hand, the idea that public service broadcasts should be commissioned from a range of providers instead of maintaining public service broadcasters, was retained.[16] The Green Paper also placed a question mark over whether public service broadcasters should be allowed to move into new areas such as the provision of on-line services.

The most important section of the Green Paper focused on the regulatory response to convergence. Three options were presented. First, building on current regulatory structures, largely at the national level; second, developing a separate regulatory model for new activities that could not be satisfactorily classified under telecommunications or broadcasting; and finally, moving towards a new regulatory model to cover the whole range of existing and new services. The preference that clearly emerged was for the third option of a new regulatory model for the entire converging communications environment. Having pointed out that this would call 'for a fundamental reassessment and reform of today's regulatory environment', the Green Paper was at pains to offer reassurance not just about the pace of any move towards the new model but also regarding its compatibility with policies aimed at addressing public interest concerns.[17]

Pressures for regulatory convergence

The forces pushing for a radical rewriting of regulatory structures were considerable. Many EU and other national telecommunications policy-makers argued that sector-based broadcasting regulation should be replaced by much greater reliance on competition policy, alongside a converged regulatory framework embracing the entire communications sector. Some went further, arguing that the increasingly trans-frontier nature of the communications industry called for more of such regulation as was still necessary to be enforced at the international or European level. For its proponents, the case for regulatory convergence had the advantage of presenting as inevitable something they themselves regarded as highly desirable. It suited EU policy-makers who wanted to see regulatory authority shifted from the national to the European level and influence within the Commission rebalanced, reinforcing DG XIII at the expense of the audio-visual Directorate, DG X. It also suited communications companies who wanted to launch new multimedia services unconstrained by what they saw as the tiresome and often conflicting obligations of national broadcasting regulation. Their hope was that European-level regulation would impose fewer constraints than national regulation while bringing more consistency. Enthusiasm for the primacy of competition policy may also have been motivated by the knowledge that DG IV was seriously understaffed.

Within the Commission, DG XIII officials and Commissioner Bangemann left little doubt that they favoured Option Three in the Convergence Green Paper. In speeches made just a couple of months before the Green Paper was published Commissioner Bangemann had expressed his desire for a complete change of approach towards communications regulation:

The future regulatory framework for communications and media in Europe . . . must be 'technology neutral', simplified, uniform, and not fragmented, so that it genuinely reflects the converged environment . . . When we come to review the European telecommunications environment in 1998, we will have to take stock of a completely different situation where it is no longer appropriate to keep telecommunications services separate from other media services. We will undoubtedly need to simplify the current framework and to design a European Communications and Media Act bringing together legislation on the provision of infrastructure, services, content . . . and on the conditions for access to that content (via TV, computer, or telephone networks) . . . For the time being we are encouraging closer co-operation between national regulatory authorities, however a single European regulatory authority for communications and media services may prove necessary.

(Bangemann 1997a)

Advocates of regulatory convergence did not have to depend just on the support of DG XIII within the European Commission. They could also turn to the OECD, whose thinking developed in a similar direction during the course of 1996–97. One OECD paper that appeared in 1997 called for the elimination of:

the traditional regulatory paradigm based on strict communication service boundaries . . . [of the] need to review content regulation, especially in terms of liberalising the provision of transborder flows of information including content [and to move at] the international level to have greater harmony between national regulatory concepts and practices.

(OECD 1997b: 7–8)

Later that year a pioneering piece of OECD work on the impact of 'webcasting' or the use of the Internet to deliver broadcast-type audio and video services appeared which concluded that:

The more webcasting comes to resemble traditional services the greater the challenge will become to the existing regulatory frameworks. This implies, if technological neutrality is to be practised, that existing regulation of traditional services needs to be reviewed in this light.

(OECD 1997c: 6)

The OECD's reflections were similar to those made by others concerned with telecoms policy-making. In the UK OFTEL had argued from as early as 1995 that 'broadcast services will become increasingly difficult to distinguish from other services [and] the traditional regulatory distinctions between broadcasting and telecommunications will be difficult to sustain' (OFTEL 1995: 4). Three years later (as noted in Chapter 6) the UK's House of Commons Select Committee on Culture, Media and Sport, recommended that there should be a single regulator and government department to deal with the entire communications sector (House of Commons 1998).

Within the EU – and in Germany – one of the most pressing concerns of new media companies was that unless they acted fast they might be subjected to broadcasting-type regulation. This fear was fuelled by the German debate between the Länder and the Federal Government over the treatment of new media services. In the EU fears focused on the attempts to expand the definition of broadcasting within the Television Without Frontiers Directive. Broadcasting was defined in the 1989 Directive as 'the initial transmission by wire or over the air, including that by satellite, in unencoded or encoded form, of television programmes intended for reception by the public . . . It does not include communication services providing items of information or other messages on individual demand such as telecopying, electronic data banks and other similar services'. When the revised draft Directive came to be discussed in the Culture Council the French and Belgium delegations tried to get the definition extended to include the phrase: 'it includes . . . communication to the public of audiovisual programmes on individual demand in return for payment'. Such attempts in the Council and the European Parliament failed, but they attracted sufficient support to persuade several industry players that there was a real threat which they needed to mobilise against. Much of the so-called convergence debate was prompted by this rather narrow concern about the degree to which broadcast-type regulation might otherwise be extended. Hence the enthusiasm of many IT companies for an approach based primarily on competition law rather than sector-specific regulation.[18]

Countervailing pressures

Advocates of regulatory convergence were naturally keen to suggest that their approach was the only reasonable response to the undoubted technological change that was underway. And yet, whilst they succeeding in launching the debate on regulatory reform in 1994–7, by 1998 radical solutions seemed far less likely to prevail than had appeared initially. Three factors led to this change. The first was that in their own reflections on regulation Member States saw far less of a pressing need for dramatic change than was identified by EU and international policy-makers. Second, the development by the Internal Market Directorate, DG XV, of a so-called transparency measure for the mutual notification of regulatory reforms weakened the case for EU-wide regulation of the entire communications sector. Third, the publication of the Convergence Green Paper helped to mobilise far more active opposition to regulatory convergence within the EU's institutions, from certain sectors of the communications industry, and on the part of Member States, than had previously been anticipated.

We have seen in Chapter 6 how very few Member States saw convergence as necessarily leading to a radical reform of existing regulatory structures. It is true that in Italy a single communications regulator was established. The governments of the UK, France and Germany were all fascinated by the opportunities for economic growth offered by convergence but there was no consensus on the pressing need for regulatory convergence. The pressures were greatest in Germany, but this largely reflected the creation of a new arena in which the struggle for competence between the Länder and the Federal Government could be played out. All three countries undertook some regulatory reform, but none established a converged regulator at national level, and they all retained regulatory rules that treated broadcasting – including video-on-demand – differently from telecoms. Each of them gave greater attention to the application of competition rules to questions of access and market power in the communications sector, but none made the logical leap proposed by some advocates of regulatory convergence, namely, that of replacing sectoral regulation for broadcasting and telecoms with a complete reliance on competition law.

Proponents of a greater EU role in regulation of the Communications sector also found difficulty in mobilising support from Member State governments. It was hardly surprising that many Member States were wary of what would amount to a corresponding decrease in their autonomy. But for the most part their natural suspicion of any extension of EU competence in the communications sector was matched by a lack of enthusiasm on the part of industry itself. Since the Commission failed to win widespread industry support for the creation of an EU telecoms regulatory authority, it seemed unlikely that industry would be any more enthusiastic about the Bangemann proposal for the creation of a Europe-wide Media and Communications authority.[19]

The transparency directive

One of the arguments that the Convergence Green Paper deployed for the creation of a greater EU regulatory role was that too great a dependence on reforming existing national regulatory frameworks would lead to fragmentation of the internal market. Similarly, the Green Paper's preference for Option Three, of a move towards regulatory convergence, was that the continuing adaptation of sectoral regulation, or the creation of a new regulatory framework for so-called new services, failed to recognise the impact of convergence in leading to the collapse of past sectoral boundaries. But, ironically, the Commission had itself created a response to both these arguments through its Directive on Regulatory Transparency for Information Society Services first proposed in 1996 and then adopted in 1998. This Internal Market measure created a new and separate category of 'Information Society services' which included neither broadcasting nor telecoms, and introduced a mutual notification procedure for changes in Member States' regulatory treatment of such services.

The 1998 Transparency Directive builds on a 1983 Internal Market Directive (Directive 83/189/EEC) requiring Member States to notify the Commission and other Member States of proposed technical rules for products in draft form. It introduced a three-month notification period for new national legislative proposals during which other Member States could lodge objections. If objections were raised the first state would have to postpone adoption of the technical regulation for six months from the date of notification, a period which could be increased to twelve months if the Commission notified it that it was itself planning to propose or adopt a Directive on the same subject, or eighteen months in certain circumstances. The possibility of exemptions from these rules were strictly limited to grounds of health and safety, the protection of animals or the protection of plants.

The 1998 Transparency Directive marks a new departure in extending a measure previously devised for technical standards in products, to the regulation of service provision (Directive 98/34/EC, 22 July 1998, *Official Journal* L 204/37, 21 July 1998). When proposing the measure in 1996 DG XV – the lead DG – justified this because of the expected upsurge in regulatory reform by Member States keen to respond to the impact of the Information Society, arguing that:

> there is every reason to believe that these new rules and regulations in the Member States will be highly divergent from one Member State to another, each of them being motivated by concerns of their own stemming from a different perception of the general interest objectives to be pursued. [As a result there is a] serious risk of refragmentation of the Internal Market, that is to say, of the introduction of new, unjustified or excessive obstacles to the free movement of services between Member States and to the freedom of establishment for the providers of such services, which might . . . have repercussions at Community level in the form of overregulation or mutually inconsistent regulations.

The Commission concluded that there was 'a clear need for co-ordination at the Community level of this future regulatory activity in order to forestall any such refragmentation of the Internal Market and to pursue more incisively (sic) general interest objectives that are worthy of protection' (EC 1996a).

At one level the Transparency Measure was in keeping with the deregulatory bias of much of the IS Programme, and it can be seen as a pre-emptive attempt at deregulation in this field as well as an internal market measure.[20] On the other hand the very existence of the draft Directive from 1996 onwards, with its mutual notification procedures, weakened the case for pan-European regulation. Moreover, the sensitivity of the subject matter meant that the Commission only felt able to propose this mutual notification procedure for a limited range of those new services 'provided at a distance by electronic means and on the individual request of a service receiver', a definition that specifically excluded broadcasting but could extend to situations where a viewer ordered a VOD film.[21] The effect was to create a new category of services, thereby undermining the case for a single, converged framework for all communications services.

The hostility aroused by the draft Transparency Directive provided an indication of the extent to which Member States would defend their freedom of action in communications regulation. When the measure was first discussed by Internal Market Ministers in October 1996 the most vocal objections came from France, but reservations were also made by Belgium, the Netherlands, Luxembourg, Denmark, Sweden, Portugal and Germany. The French objected – on cultural grounds – to regulation of cultural and some audio-visual matters simply being treated as IS services. The Swedes were concerned about the implications for national legislation on freedom of the press.[22]

Germany's objections were threefold. First, on the grounds of subsidiarity: from their perspective the loose definition of IS services could be used as a bridgehead from which Commission competence could expand without limit. As one Federal Government official objected: 'the regulation will have an inherent tendency to cover almost everything'. Second, since Germany was herself keen to move fast in creating her own legislative framework for multimedia services, the prospect of any of their proposals being delayed for eighteen months by the EU was disturbing, particularly since the Germans knew that their legislation might require later amendments which could be subject to the same delay. Finally, while the Commission was explaining to journalists that the transparency measure could prevent unnecessary national regulation on cultural or taste and decency issues for on-line services, the Germans were regarding this as either a Federal or a Länder responsibility, but not a matter which should fall to the EU.[23]

Many of these objections were resolved in discussions between Member States' representatives (in COREPER). When the proposed Directive was discussed in the Council of Ministers, the proposed six-month standstill before a disputed piece of national legislation could come into effect was reduced to a maximum of four months (*Agence Europe* 29 November 1997).[24] Other concessions by the Commission included: a reduction in the scope of the draft directive; the addition of clauses indicating that it would have no impact on national legislation on freedom of the press and general criminal law; a new provision allowing Member States to adopt a fast track procedure and legislate in exceptional circumstances for urgent reasons of public policy; and a limitation on the Commission's power to impose the maximum standstill period to those cases where provisions in a draft national rule conflicted with the Commission's own proposals. From the point of view of the broadcasting sector, the most significant concession was a specific statement that the standstill provisions would not affect any cultural policy measures.[25]

Reactions to the Convergence Green Paper

The publication of the Convergence Green Paper also played a decisive part in mobilising opinion against many of the assumptions that underpinned it. Until then, the advocates of regulatory convergence had usually made headway within the telecoms or IT policy community, or at least in areas where they found few opponents with sufficient expertise to dispute their approach. In contrast, the very ambition of the Convergence Green Paper meant that it extended across the whole communications sector, and it was only to be expected that broadcasting policy-makers would want to express their views on it. As we have seen, even before the Green Paper was published there was a vigorous battle over its contents within the Commission, with DG X fighting hard to ensure that it was genuinely consultative and not just a manifesto for regulatory convergence at the European level (*European Voice* 25 June 1998 and *The Guardian* 10 December 1997).

After publication, the Green Paper provoked a backlash against its deregulatory assumptions. Within the European Parliament Socialist MEPs such as Carole Tongue and Helmut Kuhne campaigned to ensure that questions of cultural policy, public interest regulation, and the role of public service broadcasting were properly recognised in discussions of convergence.[26] Many of the reflections by Member States, broadcasting regulators, and some industry groupings also questioned large areas of the Green Paper's approach and conclusions. Telecoms and Culture Ministers meeting in the first half of 1998, during the UK Presidency, registered the importance of convergence, but resisted any speedy endorsement of any of the options in the Convergence Green Paper. Then the April 1998 Birmingham Audiovisual Conference, which was jointly organised by DG X and the UK presidency, offered an important opportunity for DG X and those Culture Ministers who were present to reaffirm the importance of many aspects of public interest regulation – such as measures to protect pluralism, the European production industry, and the role of public service broadcasting – which advocates of regulatory convergence generally accepted more on sufferance than anything else. A combative speech during the conference by Rupert Murdoch, in which he attacked Europe's public service broadcasters, only seemed to strengthen the resolve of DG X and national officials to reject the simple deregulatory route.

The UK Presidency reported to the May Culture Council on how the Birmingham Conference had stressed the need for a partnership between cultural and commercial goals, together with strong support for the continuing centrality of PSBs. (In Birmingham, the UK Culture Secretary, Chris Smith, had commented on how public service provision might grow more, not less, important as commercial pressures intensified.) The UK Presidency also reported that there had been 'little enthusiasm for models which seek to prescribe or second guess future market developments. For this reason the Conference was not in favour as such of the third option in the Green Paper on Convergence'. The importance of subsidiarity was also stressed in the area of cultural regulation.

Similar themes appeared in the responses of some key broadcasting regulators to the Green Paper. The French CSA's response expressed doubts about the extent, timing and consequences of convergence, arguing that strong regulation will remain necessary to guarantee proper functioning of the market and the preservation of the general interest, and that the audio-visual sector should continue to be subject to specific regulation. According to the CSA, regulation should be based on the nature of the service rather than the technical means of delivery; questions of whether or not there should be a single regulator were seen as being best decided at national, rather than the EU level. Unsurprisingly the CSA endorsed the evolutionary reform option (Option One) as the only viable way forward.

The response from the UK's broadcasting regulator, the ITC, adopted a similar approach, stressing the specificity of broadcasting regulation and the need for its continuation, despite the increasing number of channels and widespread technological change. It too endorsed evolutionary rather than radical regulatory change, and opposed the introduction of any new form of EU regulation of the broadcasting sector. Interestingly this sceptical note was also contained in the response submitted by the DVB group, which represented a wide range of public service and commercial broadcasters, regulators, and consumer electronics and IT companies, and which endorsed Option One in the Green Paper. The DVB response also recognised a continuing role for content regulation and sector-specific regulation, alongside an increased role for competition policy.

When in July 1998 the Commission published its Working Paper summarising the responses to the Green Paper, it was clear that there was no consensus for radical reform (EC 1998i). A clear majority of those responding favoured an evolutionary approach to regulatory reform, supporting Option One or Two rather than Option Three. Sectoral regulation – which operating alongside competition policy rather than being replaced by it – was endorsed, and whilst there was substantial support for moving towards a common set of rules applied across all infrastructure and networks, most respondents favoured a sectoral approach for content regulation. The majority of broadcasters who responded questioned the Green Paper's assumption that public interest objectives constituted a barrier to convergence. There was no demand for the abolition of public service broadcasters, but commercial operators, and some regulators, called for greater transparency between their commercial and publicly funded operations, and some sought to curtail the range of activities undertaken by public service broadcasters.

Undeterred by this lukewarm response, the Commission announced plans to undertake a further consultation exercise, focusing on regulation of access to networks and digital gateways, on creating a framework for investment, innovation and European content production, distribution and availability, and on the future regulatory framework. The justification for this second round of consultation was that it would be more tightly focused. There must also have been the hope that it might provide more support for regulatory action by the EU rather than Member States.

By the middle of 1998 it was clear that whilst the Commission had succeeded in launching a far-reaching discussion on convergence both at the EU and national levels, it had not won support for a radical agenda of regulatory convergence. Member States were wary of Option Three, recognising that it would offer an opportunity for greatly increased EU intervention in the media sector. Similarly the cultural lobby, along with the majority of broadcasting regulators and public service broadcasters, felt that radical regulatory change was more likely to follow a telecoms or IT deregulatory approach that might cast doubt on their future utility. And finally, many commercial broadcasters recognised that whilst widespread regulatory reform might be intellectually attractive, it was also likely to launch a protracted period of political debate and regulatory uncertainty. Without a guarantee that the outcome would be the desired one, few were ready to place the future operations of their companies at the mercy of the EU political process. In short a consensus emerged that incremental change at the national level was preferable to wholesale reform at the EU level. The result was that whilst regulatory reform would undoubtedly progress, it appeared that as far as broadcasting was concerned, this was more likely to occur at the national than the EU level. The EU's role as a policy leader towards regulatory convergence across the communications sector, which had been so painstakingly established in the years immediately following on from the Bangemann Report, seemed to be on the wane.

Part IV
Conclusions

8   Convergence
New approaches

Introduction

Much of the discussion about the regulatory implications of convergence
is characterised by differing forms of determinism which assume that consumer behaviour will be led by technological change and that regulation
should follow suit. At its most extreme this view asserts that if communications technologies converge, then there must be a converged regulatory
framework across the communications sector; if digitization makes content
technically interchangeable then it too should all be regulated in the same
way; and that if new digital services are capable of crossing national boundaries then it follows that regulation must move from the national to the
international level.

Many of these assertions are highly questionable. Technological convergence itself will not be total. Many services will remain primarily national
in scope, and while some will stretch the boundaries between the broadcasting and telecoms sectors, the majority will fit within traditional
categories. Digitization will be accompanied by a convergence of networks
and of consumer devices but not of content. Consumers may use the same
networks and devices to access digitally encoded faxes, films, phone conversations or TV programmes, but they will use all these items in different
ways, and expect regulators to recognise this fact. As integrated PC/TVs
become more widely available and digital set-top boxes become increasingly like computers (with larger processors, Internet access, and in time,
integrated hard disks) the likelihood is that there will continue to be a difference in the way that consumers use the TV/PC in the living room, from
how they use the PC/TV in their office. Word processing, watching TV,
and making a phone call – even via a videophone – will all continue to be
different kinds of activity, consumed in different ways, and with different
social and hence regulatory implications.[1] And yet it is changes in consumer behaviour rather than technology that should drive the pace of
regulatory change.

Convergence does not render all existing regulatory distinctions, or indeed regulation itself, either redundant or ineffective. Instead it creates a need to review some regulatory categories, raises some new regulatory issues, and creates new problems of implementation. Similarly, whilst convergence will lead to more cross-national services it would be premature to conclude that the existing territorial basis of regulation is outdated and must immediately be replaced with EU or international level regulation (Bangemann 1997a). Europe will be too big for some issues and too small for others. Most digital TV services will still be created and operate primarily at the national level. Some Internet services on the other hand will be truly global, and their regulation, in so far as it is possible at all, may accordingly have to take place at a global rather than a regional level.

This chapter starts by assessing some of the more common arguments that are made for regulation to be relaxed in the face of convergence. It moves on to propose a regulatory agenda for digital broadcasting and to look at the ways in which this agenda might be accomplished in terms of the instruments that might be used, the regulatory structures, and the balance between sector-specific and competition regulation. Later it examines some of the ways in which regulatory responsibilities might be divided between the nation states and the EU, and offers a view of the main options for future regulation presented in the 1997 Commission Green Paper on Convergence.

The end of regulation?

Several arguments are advanced as to why convergence should lead to a reduction in the role of broadcasting regulation. Some argue that it will become redundant, others that it is undesirable, and both schools of thought agree that it will become increasingly difficult to enforce. The end of spectrum scarcity, the proliferation of channels, and changes in the way in which broadcasting is consumed, are all cited in support of the case that digitalisation will render broadcasting regulation superfluous.

Redundant regulation

Spectrum scarcity provided a useful pretext for much broadcasting regulation over the last half century. Digitalisation and compression will diminish – though not eliminate – the impact of that scarcity.[2] But to argue that scarcity was the driving force behind intervention in broadcasting is to confuse means with ends. The true rationale for broadcasting regulation lies in the uniquely influential role of a medium which helps form public opinion, provides a forum for public debate and discussion, and – in places where regulation has not intervened to prevent it – offers a unique source of commercial and political power for private media owners (Garnham 1996). As long as broadcasting continues to be influential, its content, structure and ownership will continue to be a source of concern to public policy-makers. There is no more sign of a waning of that influence in multichannel Germany or the US than there is in Britain where the average household has access to only four or five channels. Whilst convergence will lead to more channels it will also increase people's dependence on screen-based media for all their information, educational and entertainment needs. Regulatory concerns motivated by the unique influence of the medium may be expected to increase, rather than diminish. As Hoffmann-Riem points out:

> The crucial topic of regulation is the problem of use and abuse of power . . . The basic normative idea of necessary protection against the one-sided use of power, however, continues to apply, even if there is a shift in the scarcity constellation and new abuse potentials become identifiable.
>
> (Hoffmann-Riem 1996b: 333)

The market solution

Others have argued that with hundreds of channels many of the traditional concerns of broadcasting regulation – for pluralism, impartiality, a diversity of programming, and the promotion of cultural goals – will be met by the market.[3] While the operation of the digital broadcasting market will undoubtedly increase competition and choice, it will not guarantee, and it may not meet, many of these aspirations. Market disciplines will not of themselves deliver all the things we expect from broadcast media such as an extended range of high quality programming, universal access to broadcast programmes and events, and independence and diversity. As Congdon puts it: 'There is no evident connection between the conditions for pluralistic political debate and the motives of companies trying to maximise their profits in a competitive environment' (Congdon 1995: 15).

A further argument is that free-to-air 'broadcasting' will increasingly be replaced by narrowcasting and the development of on-demand, individualised pay services. According to this view the rise of direct payment and the decline of mass universal channels weakens the case for special regulation of broadcasting. If those market predictions were accurate there would be a case for relaxing some aspects of the prohibitive approach to content regulation, but not for ceasing positive public intervention in the broadcast sector. Yet most industry observers agree that in ten years' time the typical consumer experience will still be that of watching conventional networked channels, rather than calling up programmes on demand, or indeed of consumers 'producing' their own programmes at home.[4] As long as broadcasting remains a one-to-many mass medium, regulation may be expected to recognise that fact.

Regulation as an obstacle to convergence

Allied to the suggestions that broadcasting regulation is redundant, there is a series of arguments which contend that it is positively harmful and that regulation is acting as a drag on the realisation of full convergence and its accompanying benefits. Nationally and sector-based broadcasting regulation is blamed for creating regulatory inconsistencies between converging technologies and double jeopardy for firms exposed to multiple regulatory authorities, as well as for placing the EU at a competitive disadvantage to other regions with a more consistent, or simply a lower set of regulatory requirements (EC 1997d, KPMG 1996). Regulatory overlap and a lack of transparency or clarity about the rules can lead to difficulties for some firms. But there is no evidence that regulatory differences explain the relative economic performance of the US and European ICT sectors. Other factors such as the benefits of a large and linguistically homogenous home market, labour skills and mobility, access to risk capital, and the cost of local phone calls (free local calls have played an important part in the growth of the Internet in the US) are all likely to loom far larger than the regulatory framework. So far the economic case for regulatory reform has been marked by a lack of any hard evidence, or indeed any rigorous analysis of the relationship between regulation and growth to date.[5]

In the absence of a particularly powerful economic analysis, it may be that demands for regulatory reform are motivated by other reasons. The simple desire to create a more predictable and 'rational' system may offer one such motivation. But the regulatory convergence agenda also fits well with the broader ideological trend towards deregulation. It offers the basis for an alliance between policy-makers at the EU level, keen to expand their remit to take in broadcasting, and companies who believe that a converged EU regulatory system, will be less constricting, less intrusive and less 'political' than one dominated by national 'cultural' concerns. Arguments for greater consistency of rules within the EU are persuasive, but need to be balanced against the differing circumstances and regulatory objectives that prevail in each country. It is not fanciful to suggest that the search for greater regulatory consistency via a general levelling down of obligations, may be motivated more by a combination of sectional, bureaucratic and ideological interests than by any well documented economic case for regulatory reform.

The impossibility of effective regulation

Critics of broadcasting regulation often argue that what they regard as undesirable is also unachievable, and that an increasingly international media market will be impossible to regulate. Yet many of the current concerns about enforcement were first raised when satellite broadcasting started in the 1980s. Since then, national rather than Europe-wide services have been the norm, and a few Member States, notably the British, have found ways of restricting the availability of some foreign satellite channels.[6] While the advent of satellite broadcasting undoubtedly reduces the effectiveness of national licensing controls, the move towards pay television that will accompany digitalisation also presents new possibilities for regulators. Pay broadcasters will require conditional access and subscription management services, as well as ways of marketing and receiving payment for their channels. Most of these activities must take place in the country of reception rather than transmission (the set-top box which will decrypt the signal must be located in the consumer's home), and some require licensing by national authorities. Collectively they offer a new locus for enforcement by national Governments and regulators.[7]

Regulating digital broadcasting

Regulation of digital broadcasting needs to build on the objectives established for the analogue world. Existing concerns with the regulation of content and controls to ensure pluralism will remain, while coinciding with an increased focus on the regulation of access to the distribution system, and on ensuring fair competition and consumer protection within the converging communications market. One of the greatest challenges will be to ensure that, as pay services develop, television's current role in providing free, or very cheap, mass access to quality information does not decline.

Regulating content

Content regulation is one of the main features of broadcasting – as opposed to telecoms – regulation. As argued above, so long as broadcasting remains uniquely influential, policy-makers will continue to have a view on what material should be offered, and will engage in some form of content regulation. Views will differ between countries, but most concur that there are benefits in ensuring that at least some parts of the broadcasting system are obliged to offer quality programming across a range of genres, to provide impartial coverage of news and current affairs, and generally to help serve as a focus for debate and a source of common reference points within society (Graham and Davies 1997). These functions reflect television's role in both reflecting and influencing a society's values, its culture and its political behaviour.

Convergence does not remove the need for public policies to secure these objectives, but it does raise questions about how they might be best achieved. Huge increases in the numbers of channels that are available, and a greater degree of individual control over what is watched, make it unreasonable to suggest that all channels should be regulated equally vigorously; what is more, the costs involved in constantly monitoring all the available channels would be difficult to justify. Traditional forms of negative regulation, aimed at prohibiting certain kinds of programmes, at protecting young people from pornography or violence, and at preventing offence being caused to certain groups or individuals, will still be needed. But in a multichannel world viewers too will have to accept a greater sense of responsibility. Technology can offer some help here if programme providers are willing to co-operate. Viewers will find it easier to access information about a programme from their EPG rather than hunting for the correct page of a listings magazine. And it is a relatively easy process to build in user-programmable controls to limit access to certain types of programmes. Devising suitable labelling and classification systems, however, is far more complex.[8]

Viewers will also play a greater role in enforcement procedures. In the absence of constant monitoring, regulators will be increasingly dependent on viewer complaints. New delivery mechanisms, and the growth of niche and pay channels, will offer greater scope for content regulation to be both relaxed and strengthened. Rules for content regulation should be applied in a more graduated way, depending both on the degree to which the channel is available to the 'public', and the consciousness of the choice and degree of user control exercised by the viewer. In practice this reflects the long accepted approach towards the regulation of pornography, where differing levels of prohibition apply to films. These depend on the time, manner and place in which the films are shown, namely, on TV (before or after 9 p.m.), in a cinema on general release, or, for a video, on whether they are sold in a 'specialist' or a general video shop.[9] The graduated approach to content regulation would mean that some 'broadcast' content, offered on demand, or via pay per view, where the viewer makes a conscious choice to view the material, would be regulated more lightly than in the past. Programmes offered over 'telecoms' or Internet-type delivery systems, would not be exempt from broadcast regulation as many in the IT sector desire. However if, as seems likely, the services were subject to a charge, or other form of user control, then they would be subject to the lightest form of broadcast regulation.

Alongside this decline in negative content regulation for the bulk of commercial channels there will be an increased role for public service broadcasting (PSB). This will reflect a more general need for intervention in the communications market to rely increasingly on the positive promotion of public goods, rather than traditional prohibitive approaches. Public service broadcasting offers one way of ensuring that certain kinds of programming continue to be available to a mass audience. Clearly the remit and funding of these public service broadcasters should be left to Member States to determine, as provided for in the 1997 Amsterdam Protocol on PSB. There are advantages in having Member States specify that remit with a degree of clarity, thus allowing commercial operators to plan accordingly. But while the economic justification for such intervention may be market failure, the social, political and cultural justifications for the existence of public sector broadcasting demand that it is provided on more than a purely niche or residual basis.[10] With digital technology, and the growing role of pay channels, effective public service channels will need to retain a universal appeal in order to ensure that they really do provide universal access to quality free-to-air programming. 'Must carry' provisions will be needed on the new digital networks to ensure that viewers have ready access to these publicly funded channels, and that network operators are not tempted to use all their capacity for pay TV and other transactional services.[11] The increased capacity available on digital networks should also make 'must carry' requirements less onerous than in the analogue world. Similarly, as distribution technologies develop and consumer habits change, so PSBs will need to adapt to these changes and offer public service content on a range of different delivery systems.

It is the Internet rather than broadcasting which poses the most serious problems for enforcement of content regulation since, uniquely, it is a truly international service, but even here we should be wary of what has been termed the 'easily committed mistake that because regulation is not watertight we should abandon the attempt to regulate at all' (Collins and Murroni 1996: 114). It is interesting to note that the same groups who declare that Internet content regulation is impossible are often very ready to pursue vigorous enforcement of various forms of economic regulation on issues such as copyright and piracy.[12] If enforcement of intellectual property rights is possible on the Internet this would suggest that content control is not completely out of the question. What is true is that the effort involved in the enforcement of content regulation will need to be weighed carefully against the objectives that are sought. Self regulation and content rating systems will be much more important in the Internet sphere than for broadcasting, but should not be seen as a panacea either. The rapid expansion in the World Wide Web, together with the time required for rating, means that the proportion of pages with content rating declines daily.

Regulating access

The access and interconnection regulation which characterises the telecoms sector will become a feature across the converging communications industry. Regulation of access to the new digital networks and attempts at standardisation will be required to ensure that consumers can access the widest possible range of services, and that service providers and broadcasters can access whichever networks they need to reach their consumers and viewers.

There will be different ways of achieving these goals. Common and open standards offer the best way of ensuring that consumers are not tied into any one proprietary technology. Where common and open standards cannot be agreed, public authorities must have reserve powers to step in to aid moves to interoperability, and in cases where proprietary technologies become the *de facto* standard (as with Windows in the PC environment), their owners must allow third parties timely access to the specifications so that applications and services can be designed to run smoothly with them. Regulation will also be required to guarantee fair, reasonable and non-discriminatory access to digital networks, as provided for in the 1995 Television Standards Directive (see Chapter 4). With convergence, these access obligations need to be drawn more widely, and extend beyond the TV environment to include other interactive and on-line services. Since new digital gateways are emerging all the time, the regulatory framework should focus on behaviour as much as on any specific pieces of technology. A presumption that the entire digital gateway constitutes an 'essential facility' or 'bottleneck' to which access should be granted, would minimise the risks of operators circumventing specific access regulation through the use of new, and as yet unspecified, access devices (Murroni and Irvine 1998, OFTEL 1998c).[13]

Judgements of what constitutes 'reasonable' terms for access to such facilities will call for regulators with deep knowledge of the industry. In cases where detailed regulation of prices and access (of the kind already started by OFTEL in the UK) becomes unduly onerous (either for the regulator or the network operator), an alternative could be considered involving structural separation of vertically integrated broadcasters/network operators, with a view to reducing their incentives to exert leverage for dominance across market sectors. In the UK context structural separation might, for example, require BSkyB to choose between being a broadcaster or a network operator and supplier of conditional access services. Similar questions have been raised by DG IV over BT's (admittedly limited) involvement in the UK cable industry.

Pluralism, competition and consumer protection

Broadcasting is characterised by substantial economies of scope and scale which, unchecked, create pressures towards concentration (Graham and Davies 1997). Digital technology increases these pressures as operators seek to gain control of the most attractive content and the delivery systems which provide access to the customer. Regulation will be required to avoid the creation of monopolies in either content provision or carriage. Competition rules will need to be enforced rigorously across the industry, whilst not deterring companies from investing in the creation of new content and delivery systems. Competition will be helped if limits are imposed on the ability of any player to monopolise ownership of premium content (such as key sport and film rights), if multiple delivery systems are encouraged, and if interoperability between delivery systems emerges.

Given the special nature of the media there will also be a case for intervention to protect diversity of programming as well as simple competition.

As the UK Government pointed out in 1995, 'special media ownership rules, which exist in all major media markets, are needed . . . to provide the safeguards necessary to maintain diversity and plurality' (DNH 1995 para. 1.4). Hoffmann-Riem justifies intervention to achieve pluralism in the following terms: 'Anyone who makes the provision of communication the purpose of business activities and thus shapes the opinion of society as a whole must themselves become the object of this public opinion, with respect to internal structures too' (Hoffmann-Riem 1996b: 341). In the digital environment, media ownership regulation will be a necessary part of measures to promote pluralism and competition, but it will not be sufficient to guarantee either objective.

New consumer protection issues will arise as digital services develop. As viewers interact more with their TVs, ever more sophisticated customer profiles will be created, and thought will need to be given to the privacy issues that arise, and to who owns the customer information that is generated by each transaction. If consumers themselves are not allowed to own their own customer information and profile (rather than just simply granting or withholding consent for its generation) then they will find that changing their service provider or network operator will be extremely difficult.[14] On digital networks, consumers will also find it far harder to know whether what they are viewing is really what it purports to be, and there may be a need for new methods of confirming the origin of channels, programmes and services.[15] Content producers and consumers alike will have an interest in secure authentication systems, the first group in order to protect their intellectual property, and the second to confirm the reliability of the information or programmes they are accessing.

Industrial and cultural policy

Television is unusual in that, in the absence of any market intervention, Europe's adverse balance of trade with the US will continue to deteriorate. The growth of satellite broadcasting has had a very direct and adverse impact on the balance of the audio-visual sector's balance of payments with the US (Tongue 1998). The reasons for this are many, and policy-makers need to decide whether they are happy for the trend to continue or whether instead they advocate some intervention to reverse it. The influence of television on mass culture means that this is a cultural and social as well as economic issue. But policy-makers need to be more specific about when they seek to intervene for cultural reasons and when for economic reasons. A failure to make this distinction can lead to confused policies, which achieve neither aim, a fate which has befallen some of the EU's own interventions in this area. Broadcast quotas, of the kind provided for in Television Without Frontiers, have not been a particularly effective way of increasing investment in the European production industry.[16] The same is true of the various EU support measures which have been tried to date.

The paradox of European audio-visual policy is that so far there has been more industry support at the national rather than the European level. Europe's PSBs together invest more each year in original audio-visual production than either the film sector or all the EU support money that has been spent since EU intervention began. There are strong arguments for including the obligation to invest in original national and European productions within the remit of PSBs, rather than imposing quotas on the industry as a whole. Since the most popular programmes in every European country are themselves domestically produced, a production obligation on PSBs will have a beneficial spill-over effect on the rest of the market.

Reforming regulatory structures

Regulatory objectives should be reflected in the regulatory instruments and structures that are used. But proposals to alter existing structures need to ensure that they do not create greater regulatory uncertainty than it was their intention to dispel. Given the uncertainties about the development of the market, the search for the perfect regulatory structure for the converging communications industry is destined to prove illusory. Much of the debate on regulatory structures has focused on three interlinked themes: the move towards a horizontal regulatory approach focused on carriage and content rather than sectoral distinctions; the arguments for a greater focus on competition-based rules rather than sector-specific regulation; and the contention that a single regulator for telecoms and broadcasting would offer the most effective solution (KPMG 1996, Murroni 1997, Collins and Murroni 1996). This section examines the case for each of these proposals.

Horizontal versus sectoral regulation

It is possible to view many, but not all regulatory objectives in terms of those that relate to the economic issues of carriage and infrastructure, and those that relate essentially to the political and cultural issues raised within content regulation.

There are undoubted attractions in moving towards a horizontal approach based on these distinctions instead of the existing sectoral distinctions based on the delivery system that is used. Convergence places traditional sectoral categories such as 'broadcasting' or 'telecoms' under strain, since some new services will emerge that do not fit easily into either category.

Broadcasting has traditionally been defined in terms of communication from one to many, and as such the nature of the content that has been transmitted has concerned policy-makers far more than in telecoms, where most communication is one to one. Some new services such as VOD will contain elements of both – one to many communication when a VOD film is received, and one to one communication when it is ordered. Borderline services such as these could be placed in either category, hence the attraction of transcending existing sectoral definitions and creating a new set of horizontal regulatory structures. Yet even the content/carriage distinction is far from watertight. Many aspects of content regulation, such as the promotion of a national production industry, the desire to encourage large industry players, and the regulation of access to national sporting events, are either motivated by, or impact on, economic as much as cultural considerations. Similarly, many aspects of carriage regulation accomplished by existing regulators, such as access to spectrum, licensing and so on, provide useful levers through which regulators can secure compliance with content-related objectives (Murroni 1997: 7). Attempts to categorise all regulatory issues as being either content or infrastructure related must address these complicating factors.

An alternative approach would be to build on existing regulatory structures, extending the remit of broadcasting regulators to cover content on new distribution systems, whilst relaxing regulation to reflect the very differing circumstances in which such content is consumed. Similarly, telecoms regulators should extend their remit to include access to networks and distribution systems in the broadcast and on-line as well as telecoms environment. The consequence would be that some services – such as VOD – might be subject to dual regulation, both of content and infrastructure. This should not be dismissed as an unworkable or 'untidy' solution, but rather recognised as reflecting the varied regulatory issues that such services raise.

The UK regulatory framework has started to evolve in this direction over the last few years. The telecoms regulator, OFTEL, has become more involved in regulating access to broadcast as well as telecoms networks, primarily through its regulations on conditional access. Similarly the broadcasting regulator, the ITC, has become more willing to use its powers to ensure 'fair and effective competition' (under the 1990 Broadcasting Act) to examine the ways in which channels are 'bundled' together and to produce a code of conduct on the operation of electronic programme guides (ITC 1997b, 1998a). This approach seems to make best use of the skills that differing regulators possess, and has the flexibility to recognise that differing aspects of the same service may raise access and content-related issues.

Competition versus sector-specific regulation

The arguments for the replacement of sector-specific regulation by the operation of competition law have developed considerable support – primarily amongst pay broadcasters, telecoms companies and from the IT sector – in recent years. Those who argue in favour hold that such a move would overcome the definitional issues raised by convergence, reflect the way in which communications as a whole is becoming a sector like any other, and remove the excessive political interference which is often a feature of broadcasting regulation.[17]

The arguments for the pure competition-based approach appear weak. The fact that broadcasting regulation is subject to political intervention simply reflects the political importance of the sector. The assumption that a simple structural change – whereby broadcasting regulation would be transferred to a competition authority – would reduce the incentive for such intervention is a naïve one. Clearly, broadcast content regulation requires essentially qualitative and subjective judgements that can best be taken by specialists in the subject, even if that will prove no guarantee of immunity from controversy. Regulation of access issues in broadcasting might appear the most fruitful area where competition policy could replace sector-specific regulation. Competition policy can play a valuable role in establishing clear principles in areas such as the treatment of new digital networks as essential facilities or bottlenecks, enforcing structural separation where necessary, and acting as an additional safeguard standing behind sector-specific regulation. But specific access regulation is needed for detailed matters such as the terms for interconnection and interoperability, of access to networks, and for the ways in which the new navigation devices will guide viewers through a range of channels.

In each of these cases regulation needs to be established early on, both to prevent abuses before they occur and to create the greatest possible regulatory certainty for investors in new services. A sector-specific regulator, or a regulator of carriage issues across the communications sector, can in this way establish expertise in one area, and build up precedents that can help create greater predictability in the regulatory process than is possible simply through the operation of competition law. The EU competition regime offers a very valuable point of appeal in the case of abuse. However, other than in the case of merger control, it suffers from severe overload, long delay, and retrospective implementation, all of which pose severe problems in a fast moving industry.[18]

Against the advantages that flow from the operation of specialised regulation of this kind, must be set the risk of regulatory capture. The solution – rather than relying exclusively on a competition-based approach – is to create regulatory bodies that are both expert in their field and rigorously independent. A comparison of the relative effectiveness of the UK Office of Fair Trading as against that of OFTEL suggests that the quality of the regulator, and its ability to resist political and commercial pressures, are not necessarily linked to whether it is a sector-specific or general competition agency.

A single regulator?

The most radical proposal for regulatory reform is that there should be a single communications regulator – an Office of Communications (OFCOM) at national level, or even a EUROCOM at the European level (Bangemann 1997a, Labour Party 1995, Collins and Murroni 1996). This idea is intellectually appealing and appears to offer a simple solution to the many problems of overlapping jurisdictions and shifting definitional boundaries that are identified by proponents of regulatory convergence. But the complicating factor in broadcasting is not so much the multiplicity of regulatory bodies as of regulatory objectives. After all, broadcasting attracts attention at differing times, as a major sector of the economy, a generator of jobs, a source of competitive advantage, a cultural product, an educational instrument, a forum for political debate, a window on the world, and a key component in cultural and political socialisation.

The creation of a single regulator would do nothing of itself to reduce the number of these multiple and sometimes contradictory objectives. The key question is whether the inevitable trade-offs between these differing objectives would be better accomplished within a single communications regulatory body, or through constant negotiation between the regulators and the government departments that are charged with pursuing them. The first option would create the illusion of coherence, since the most difficult decisions would be taken behind closed doors, whereas the second option gains in transparency what it loses in coherence. Neither solution is perfect; the single regulator risks substituting bureaucratic infighting for the less seemly public disagreements that will inevitably surface between rival regulators. Arguably if the key decisions about the balance between conflicting regulatory objectives are essentially political, there are advantages in a system that ensures that such debates are brought out into the open.[19]

National and EU regulation

What balance should there be between national and EU or international regulation under convergence, and to what extent should the creation of international services lead to regulation moving beyond the purely national level? The best guide to where regulatory responsibility should lie must depend not on what is techologically possible, but rather on whether services are offered on a national or Europe-wide basis, and on the extent to which regulatory objectives are determined at the national or the European level. For broadcasting it is the nation state rather than the EU which still counts for most. Television operates predominantly along individual national markets rather than on a Europe-wide basis. Regulation likewise reflects specific national preferences.

Content regulation is clearly the most difficult candidate for Europe-wide treatment, although it was included in Commissioner Bangemann's call for the creation of a single European regulatory authority for communications and media services.[20] There will be cases with a truly international communications network, such as the Internet, where some agreement on international norms will be helpful, even though it can never be comprehensive.[21] But it is questionable whether that approach offers the best method of content regulation in media such as the press and broadcasting which are essentially national in scope. While the technical possibility of engaging in trans-frontier broadcasting has been available for more than a decade, the reality is that most broadcasting – even via satellite – is still targeted at specific countries or linguistic regions. As long as that remains the case, the strong political, social and cultural concerns of most content regulation dictate that it should be conducted at the national rather than the EU level. The mutual recognition procedures of the Television Without Frontiers Directive should remain adequate to cover those cases where services licensed in one country target another. If the balance in service provision were to change, so that most channels were offered and consumed on a pan-European level, then there would be a case for following the Internet model and aiming for EU or international rather than national regulation, but that moment seems very far off at this point in time.

Access and economic regulation more generally might seem to offer greater potential for European-level regulation. In telecoms the EU has played an important part in establishing a regulatory framework, but so far there has been no substantial support for the creation of a Europe-wide telecoms regulatory authority. Most studies on this question have identified a rather mixed picture as regards the enthusiasm of industry players and regulators, the legal competence of the Commission to create anything that had policy-making or enforcement powers (as a national telecommunications regulator such as OFTEL has in practice), and indeed the range of activities that it might usefully carry out (Cave and Crowther 1996). Even in telecoms regulation there are many issues, relating for example to the allocation of radio frequencies, pricing and consumer protection, where any European regulatory involvement would seem likely to be rejected by – or at best be unwelcome to – the majority of industry players (NERA 1997: 43).

Many of the difficulties involved in the creation of a European telecommunications regulator will also apply to any attempt to create a European Regulator for all access issues across the converging communications sector. Whilst there is a good case for greater EU co-ordination, there are several areas (such as the use of spectrum, licensing procedures, and some competition issues) where Member States may be unwilling to relinquish control to a European authority. On the other hand, so far there have been wide variations in the degree of interest and competence that Member States have shown in regulating conditional access systems and other gateways, and there would be benefits in having the EU – at the very least – establish a rather more prescriptive framework within which access regulation could be treated. This could take the form of a committee of European communications regulators, or a putative authority, and it would need to be complemented by mutual notification procedures of the sort established by the Transparency Directive for Information Society Services (see Chapter 7). Whether in the longer term the main contribution of this kind of European co-ordination would be to improve the quality of national policy-making, or lead to the transfer of competence to the European level, would depend on the degree to which there was agreement on the regulatory objectives.[22] What is clear, however, is that in telecoms and the communications sector more generally, infrastructure regulation benefits from detailed knowledge of local circumstances, knowledge that is more likely to be available at the national than the European level.

Options for regulatory reform

The 1997 Convergence Green Paper (EC 1997d) proposes three options for regulatory reform: building on current structures, developing a separate regulatory model for new activities to coexist with telecoms and broadcasting – as is the case with the current EU Transparency Measure for Information Society services – or progressively introducing a new regulatory model to cover the whole range of existing and new services.

None of these models can resolve *all* the problems raised by convergence. The third option, favoured by the Commission itself, seems unlikely to create the perfectly 'rational' regulatory system that is desired, but rather a protracted period of regulatory uncertainty as differing interests try to influence the outcome. The end result would be probably be an untidy political compromise. The second option is worth serious consideration, but runs the risk of creating a more complicated regulatory structure, and of leading to constant battles over where jurisdiction should lie for each 'new service'. While such battles are inevitable they would only be complicated by the additional category of 'new services' to add to the existing categories of 'telecoms' and broadcasting'.

Of all the options, the first, of adapting current structures, seems to offer the best way of creating the regulatory flexibility that is necessary in a dynamic and fast changing market, without prejudging future development or undermining the regulatory stability that is needed for secure investment. But this evolutionary process should have a clear sense of direction, moving towards a more horizontal approach to regulation, albeit one based around existing regulatory traditions, where a graduated approach to content regulation is combined with the continuance of public service broadcasting, and the adoption of more vigorous competition safeguards and infrastructure regulation.

One of the risks with building on current structures – and one which is alluded to in the Green Paper – is that it 'might leave in place certain anomalies which today deter investment' and that without sufficient co-ordination at a European level it 'could risk creating significant new barriers between Member States and slowing the transition to the Information Society'.

These are valid concerns but they are less than overwhelming. As mentioned above, it is false to see regulation itself as either the prime facilitator of, or obstacle to, convergence. In so far as there are regulatory obstacles these should be discussed at national level, where policy-makers must decide whether there are better ways of achieving their regulatory objectives, or indeed whether some may no longer be required. Similarly, any potential regulatory fragmentation of the internal market can be dealt with through a variety of responses. Greater contact between national infrastructure regulators can help develop a greater understanding of good practice, and the Transparency Measure for Information Society Services can play an important role in ensuring the prior notification of changes in key national legislation. Similarly, the Contact Committee of representatives of Member States, which was established under the 1997 revision of the Television Without Frontiers Directive, will also allow for the exchange of experiences concerning developments in the sector. All these fora provide opportunities to facilitate such information exchanges and avoid the creation of new barriers to the internal market. Close co-operation between the EU competition authorities and national competition and infrastructure regulators will continue to be important. In time, there may well be a role for greater EU co-ordination in the regulation of carriage, and the EU's intervention in telecoms infrastructure regulation and the Advanced Television Standards Directive have both set useful precedents in this area.

Convergence clearly does create challenges for existing regulatory structures and approaches. But the argument that sees the solution as removing regulation altogether, moving it to another territorial level, or creating a new Europe-wide light touch regulatory framework, is far from proven. Regulation must adapt rather than wither away. Access regulation will be more important than ever to ensure that broadcasters can access the distribution networks, and that consumers can have guaranteed access to the widest possible range of material – both on a pay per view and a free-to-air basis. Given the social, political and cultural dimensions of the media, content regulation will also remain necessary, even if it is conducted in a more flexible way. Subject to that flexibility, however, the case for such regulation being conducted primarily at the national rather than the European level, albeit with systems of mutual recognition of national licensing procedures, simply becomes stronger.

9 Broadcasting regulation, the nation state and the European policy process

Introduction

Much of the recent literature on decision-making within the EU has polarised between those who draw on international relations approaches and depict EU policy as predominantly the result of intergovernmental negotiation, and those who build on neo-functionalist interpretations highlighting the integrationist dynamic within the EU. In the second camp are analysts who depict the EU variously as a policy-making or regulatory state, where a tissue of policy networks and communities helps determine policy outcomes, and where nation states acquiesce or connive at a transfer of decision-making power from the more politicised and constrained national arena to the largely technocratic environment which characterises much EU decision-making (Majone 1996). Richardson provides a particularly striking critique of the limitations of intergovernmentalist interpretations in explaining how much policy now gets made in the EU:

> Put simply, the traditional 'clients' of national governments have become transnationally promiscuous in their relationships. Second, the 'politics of expertise' has become especially important in situations of loose networks and high uncertainty. This also weakens national sovereignty because of the increasingly cross-national nature of expertise and the ability of other EU policy actors – particularly the Commission – to choose which body of expertise to mobilise at any one time. Hence our suggestion that the concept of epistemic communities is especially useful at the EU level in understanding how policy problems emerge and come to be 'framed' for official policy-makers.
>
> (Richardson 1996: 20)

This analysis is useful in understanding the bulk of the EU policy-making process. The approach taken in this book assumes that in the broadcasting sector, as in many others, the Commission has aspired to act as a 'policy entrepreneur' seeking to intervene through a transfer of regulatory competence from the nation state to Brussels. As Majone explains 'what the European

Commission attempts to maximise is its influence, as measured by the scope of its competence' (Majone 1996: 65). Laura Cram's recent analysis of EU policy-making takes a similar view of the Commission's ambitions:

> much of the activity of the European Commission might well be interpreted as an attempt to gradually expand the scope of its competence without alienating national governments or powerful sectoral interests. The Commission of the EU, acting within the many constraints upon it, has played an important role in shaping the environment in which policies are developed, in justifying a role for the EU, mobilising support for its action, and in selecting the types of policy intervention pursued by the EU.
>
> (Cram 1997: 6)

One of the problems that this chapter seeks to resolve is why (other than in the case of competition policy) the broadcasting sector proved so resistant to such ambitions, and why such limited progress was made by the Commission, whether in terms of setting the policy agenda, in transferring increased competence to Brussels, or in imposing regulatory solutions at the EU level that had a substantial impact on the shape and behaviour of the emerging digital TV market. The answer lies, in part at least, in the desire of Member States to keep control of such a politically sensitive area.

Thirty years ago Hoffmann drew a distinction between areas of 'low politics', such as economic and welfare policies, where national governments would be willing to delegate power, and the key areas of 'high politics', primarily foreign policy and defence, where governments would be far less willing to do so (Hoffmann 1966, Cram 1996: 49). Broadcasting, however, is one of several policy areas which clearly belong in Hoffmann's 'low politics' category, but where the delegation of power is frequently problematic.

In this context, John Peterson's three-level analysis of EU decision-making is more helpful. He identifies a top level of 'history making decisions' taken at a super-systemic level which may 'alter the Union's legislative procedures, rebalance the relative powers of the EU institutions, or change the EU's remit'. He then replaces Hoffmann's very broad category of 'low politics' with a more sophisticated distinction between 'policy-setting decisions' taken at a systemic level, where the Council of Ministers rather than the Commission is often the dominant actor, and 'policy-shaping decisions' that focus primarily on the question of 'how do we do it?'. Most sectoral policy-making in, for example, the telecoms and IT sectors, fits in with Peterson's 'policy-shaping' decisions where, as he puts it, 'technocratic rationality, based on specialized or technical knowledge, often dominates', decision-making is characterised by a general weakness of political controls, informal bargaining and a wider variety of actors than in national sectoral policy-making, and policy outputs tend to be determined at 'the relatively early stages of the EU policy process' (Peterson 1996: 72–5).

But one of the complicating factors in EU broadcasting policy was the way in which the subject could drift between Peterson's two levels of 'policy-setting' and 'policy-shaping'. Issues might start as classic technical problems, where policy-shaping approaches were clearly appropriate. But there was always the risk (and in broadcasting these risks were greater than in many other sectors), that such 'technical' issues would suddenly attract the attention of national or European Parliament politicians, and that more political modes of decision-making would then intrude on the closed and consensual world of policy and technical expertise. This volatility made it particularly difficult for EU policy-makers to establish stable policy communities, identify all the key stakeholders in advance, and decide on the most effective approach to policy formation. A familiar complaint of both national and EU policy-makers about the broadcasting sector was that whilst there was no shortage of experts, at times it appeared that *everybody* had a view about key policy choices.

The limited impact of EU intervention in the broadcasting industry

Whereas many of the recent studies of EU policy-making are studies in success, one of the main conclusions of the previous chapters is that broadcasting is an area where, despite huge technological change, the Commission's ambitions have only been partially realised. EU intervention has been relatively successful in establishing a framework for the regulation of access to digital networks, through the Advanced TV Standards Directive, and potentially through DG IV's guidelines on access agreements in telecommunications (EC 1998e, Ungerer 1998a). Similarly, the operation of Competition and Merger policy has had far-reaching implications for the ways in which programme rights are purchased, digital TV alliances are formed and, potentially, for the funding arrangements of public service broadcasters. But in several of the other areas examined there has been far less success. Television Without Frontiers was dogged by confused objectives, and its moves to open up the European TV market to cross-frontier services primarily benefited the US-controlled and UK-registered channels such as CNN, MTV and TNT Cartoon network, together with national channels seeking to escape domestic licensing constraints. TVWF's European content quotas and EU support measures such as the MEDIA programmes often seemed to dominate debate on EU broadcasting policy, but only ever had a very limited impact on the overall competitiveness of the European TV industry (EC 1998j: 7–8).[1]

Commission proposals for European regulation of media ownership have been even less successful, failing to win sufficient support – either within the Commission itself or from Member States – to allow a draft Directive to be proposed. Finally, DG XIII's desire to respond to techno-logical convergence by creating a converged European-level regulatory approach to broadcasting and telecoms has so far failed to bear fruit. Although the regulatory convergence agenda has only been articulated in the vaguest of forms in official documents (the tone of the Convergence Green Paper is far more tentative than the proposals contained in Martin Bangemann's September 1997 speech, or indeed in earlier drafts of the Green Paper), it follows on logically from much of what the EU has achieved in telecoms, and there is strong evidence that it is favoured by some elements in the Commission and in parts of the IT and telecoms industries. However, since regulatory convergence at European level would represent a rebalancing of power within the Commission and a very dra-matic transfer of power from Member States to the EU, it has encountered substantial resistance from several Member States, from the majority of the broadcasting industry, and from some forces within the EP and the Commission.

The obstacles: broadcasting as a hard case for Commission activism

The obstacles to Commission activism in the broadcasting sphere are sub-stantial. The first such obstacle lies in the peculiarly multi-layered nature of broadcasting policy, where national governments have long pursued a multiplicity of cultural, political, economic and industrial goals. These conflicting goals simply reflected the dual nature of broadcasting – as both a commercial industry likely to expand with increased competition and technological change, and a cultural product which is a powerful reflec-tion and generator of political and cultural values.

As a result, broadcasting attracted the attentions of a peculiarly large number of departments, and regulatory bodies within each Member State. Their proliferation injected new bureaucratic (and, in Germany, territor-ial) rivalries to compound the problem of multiple policy goals. Since each Member State resolved these tensions in different ways, there was no obvi-ous route to the creation of a Europe-wide regulatory system. In addition, the diffuse nature of broadcasting meant that it was dealt with by several different Commission DG's; as each added their own concerns into the European debate, they themselves often reduced the chances of a consen-sus emerging over the key priorities for any EU audio-visual policy.

The Commission's lack of competence to regulate for broadcasting, at least until the introduction of the limited cultural provisions of the Maastricht Treaty (Article 128), posed it with a second problem. On its own this was not too serious, since the multifaceted nature of broadcasting meant that a great deal of policy for the broadcast sector could be developed through the application of the internal market and competition provisions of the Treaties. But the initial lack of competence in respect of broadcasting, and the requirement for unanimity in the use of Article 128, and for the various financial support measures that were proposed, reflected a powerful political reality. Member States accorded such great political importance to broadcasting that many of them started from a position of suspicion towards any EU attempts at intervention. Each state regulated its industry differently, and such diversity, they agreed, required subsidiarity to be the rule rather than the exception in broadcasting.[2]

Faced with these and other difficulties the Commission advanced arguments similar to those used in other sectors to justify greater EU intervention in broadcasting. Common themes included the need to build the internal market, the increasing internationalisation of the broadcasting industry, and the challenge of technological change and particularly of convergence between telecommunications, computing and broadcasting. All these arguments carried some weight, but once again Member State responses tended to diverge. Views differed about the extent to which changes in technology and the external environment offered a convincing case for regulation at the EU as opposed to the national level. Similarly, whilst there was general agreement on the problems posed by a deteriorating audio-visual deficit with the US, and the difficult issues posed by technological change, neither of these translated into agreement on the solutions.

When it was passed, the 1989 Television Without Frontiers Directive appeared to meet the needs of an internationalising industry keen to operate on a pan-European level, together with the concerns of those who feared increased US penetration of the European film and TV market. But even in 1989 its acceptance was eased by the fact that the prescriptive elements of the Directive were relatively limited, with the greatest emphasis on mutual recognition of national licensing regimes. Between 1989 and renewal of the Directive in 1997 there was only limited development of pan-European channels; it became clear that the TV markets of the major Member States were primarily national rather than European, and that quota provisions had done nothing to redress the growing audio-visual trade deficit with the USA.[3] And whereas some countries wanted to redress the trade imbalance by limiting US imports, others such as the UK were both more ideologically attached to free trade and wary of measures that, if they were to rebound, could limit the scope for their own TV exports to the US. It was notable that the most significant new element of the 1997 TVWF was permissive rather than prescriptive; under the new Article 3 Member States were allowed to draw up lists of protected sporting events, together with measures to ensure that neighbouring EU countries could not be used as bases from which subscription broadcasters could circumvent such restrictions.

In many other sectors the combination of internationalisation and technological change often created favourable conditions for greater EU intervention. Sometimes national regulatory reforms led to a narrowing of differences between national policies. On other occasions, as we have seen, the EU itself seized on technological change as justifying an EU-wide approach to policy-making. In recent years a substantial literature has developed on this process of policy transfer or convergence between countries, often in response to a specific technological change. Bennett's detailed study of data protection legislation led him to identify four different ways in which political actors typically come to adopt converging policies: through 'emulation', through elite networking and the growth of policy communities, through 'harmonisation' induced by interdependence, and finally through 'penetration', where countries 'are forced to conform to actions taken elsewhere by external actors', either through pressures from multi-national companies seeking a common regulatory framework, or through the activities of international organisations seeking to force laggards to conform to the rules adopted by other members of the club (Bennett 1991a).

Yet, as Chapter 6 has shown, extensive national broadcasting reforms in France, Germany and the UK, did not necessarily produce a greater similarity of outcomes. Even when policy agendas converged, as was the case in questions of media ownership control, or in the implementation of a European directive on conditional access, policy outcomes diverged considerably in response to differing political circumstances and preoccupations. Broadcasting seemed peculiarly resistant to the processes of policy transfer identified by Bennett. Thus, while elite networking in the telecommunications policy community helped launch a debate on a new regulatory agenda, it left broadcasting policy itself relatively unchanged. Harmonisation and increased interdependence may explain a common move to relax media ownership restrictions but do not help us understand the widely differing ways in which such policies were devised. Similarly, policy penetration – in response to the EU Advanced Television Standards directive – explains why Member States introduced regulations on the use of conditional access systems, but not the wide variations in the enthusiasm with which they approached this task.

Different issues – different outcomes

The Commission's relative lack of success in offering policy leadership in broadcasting was even more surprising given its impressive track record in the telecoms and IT sectors, and the moves towards the convergence of the three sectors. Telecoms was a sector where the Commission's policy leadership was well established. The Commission:

> succeeded in transforming an initially national issue into a European one, pushing the Member States towards the harmonization of their policies and, moreover, setting the pace for a constant and convergent

development of their legislation into the direction defined by the Commission itself.

(Schneider *et al.* 1994: 494)

Cram's analysis of European IT policy paints a similarly striking picture of Commission intervention:

> having already softened up the policy area, mobilised the key actors and, crucially, having developed a clear institutional identity in the ICT field, the Commission was able to capitalise on the legitimising concept of the Single Market and the 1992 project, in the mid 1980s. Viewed over time, it becomes clear that a crucial aspect of any interpretation of the development of an EU ICT policy is the gradual institutionalisation of the Commission's central role in the ICT sector.
>
> (Cram 1997: 69)

It would be wrong, however, to assume that there was anything inevitable about such Commission policy leadership. Suzanne Schmidt's comparison of the approaches to regulation of the telecoms and electricity sectors highlights the near impossibility of Commission action in the absence of some support from Member States and industry. Since her study focuses on the use of Article 90, under which the Commission has power to act unilaterally, her findings are particularly striking (Schmidt 1998). For EU policy leadership to become a reality, several conditions needed to be met. First there had to be a convincing set of reasons why EU-level regulation was preferable to national regulation. Second, Member States had to be prepared to acquiesce in such a transfer of responsibility. And third, it helped if the nature of the sector and the issues it raised were such as to allow the creation of stable policy communities, to provide the Commission with a source of expertise, to engage in an EU policy process, and to help in mobilising industry support for Commission action.

In most areas of the broadcasting sector many of the traditional reasons for Commission, rather than national regulation, either did not apply, or else appeared less convincing than in other sectors. The forces for what some have termed 'negative integration' were not particularly strong (Scharpf 1996). National governments were not being overwhelmed by the impossibility of imposing their will, nor were they unduly exposed to pressures towards competitive deregulation. Similarly, while the operation of the internal market, state aid and competition provisions of the Treaties impacted on national broadcasting policies, they had not made them unsustainable. The merger regulations set strict limits on the types of digital alliances that could be pursued, but the right of Member States to support public broadcasters was reinforced with the introduction of the Amsterdam Protocol on public service broadcasting – even if its interpretation was subsequently much disputed. In an industry where programming and advertising markets were predominantly national, the majority of Member States saw no pressing reasons for a greater European role in broadcasting as such. Many technical issues, however, closely allied with broadcasting, such as copyright legislation and standards setting, were seen as benefiting from a Europe-wide approach.

Member State willingness to see regulatory responsibility transfer to the EU could be increased by two different, and in some respects contradictory, factors. New policy issues and problems where Member States had only limited knowledge, and no regulatory traditions or institutions of their own, were often among the easiest areas to delegate. Pollack comments on how:

> The Commission's influence as policy entrepreneur . . . seems to depend largely upon member-state uncertainty regarding the problems and policies confronting them, and on the Commission's acuity in identifying problems and policies which can rally the necessary consensus among member states in search of solutions to their policy problems.
>
> (Pollack 1996: 450–1)

Countries were far readier to see EU policy leadership in areas such as Internet regulation and electronic commerce than in broadcasting itself, where there was no shortage of expertise at the national level. Whilst there were disagreements about whether the EU or the OECD or some other international organisation would be best suited to take the lead role in these new policy areas, there were relatively few Member States that sought to keep regulatory responsibility exclusively at the national level.

The second factor that could encourage the desire to delegate issues was where Member States thought there were benefits in ensuring that regulation operated at one remove from the political context. This could be reflected in the creation of independent regulatory agencies at national and European level, and in the transfer of some policy-making responsibilities to the EU level (Majone 1996). This consideration may have applied in the case of telecoms liberalisation. Arguably it can also be said to explain why states were willing to see the emergence of a strong EU competition regime (Allen 1996, Majone 1997). With some controversial issues there were attractions in this form of delegation. But with broadcasting, it was precisely because of the intense politicisation of the issue and the cultural and political importance of the sector that Member States were reluctant to relinquish control. These arguments were particularly important in the area of media ownership, where national regulations were keenly crafted with an acute awareness of their impact on the key players.

Finally, as noted above, the nature of a great deal of broadcasting policy was not conducive to the creation of stable policy networks. Richardson describes their importance generally within the EU policy process:

> By drawing other policy actors into the policy process, the Commission may be able to build coalitions in favour of its own notions of desirable policy change. By assisting the formation of networks of 'relevant' state and non-state actors, or by 'massaging' the way that these networks operate, the Commission can maintain its position as an 'independent' policy-making institution and can increase its leverage with the Council of Ministers and the European Parliament. Information and ideas are important building blocks in this process.
>
> (Richardson 1996: 15)

There were attempts at constructing such policy networks within the broadcasting field, but they met with varied success. DG XV saw one of the benefits of its protracted consultations on media ownership regulation as being the creation of such a network (see Chapter 3 above). But the impact of such a network of specialists could only ever be very limited in this area. The political sensitivity of legislation on media ownership meant that, whilst the detailed principles of regulation might initially only be of interest to specialists, decision-making was always going to be guided more by political considerations than by experts alone.

The whole Information Society programme of the Commission tended to spawn large numbers of new expert groups and policy networks. This process was helped by the mismatch between the levels of economic and social importance and public understanding associated with many of the key technological developments in the IS. Within broadcasting one area where EU decision-making for the broadcasting sector came closest to the policy network model was in the framing of the Advanced TV Standards Directive, and in the Commission's privileged relations with the DVB Group. Initially many key decisions were delegated to the industry, as represented through the DVB. While the DVB played an important role in facilitating agreement on some key standards, it could never be the proper vehicle for the devising of a regulatory strategy for digital TV. But it was not until the question of conditional access regulation moved to the political level – through the European Parliament – that the regulatory agenda began to be decided outside an expert community.

Convergence between broadcasting, telecoms and computing did not eradicate the political imperatives that guided broadcasting policy, but it did raise new issues and bring new players, networks and policy styles into discussions of broadcasting regulation. Increasingly a new policy community emerged which favoured the creation of a single regulatory structure for the communications sector and saw sector-specific broadcasting regulation as a major obstacle to change. Debate was initiated and often guided by telecommunications policy-makers in the Commission (DG XIII and

DG IV) or the OECD. Naturally these groups were most inclined to test out their views on the players and officials they knew best, namely telecommunications companies, manufacturers, and national officials from the Ministries of telecoms and industry rather than officials from the Länder or the national Ministries of Culture or National Heritage.[4] This policy community was attracted by the idea that as broadcasting and telecommunications converged so broadcasting could benefit from a wave of deregulation and Europeanisation similar to that seen in telecommunications.

While the case for regulatory convergence was often presented as the inevitable result of technological change it could also be used to mask the political agendas of its advocates: of national industry officials keen to gain influence at the expense of culture ministries, of EU officials seeking to boost the importance of their Directorate General and extend the competence of the Commission, and of those new media companies who believed a European-level converged regulatory framework would subject them to fewer and less onerous obligations than would national broadcasting and culture regulators. But this conjunction of technological change, support from some sections of industry, and vigorous Commission policy entrepreneurship, could not transfer to broadcasting many of the lessons and policy successes established elsewhere in EU ICT and telecommunications policy. Digitalisation created a common coding system and common systems of transmission across the communications sector. But consensus on the realities of such technological convergence has so far had no impact on policy-makers' and politicians' awareness of the specificity of broadcasting and above all of its unique cultural and political importance within each Member State. That unique role must disappear and broadcasting must develop as a truly pan-European industry before EU policy leadership will be a realistic possibility.

Notes

1 Converging technologies, changing markets

1 G. Moore was the co-founder of Intel, who manufacture the majority of processors in PCs.
2 Initially BSkyB are offering 140 channels, including their near video-on-demand service.
3 The BBC predicts that by 2005 in the UK the major, well-funded networks (BBC, ITV, Channel 4 and Channel 5) are likely to have a 65–75 per cent share of total audience viewing, new themed specialist channels could have a share of 15–25 per cent, and interactive, on-demand services might have around 5–10 per cent (BBC 1996).
4 Ten NVOD films starting at quarter of an hour intervals could on their own occupy sixty to eighty channels. DirectTV in the US allocates fifty to sixty channels to offering NVOD films at thirty-minute intervals. Its services sell an average of two films per month to each subscribing household as against the slightly more than four per year sold on traditional US pay per view networks (*Screen Digest* 1996: 184).
5 By the end of February 1997 Telepui had 47,000 subscribers to its digital football 'season ticket' service at a time when subscribers were required to buy a very expensive (£740) digital decoder. It was thought that subscriptions would increase if the decoders became cheaper or could be rented rather than bought (Westcott 1997: 5).
6 The sample size for this survey – 300 – was too small for it to be viewed as wholly reliable. Baskerville (1996) predicted that each UK digital home would generate on average $228 in PPV soccer revenues alone by 2005.
7 It is significant that Kirch and Bertelsmann's CLT-UFA have both started moves to get the definition of pornography (which is prohibited from German TV) relaxed (*Le Figaro* 5 August 1997). UK cable operators criticised new rules from the UK regulator, the ITC, for not allowing violent or sexually explicit films to be shown at any time of the day on a ppv basis, rather than only after 8pm as proposed by the ITC (New Media Markets, vol. 15, no. 25, 10 July 1997).
8 CLT/UFA's holdings include stakes in Channel 5 in the UK, M6, TPS and RTL in France, as well as control of the German pay TV company Premiere and the advertising funded channels RTL, RTL2 and Super RTL.
9 SECA is in fact a Canal Plus/Bertelsmann joint venture, Irdeto is a NetHold subsidiary.
10 Deutsche Telekom also owns a share in the dominant European satellite company SES-Astra. DT's control of the German cable industry later led to pressure from the European Commission for them to sell off their stake.
11 The DT, Bertelsmann and Kirch agreement was overturned by the EU competition authorities in May 1998 (Commission Press release ip/98/477: 27 May

1997). Bertelsmann has also moved beyond its traditional publishing and TV interests, establishing Bertelsmann New Media which, among other things, operates the America On Line company in Western Europe.

12 The API is akin to a computer operating system. Even basic interactive TV applications – such as teletext – will only operate satisfactorily if they can access and function with the API that is located within the set-top box or integrated digital TV. (This issue is discussed in more detail in Chapter 4.)

2 National regulatory traditions

1 Between 1972 and 1998 – when a new law was proposed – there were seven major changes in French broadcasting law (1972, 1974, 1982, 1986, 1989, 1992 and 1994). The key 1986 text on 'Freedom of Communication' was modified twenty-in its first eleven years (*Le Monde* 11 November 1998, Cathodon 1995: 266, *Le Monde* 19 February 1997). A law-baed approach is the norm in France and Germany, in contast to the UK where regulation plays a much greater role.

2 The CSA was created in 1989, succeeding the CNC under the audio-visual law of 17 January 1989. Of the nine members of the CSA Council three are appointed by the President of the Republic, three by the President of the National Assembly, and three by the President of the Senate, each for a non-renewable six-year term. It is an administrative authority whose task is to appoint the heads of public service broadcasters, set and monitor the licence conditions for private broadcasters, and monitor the compliance of all channels with the legislation in force on matters such as taste and decency (see KPMG 1996: Appendices 117).

3 Although the UK film industry is now more buoyant and occupies a more central place in UK media policy than for many years (DCMS 1998a).

4 One 1998 study by the European Audiovisual Observatory found that of the 500 million ECU spent annually on subsidising the film industry in Europe, more than half came from France, with Germany in second place. Interestingly while 64 per cent of German funding came from the Länder, only 2 per cent of French funding came from the Regional authorities (*Tech Europe* June 1998).

5 Canal Plus was allowed to broadcast 416 films per annum (as against the 192 permitted the other channels) and allowed to show films one year after release, compared to the two or three years that other terrestrial channels had to wait (KPMG 1996).

6 Canal Plus, 1995 Annual Report, comments on how Studio Canal Plus had 'refocused its activities on European and French products' and suggested that output from Studio Canal Plus had contributed to an increase in cinema admissions to French films during 1995 (up from 27.8 per cent in 1994 to 35 per cent in 1995).

7 The launch of two commercial channels – TV 6 and La Cinq – in 1985–86 was motivated, however, more by political considerations than cultural or industrial policy, and subjected those policies to great pressure (Kuhn 1995 184).

8 In the three years 1993, 1994 and 1995, TF1 had missed its quota by 238, 87 and 65 hours respectively, and had had similar 'non-fines' imposed of 18 million, 15.5 million and then 45 million francs. The increase in the size of the penalty may have been seen as a warning to TF1, but the company had its licence renewed later in 1996 without any trouble (*Le Monde* 21 February 1996, *La Lettre du CSA* no. 83, August 1996: 1–3).

9 It is also part of a wider reliance on law as a means of regulation. Cf. N. Johnson's comment: 'the law is unambiguously in politics both as a structuring instrument defining institutions and the rights and duties of citizens, and equally in the guise of a statement of political and social values to which society as a whole is committed and to promotion of which those active in politics are held to be especially bound' (cited in Dyson ed. 1992: 65).

10 One observer characterises the Constitutional Court as acting 'much like a

legislature' in the way in which it establishes basic guidelines for the industry (Hoffmann-Riem 1996: 119).

11 Given their political divisions even this arrangement does not always succeed in representing a collective Länder view.

12 There are in fact sixteen Länder, but the Berlin-Brandenburg authority covers both the city of Berlin and the State of Brandenburg.

13 Primarily through its fourth TV judgement of 4 November 1996 on the Lower Saxony broadcasting law, and its sixth TV judgement, the so-called North Rhine-Westphalia Ruling of 5 February 1991. See Humphreys (1994: 338–42) for details on all the key Constitutional Court rulings.

14 North Rhine-Westphalia's population of close to eighteen million makes it the largest Land in Germany, and a more significant media market than that of many European countries. Its media and cultural sector employs 230,000 people and has an annual turnover of DM 60 billion.

15 Interviews with Hamburg, and North Rhine-Westphalia LMAs.

16 Hoffmann-Riem has remarked how while on occasions broadcasters 'invoke lofty ideals of freedom' and complain about the onerous regulations to which they are subjected they are also 'well aware that the norms also act as a protective shield for broadcasters once they are established. Even commercial broadcasters have learned to live within these norms, realising that the legal restrictions also make it difficult for new competitors to receive licences and prevail in the market' (Hoffmann-Riem 1997: 59).

17 More than ten billion DM was spent on building the cable system during the 1980s. One estimate put the cost at an average of DM613 per household by 1989 (Schulz 1992: 33, Woldt cited in Dyson 1992: 91–2).

18 Recent complaints by the German private broadcasters' association, the VPRT, against the launch of thematic channels by ARD/ZDF have focused on this point.

19 The question of whether the Federal Government had had the authority to sign the 1989 Television Without Frontiers Directive was discussed in the German Courts for several years.

20 Humphreys (1996: 182–5) describes the UK case in terms of 'marketisation of duopoly' and this section draws on his analysis.

21 The most obvious example of the favourable treatment of the cable industry was the prohibiting until 2000 of British Telecom from providing broadcast entertainment services on its telephone network.

22 Such as some Scandinavian channels keen to avoid local restrictions on advertising aimed at children, and TNT Cartoon network which wanted to avoid European content restrictions.

23 Hence the willingness of the Government to incorporate a reinforced 'quality threshold' into the new auction-based licensing procedure for commercial TV. One effect was to make the ITC much less of a light-touch regulator than originally intended (Goodwin 1998: 103–8).

24 With the exception of the privatisation of the BBC's transmission network, which was announced in the 1994 White Paper on the Future of the BBC and accomplished in 1997. The BBC was also allowed to keep the bulk of the proceeds to invest in the transition to digital TV.

25 The 1990 Act had opened the way for cable companies to hold licences that had no 'must carry' obligations.

26 See Chapter 6 for a fuller account of UK approaches to digital regulation.

3 European Regulation

1 But so far intervention 'on the basis of article 128 [has been] . . . strictly limited. It consists solely of measures to encourage cooperation among the member states. Article 128 can be used as the legal basis for harmonising national

legislative provisions, and can lead to recommendations, only by the unanimous vote of the Council' (Machet and Robillard 1998: 33).

2 The most significant cases were Sacchi, (1974), where the ECJ ruled that the transmission of TV signals was a 'service' under Community law, and the Coditel and Debauve cases (1980) which confirmed the Sacchi ruling and 'established a body of European law treating broadcasting as a tradeable service' (see Barendt 1995: 230, Humphreys 1996: 262, and Machet and Robillard 1998: 36–7 for a complete list of such cases).

3 Fraser (1996b: 11) comments on how the debate over quotas opposed 'les "créateurs" européens aux entreprises transnationales, les dirigistes aux libre échangistes, les Etats protectionnistes (surtout la France) aux Etats libéraux (surtout la Grande Bretagne), les instances communautaires aux instances nationales'.

4 See the EP's Hahn 1982 'Report on Radio and Television Broadcasting in the European Community', the 1983 Commission Communication on 'Trends in broadcasting in Europe: Perspectives and Options', and the 1984 Commission Green Paper on 'Television Without Frontiers' (Verhulst and Goldberg 1997: 2–3, Collins 1996, Maggiore 1990: 32–3).

5 The Green Paper took up the ideas of the EP's 1982 Hahn Report which had stated that:

> Europe's future is, of course, not only a question of economics . . . this political community will not be created without a common political will . . . without action by the Member States, without the involvement of the citizens of Europe, without cultural projects or an information policy, these high flown ambitions will probably only be short-lived.
>
> (cited by Collins 1994b: 40).

6 At the Assises de l'Audiovisuel in Paris in October 1989, just days before the TVWF Directive was approved by the Council, Delors reiterated this position: 'culture is not a set of goods like any other. We cannot deal with it as we do with refrigerators or cars' and 'I refuse to speak about the free circulation of productions. I want to speak of organizing the audiovisual space' (cited in Maggiore 1990).

7 DG X, the audio-visual Directorate, only became involved from 1994 to 1997 in monitoring implementation of the 1989 Directive, but took charge of preparations for the Directive's renewal.

8 The Directive's provisions on advertising, allowing up to 15 per cent of daily transmission time or 20 per cent in any single hour, were far more liberal than the rules in force in France, Britain or Germany.

9 Section 177 of the UK 1990 Broadcasting Act allows the Secretary of State to proscribe a foreign satellite service in accordance with Article 22 of TV Without Frontiers. Once such a decision has been made the sale of decoders and the promotion of the channel in the UK can be prohibited. By the end of 1998 proscription orders had been issued against five satellite pornography services (Red Hot Television, TV erotica, Rendez-Vous Television, Satisfaction Club TV and Eurotica Rendez-Vous) with action pending against a further channel – Eros TV (DCMS Press Release 264/98 2 November 1998). The European Court has ruled against countries that argued that non-compliance with the Directive by broadcasters licensed in another country gave grounds for blocking reception or retransmission in their country.

10 The Germans went further and obtained a written statement from the Council and the Commission that the provisions on quotas should be seen only as 'politically binding', thus making the likelihood of their enforcement still more remote (Maggiore 1990: 35).

11 It was the EP which decided to increase the Commission's proposed independent production quota of 5 per cent to 10 per cent (Papathanassopoulos 1990: 120).

12 Adding with good reason that the Directive reflects more the continuing

divergence of national policy styles and preoccupations than any convergence.

13 In Germany, for example, since it was the Ministry of the Interior which was expected to reply to the Commission's request for information and the Land Media authorities who carried out the monitoring, neither party felt any great responsibility for the figures that were submitted. In the case of other countries Commission officials acknowledge that the figures submitted were far from robust.

14 BSkyB evidence to the same committee was even more critical, and drew attention to:

> the contradiction within the Green Paper, which wishes to protect individual national cultures (a legitimate ambition, which individual governments are best able to manage) whilst nurturing a barely existent 'European' culture (presumably because this gives the Commission an entry point for its interventionist instincts).
>
> (House of Lords 1995: 172–3)

15 This study on *Parental Control of Television Broadcasting* was started in the course of 1998 and published by DG X in 1999.

16 See 'Television without frontiers and major (sports) events : Commission Communication' IP/97/85, Brussels, 5 February 1997 for the Commission response to the Parliament's vote.

The Commission pointed out that the 'advent of digital transmission technology, and in particular the emergence of multi-channel digital packages transmitted by satellite' had 'brought a new, transnational dimension, to the practice of buying and selling sports rights'. Eight countries had already adopted some national measures to protect the availability of sporting events, and another three were considering them. According to the Commission this 'developing "corpus" of national law, the legal uncertainty that flows from this at Community level and the potential for market distortions' justified including provisions within TVWF.

17 A majority of those MEPs voting supported strengthened quotas, but under EP rules a majority of those eligible to vote was needed to reject a Council of Ministers agreement. There was some pressure from Member States. On the eve of the vote, Lord Inglewood, the British Minister for National Heritage and himself a former MEP, distributed a letter to MEPs urging against reinforcing quotas (*Financial Times* 7 November 1996). German Christian Democrat MEPs may also have come under pressure from Bonn not to vote for the position they had previously supported in the EP.

18 While protection for certain sporting events can be seen as a form of intervention, the approach taken by the Directive was not prescriptive on this matter; member states were left free to draw up national lists if they desired. From the beginning of the discussions a majority within the Council had supported Commission proposals to ensure that broadcasters were obliged to maintain their headquarters in the country in which they sought a licence.

19 The protocol followed on from an important EP resolution on public service broadcasting drafted by Carole Tongue MEP. The key passage of the protocol states that: 'the system of public broadcasting in the Member States is directly related to the democratic, social and cultural needs of each society' and stresses that it is within:

> the competence of Member States to provide for the funding of public service broadcasting in so far as such funding is granted to broadcasting organizations for the fulfilment of the public service remit as conferred, defined and organized by each Member State, and that such funding does not affect trading conditions and competition in the Community to an extent which would be contrary to the common interest, while the realization of that public service shall be taken into account.

The impact of the protocol on the way in which competition provisions would be applied to public service broadcasters has yet to be tested by the Court of Justice. See Chapter 5.

20 Between 1989 and 1990, there were eighty-one mergers and acquisitions announced in the EC media industry; thirty-seven of these affected the TV sector (Hitchens 1994: 586, citing Booz-Allen and Hamilton study conducted for the Commission).

21 DG XV proposals that were brought to the Commission were referred for further work in September 1994, September 1996 and then again in March 1997 ('Brussels setback for media owners', *Financial Times* 22 September 1994, *Agence Europe*, nos 6802 and 6804 2 September1996 and 5 September 1996, and no. 6939 21 March 1997).

22 The 1994 Communication explained that the ' Community objective justifying action at Community level is the guaranteeing of the function of the Internal Market while safeguarding the requirement to preserve pluralism by fixing certain limits on media ownership' (EC 1994a: 32). Similarly, the preamble to the 1996 draft referred to: the 'obstacles to the free movement of . . . broadcasting goods and daily newspapers, and . . . distortions of competition' created by the disparity in national media ownership rules; the need to remove those obstacles to achieve the objectives of the Internal Market; and how Community action in this area was needed to 'encourage investment and the growth and competitiveness of the European media industry and protect pluralism in a way which is both suited to the international dimension of the media and more effective than would be national protection alone' (CEC 1996 unpublished draft 1). Articles 57(2) aimed at facilitating the establishment by nationals of one Member State in another, Article 66 applies the same legislative powers relating to freedom of establishment into the Chapter on freedom to provide services and Article 100a offers a more general provision for the Commission to take action to promote the Internal Market.

23 There were seventy written responses to the Green Paper and the additional questionnaire which was sent out in 1993. Twenty-five of these were from European federations or associations and the rest from individual media companies, national federations or interested individuals, largely from the UK, Germany and Italy. (It is worth noting that the UK's consultative paper Media Ownership: The Government's Proposals Cm 2872 1995 produced sixty-four written responses.) The views of groups such as Fininvest and News International may have been unduly represented in the responses to the Green Paper. News International's views, for example, were included in its own response, in that of BSkyB, through the ACT and the European Newspapers and Periodicals Association, ENPA (Kaitatzi-Whitlock 1996: 471).

24 ITV complained that British rules allowed Rupert Murdoch to own 35 per cent of national newspaper circulation and a 50 per cent stake in the satellite broadcaster BSkyB, whilst ITV companies were limited to owning 20 per cent of a national newspaper or 20 per cent of a satellite broadcaster. Similarly, the Italian newspaper group, Editoriale l'Espresso complained about the activities of Berlusconi's Fininvest.

25 Sir Leslie Hill, then Chairman of the ITV Association, wrote as follows:

> The 1990 Broadcasting Act permits 100 per cent ownership of an ITV company by any European organisation. That makes the current UK commercial television ownership rules unique in Europe. It is impossible for a British company to acquire 100 per cent of a television station in any other part of Europe. National regulations vary, but the thrust of them, particularly in main markets such as Germany, France and Italy, is to make it impossible for a UK company to gain total control. Media ownership rules should be consistent throughout the EU, and the Commission should concentrate on this issue.
>
> *(Financial Times* 24 November 1994)

These sentiments from ITV were valuable to the Commission as it tried to build support for a Directive (EC 1994a: 18).

26 Owners of *La Republica* and shareholders in the UK newspaper, *'The Independent'*.

27 This determination to portray industry as supportive tends to reinforce Beltrame's observation on the relationship between the Commission and private firms:

> Whereas the Commission is usually seen as the passive victim of lobbying, in this particular case at least, the picture is quite different. Here, the Commission has had to put considerable effort in mobilising and creating interest, pointing to the necessity of a more dynamic view of interests in the Union's legislative process.
>
> (Beltrame 1996: 174).

28 Similar arguments were to re-emerge frequently during the debate on regulatory convergence.

29 Convergence, as defined, implies the removal of scarcity in distribution and a diversity of new services. This will permit a broader range of news and opinion to be made available to the public. Convergence therefore reduces the risk that pluralism objectives will not be met and it may become a self-fulfilling ambition that requires little regulatory oversight. Nevertheless, we must guard against over-simplification. Some media are likely to have a dominant impact on public opinion and governments need to ensure that these are not controlled by a single company, individual or group.

> (KPMG 1996: 217)

According to Harcourt:

> the basic source of infra-organisational conflict . . . is that DG XV views media concentration as a 'traditional internal market problem' which requires the 'harmonisation of national rules concerning media concentration' whereas DG XIII and III view the media market as a long-overdue case for liberalisation.
>
> (Harcourt 1996: 208)

30 CLT (along with News International) undertook a vigorous lobbying campaign against the DG XV proposals. Their contacts with President Santer, who had been Prime Minister of Luxembourg from 1984 to 1994 and held the Cultural Affairs portfolio from 1989 to 1994, are likely to have proved useful.

31 Interview with private broadcaster, Hamburg, February 1997. The French Government was similarly unenthusiastic about Community action.

32 Speaking to the EP in September 1996 Commissioner Monti confirmed his commitment to continuing with an initiative on media concentration. Commissioner Bangemann supported him in this describing himself as among 'the most determined supporters' of controlling media concentration, but adding that at the Commission's discussions on the matter it had emerged that 'most Commissioners consider the problem of concentration in the media to come under the competence of the Member States' (*Agence Europe* 18 September 1996). Leon Brittan consistently opposed Community action in this area (Johnstone 1998: 1).

33 For further information about this issue see Harcourt 1998a and 1998b and Doyle 1998.

34 Canal Plus was an unusual case of a pay broadcaster which did not campaign against European content quotas.

35 The UK provides one of the most striking cases of approaches to media ownership regulation being affected by the attitude of the largest media groups towards the Government of the day.

4 Regulating access

An earlier version of this chapter was published as Levy 1997a.

1 While an early Commission document (EC 1993b: 14) stressed the single market arguments for regulation, these were not fully reflected in the subsequent Council/Commission regulatory proposals.

2 Currently most analogue pan-European channels survive with relatively low market shares across the EU. In 1996, of fourteen pan-European channels only four had a daily reach of more than 2 per cent: Arte, CNN, Euronews and Eurosport. The prospects for digital pay channels with 0.5 or 1 per cent penetration, outside the home market for their chosen conditional access system, do not look good (*Multichannel News* July 1996).

3 Although the Directive forbids operators from prohibiting manufacturers from including a common interface, in practice, since many boxes will be subsidised by operators, it will be the conditional access operators rather than manufacturers who will decide on the specifications for the bulk of the boxes sold.

4 A fuller description of the background to the Directive as a whole is in Levy 1997a.

5 In 1988 Rupert Murdoch announced his intention to start broadcasting in February 1989, using PAL. Later in 1989, four German channels also decided to broadcast in PAL from ASTRA (Peterson 1993: 184).

6 For more detail on the DVB's role see Levy 1997a, Cowie 1996 and Cave and Cowie 1996 and European Commission, *Technical Papers on DVB*, 1993, includes DVB Memorandum of Understanding: 416–28.

7 The UK, France and Germany were particularly opposed to any vigorous regulation of conditional access.

8 One MEP commented on how 'the number of lobbyists involved in this game of poker has mushroomed almost out of control' (Hoppenstalt, European Parliament Debates no 4–464/7, 12 June 1995).

9 The Directive (95/47/EC) was adopted by a Council of Ministers meeting in July, but only published in the *Official Journal* in November 1995 (*Official Journal* 23 November 1995 no. L: 281).

10 CSD and Via Digital were later to reach a commercial agreement to share the pay per view football rights.

11 The Commission imposed strict limits on the way in which the Spanish regulated conditional access. The Spanish requirement for prior approval of decoders was only acceptable if it was a simple declaratory procedure and was not applied to operators broadcasting from other Member States, and the Government was not allowed to fix prices for conditional access services (*Agence Europe* no. 7076 10 October 1997).

12 For a full description of the UK regime for conditional access regulation see Chapter 6 below, DTI, *The Regulation of Conditional Access services for Digital Television: Final Consultation Paper on Detailed Implementation Proposals*, London, 27 November 1996 (and previous drafts of January and June 1996). See also OFTEL, *The Regulation of Conditional Access for Digital Television Services: OFTEL Guidelines*, London, OFTEL, March 1997.

13 Reuters 10 June 1996. According to *Les Echos*, 12 June 1996, the meeting took place on 8 June 1996 and included representatives of Canal Plus, BSkyB, Bertelsmann, Kirch, Deutsche Telekom and Vebacom.

14 See also:

> Without agreement on such systems and their common implementation, the compatibility may be jeopardized and markets segmented . . . It remains to be seen if the common implementation of . . . standards in set-top boxes can be quickly achieved with the help of all economic actors. The importance of the stake explains the interest of the Community to ensure equality of access and interoperation of systems.

15 In June 1997 the ITC went further and issued a consultation paper on interoperability in UK Digital Broadcasting which proposed mandating a single technical transmission standard for all UK digital broadcasters, together with a requirement that all APIs for interactive services, should be interoperable with that chosen for UK DTT services. These proposals aroused the opposition of the UK Government and BSkyB as well as some others. They were effectively withdrawn in the Autumn of 1998.

16 See comment by Marc-André Feffer, Deputy Chairman of Canal Plus:

> We want the TV to become the focal point of the front room. With digital technology, viewers will be able to fully interact with their TV sets and use them for a full range of multimedia services . . . We think standardisation should happen at an international level . . . Everyone is agreed that we should be working towards one single box for the consumer. The present generation of boxes have no standardised access control systems, and there is no bridge to the Internet or PCs.
>
> (*Broadcast* 12 December 1997)

See also *TV International,* 15 December 1997, 'Canal+, Open TV push for next Euro digital settop standard'.

17 It is also the case that generally national and EU policy-makers were slower than the industry itself to recognise the full anti-competitive potential of the various gateway technologies.

5 Impact of European competition policy

1 See Nihoul (1998) and McCallum (1999) for a discussion of many of the issues addressed in this chapter.

2 See Chapter 8.

3 After complaints by broadcasters not within the EBU this Commission Decision was subsequently challenged by the Court of First Instance (judgement dated 11 July 1996) and an appeal is pending at the time of writing. Interestingly, it appears that DG IV has been keen to defend the original exemption, but the EBU has been obliged to tighten up the membership criteria for its 'Eurovision' collective purchasing arrangement.

4 Collins 1994b: 150 (citing Porter and Hasselbach 1991: 159) suggests that the Commission was more tolerant of collective purchase of rights by commercial TV companies than by public service ones.

5 See section on 'Funding of public broadcasting' in this chapter.

6 In a clear reference to the EBU the Commission stated that 'where rights are jointly acquired by members of multinational associations, it must be ensured that non-members have appropriate access to the relevant programme material. This can be achieved through limitations on exclusivity or through the granting of sub-licences' (EC 1990: 20).

7 When van Miert appeared before the Culture Committee of the European Parliament together with Commissioner Monti on 27 September 1995 he spoke of public service broadcasting as an essential tool in preserving pluralism in most Member States and of the need to ensure at Community level that the conditions for its continued existence were maintained. See also van Miert speech (1997a) where he remarked that 'of course, the issues of media pluralism and culture cannot be ignored in relation to the television market'.

8 The timing of the notification to Formula One was particularly sensitive. After representations from Formula One the UK Government had recently argued that Formula One should be exempt from tough rules on tobacco sponsorship for a transitional period. Bernie Ecclestone was about to float his Formula One

Holdings Company which held the rights. The Commission also informed the FIA that it believed that Mr Ecclestone's other principal role, as Vice President of the FIA in charge of commercial activities, was 'clearly a conflict of interest' (*Financial Times* 23 January 1998). For a fuller discussion of the competition issues raised by television sports rights see Cowie and Williams 1997.

9 If, for example, DG IV were to produce market definitions which recognised that there were separate pay and free-to-air markets for the rights in the most popular sports – football and Formula One motor racing – there was the possibility that competition policy might accomplish what several Member States had contemplated, but failed to do by legislation, namely to ensure that where key events were shown live on pay television, delayed highlights at least would be available on free-to-air TV.

10 John Temple Lang is Director of the Information, Communications and Multimedia Directorate within DG IV and a key European exponent of the essential facilities doctrine.

11 Temple Lang (1997: 70) points out that 'the question has often been asked informally in Europe: can television decoding systems ("set-top boxes" and their related systems) be essential facilities to which competitors are entitled to have access, and if so in what circumstances?' This section is drawn from his discussion, which sets a fairly high threshold of proof that would need to be met (ibid.: 70–9).

12 The Head of the DG IV Telecommunications Unit, Herbert Ungerer, voiced similar sentiments:

> The central problem will without doubt be that, given the evolving market structure, the telecommunications/media/information technology sector will in many areas depend on ensuring access to bottle-neck/essential facilities – such as networks – which are essential for reaching customers and cannot be replicated in a reasonable manner by other means . . . The issue of access and interconnection in the telecommunications, media, and information technology sector will become without doubt a major test for the application of the essential facilities doctrine under EC competition law.
>
> (Ungerer 1995: 66–7).

13 The notice lists the conditions in which access would be required, including situations where:

> access to the facility in question is generally essential in order for companies to compete on that related market . . . there is sufficient capacity available to provide access; the facility owner fails to satisfy demand . . . the company requiring access is prepared to pay reasonable and non-discriminatory price and . . . where there is no objective justification for refusing to provide access.
>
> (EC 1998e: 21)

On the question of when access is essential the notice comments:

> it will not be sufficient that the position of the company requesting access would be more advantageous if access were granted – but refusal of access must lead to the proposed activities being made either impossible or seriously and unavoidably uneconomic.
>
> (Ibid.)

14 In the well known case of Magill, although the Court found in favour of the defendant, by the time the decision came Magill had in fact gone out of business.

15 See also OFTEL's reflections on bottleneck regulation in their response to the EU Convergence Green Paper follow-up consultation (OFTEL 1998c).

16 MSG Media Service *Official Journal* no. L: 364/1, 31 December 1994. This was a

proposed joint venture between Deutsche Telekom, the German national telecommunications company and operator of 90 per cent of the cable network in Germany, Bertelsmann, a leading German book, music, sound recording and TV company, and Kirch, an important supplier of feature films and TV programmes.

17 Nordic Satellite Distribution was a joint venture between Norsk Telekom and Tele Danmark, the national telecoms operators for Norway and Denmark, and Kinnevik, which is a leading Scandinavian TV, media and telecoms company involved in satellite TV and radio broadcasting (*Official Journal* no. L: 53/20, 2 March 1996). RTL-Veronica-Endemol was a proposed joint venture between RTL, a Dutch language TV and radio broadcaster, Veronica, a Dutch public service broadcaster, and Endemol, the major producer of TV programmes in Holland (*Official Journal* no. L: 134/32ff., 5 June 1996).

18 MSG Media Service (*Official Journal* no. L: 364, 31 December 1994. Paragraph 47.

19 BDB, Case No IV/36.586 *Official Journal* 97/C 291/07 25 September 1997 and BIB Case No IV/36.539 *Official Journal* 97/C 259/04 26 August 1997

20 The ITC specifically stated that conditions were imposed as a result of its discussions with DG IV (ITC Press release 19 December 1997 107/97 'ITC Grant of Multiplex licence clears way for start of Digital Terrestrial TV in 1998').

21 Premiere was jointly owned by Bertelsmann/CLT/UFA 37.5 per cent, Canal Plus 37.5 per cent and Kirch 25 per cent. Under the proposed merger, Kirch would acquire the Canal Plus stake in Premiere and divide it with Bertelsmann, so that each German group would own equal stakes in Premiere. Canal Plus would buy Kirch's 45 per cent stake in the Italian pay channel Telepui, to add to its existing 45 per cent stake, giving it 90 per cent control of Italy's only pay broadcaster.

22   Economically, today's media involve content, carriage and software. But the companies involved no longer fall neatly into these three categories, and there is much 'convergence'. Antitrust problems arise when a company which is dominant in one of these areas makes use of or extends its dominance into another, especially by a joint venture with another company which is itself dominant in the second area.

(Temple Lang 1997: 5)

23 Court of First Instance Judgement of 15 September 1998 in Case T–95/96 Gestevision Telecinco SA.

24 Commissioner van Miert's statement after the meeting (van Miert 1998) pointed out that whilst Member States had opposed guidelines 'a vast majority of Member States seems to accept that more transparency is required in relation to the funding of public service broadcasters'. He went on to give his position on the Amsterdam protocol on public service broadcasting:

> This protocol confirms the principle that it is for Member States to define the scope of the public service remit and to grant funding to broadcasting organisations. However, this protocol does not affect the Commission's responsibility to ensure that such funding does not affect trading conditions and competition in the Community to an extent which would be contrary to the common interest, while the realisation of the remit of the public broadcasting service shall be taken into account.

The question of how the balance should be drawn between the different objectives within that final sentence, itself drawn from the Protocol, remains open.

25 Effectively imposing a potential five month standstill period on marketing of a conditional access system in Germany, that it would have been perfectly legal to market elsewhere (*Financial Times* December 1997). This case stands in marked contrast to the Spanish situation where legislation to ban the marketing of a proprietary conditional access system was ruled unlawful by the Commission.

26 This is not to suggest that the decisions of DG IV were not controversial. The pressures were obvious in discussions of funding for public broadcasting. In addition, as we have shown above, many of the media cases dealt with by DG IV were particularly high profile, and attracted a great deal of criticism and political pressure, both from other Commissioners, and from industry and national governments (see e.g. *TV Express* 23 July 1998 for accounts of criticisms from Commissioners Bangemann and Oreja). It was partly in response to such criticisms that DG IV often tried to emphasise how many media mergers it had allowed, as well as focusing on the ones it had vetoed. In summer 1998 Commission officials cited the clearance of BIB and a French interactive services alliance between Cegetel, Canal Plus, America Online and Bertelsmann, as evidence of their concern to see the launch of new services (see Pons 1998a, Commission Press Release IP/98/755 for details of the French case, and McCallum 1999 for a defence of DG IV decisions).

27 The case of public broadcasting is an obvious exception, where Member States have instead been keen to see the competition provisions of the Treaty interpreted in a way which recognises the specific cultural and political significance of broadcasting, and the distinct role of public intervention in this sector.

6 National approaches to digital regulation

1 At the end of 1997 there were more digital subscribers in France than anywhere else in the EU. Canal Satellite claimed 640,000 subscribers, Télévision par Satellite (TPS) 320,000, and AB-Sat 50,000 (*Cable and Satellite Europe* February 1998).

2 Previously France had not had any listed-events-type legislation, but under its 1995 licence from the CSA, Canal Plus, as the only pay TV channel, had agreed not to acquire exclusive rights to specific major sporting events.

3 The CSA had already decided to act unilaterally in response to the European Court decision and announced a decision to loosen its cable licensing requirements in November 1997 before the measures were announced in the Broadcasting Bill (*New Media Markets* 27 November 1997).

4 Delays in introducing the French Broadcasting Bill meant that the French came in for further condemnation from the Commission. By December 1998 six years had passed since the Commission had started their infringement procedures against the French for failing to comply with TVWF in not recognising the validity of broadcasting licenses granted in other Member States for retransmission in France. The Commission then applied to the European Court of Justice for action to be taken against France (Commission Press release IP/98/1067 7 December 1998).

5 The 1990 Broadcasting Act had opened the way for the previous 'must carry' regime for analogue cable services to be phased out.

6 A multiplex is a block of spectrum (equivalent to an existing UHF channel) which can accommodate an average of four digital channels, together with data services.

7 OFTEL opposed the award to BDB arguing that 'the participation of BSkyB either as a consortium member or as a long term supplier of certain pay TV services, in particular sports programming, raised substantial competition concerns in the pay TV network and conditional access market' (OFTEL Press Release 24 June 1997). See also Chapter 4.

8 At current prices the idea of subsidised boxes for large numbers of households would be difficult to justify economically. If the subsidy was reserved for the last 10 per cent of households, early adopters of digital TV would feel justifiably aggrieved, whilst many others would delay converting to digital in the hope that a government subsidy might be on offer.

9 Almost eighteen months elapsed after the announcement of a media ownership

review in January 1994 before the Government's first proposals were produced. These then had to be refined before publication of the Broadcasting Bill at the end of 1995.

10 More than 650,000 homes paid a minimum of £9.95 to watch the Tyson-Bruno fight at 5 a.m. (*Financial Times* 25 March 1996).

11 Article 2, Information and Communication Services Act, 1997.

12 Laws on cross-ownership differed greatly between the states. Thus in Hesse the publisher of a newspaper with a dominant position was forbidden from owning a stake in any radio or TV general interest programme, but in Lower Saxony a newspaper publisher who was equally dominant would be allowed to take a shareholding of up to 25 per cent in a radio or TV station, and in Baden Wurttemburg a newspaper publisher with a market share of more than 50 per cent could be granted a licence to run a TV or radio station as long as measures such as the creation of a pluralistically composed board were taken to ensure an internal pluralism of programming (European Publishers Council 1995 Germany: 9–10).

13 On the subject of the CLT/UFA merger, Humphreys writes that 'Germany's most recent ownership rules seem designed to accommodate precisely this kind of "mega-merger"'.

14 The events include the Summer and Winter Olympics, matches involving the German team in the European and world football championships as well as the opening, semi-final and final matches, together with German football federation semi-final and final matches (*European Television Analyst* 26 March 1998).

15 Canal Satellite, Télévision par Satellite, and AB SAT.

16 *Journal Officiel*, Sénat, *Débats Parlementaires*, séance du 19 fevrier 1997: 875.

7 From the European IS to convergence

1 The White Paper predicted that telecommunications would require investment of 150 billion ECU's over the following decade, and would account for 6 per cent of EU GDP by the year 2000 (Federal Trust 1995: 39–40).

2 Although the Commission's Action Plan on 'Europe's Way to the Information Society' of 19 July 1994 which followed on from the Bangemann Report did try to redress the Report's impatient approach to the audio-visual sector with its comment that 'cultural goods, especially cinema and television programmes, cannot be treated like other products: they are the privileged mediums of identity, pluralism and integration'.

3 Arguing for co-ordinated action in the policy field, the report stated that 'the only question is whether this will be a strategic creation for the whole Union, or a more fragmented and much less effective amalgam of individual initiatives by Member States' (EC 1994c: 5).

4 The Licensing Directive, Directive 97/13/EC on a common framework for general authorisations and individual licences in the field of telecommunications services, proscribed certain kinds of licensing conditions, and obliged national authorities to adopt the least onerous licensing system possible (*Official Journal* no. L 117, 07 May 1997).

5 For a summary of Commission initiatives on universal service and all telecommunications legislation (EC 1998h).

6 An early draft of the Convergence Green Paper that was circulated unofficially took this approach. It commented on how:

> in contrast to the telecommunications sector, the regulation of broadcasting is essentially determined at national level . . . aspects of the regulatory tradition originating in the era of scarcity persist today . . . there is no concept of a general or class licence such as those which exist for most telecommunications services.
>
> (Convergence Draft Green Paper 1997 Chapter 2)

7 The areas of encryption and copyright were unusual in that the US regulated before most EU countries, with strong controls on the export of encryption technology and the introduction of the No Electronic Theft Act (NET) in 1997 making on-line piracy an offence.

8 EC 1996g, 1997f, 1997g, 1997h. See also EC, 1998k.

9 See text at http://www2.echo.lu/bonn/industry.htm

10 The Communication promised that some of the questions about the role of audio-visual regulation in a converging industry would be addressed by the Commission 'in the context of its Communication on Information Society Services: Building a regulatory framework of 17 March 1995, SEC(95) 444'. This document, drawn up by the services of Commissioners Monti, Oreja and Bangemann, and referred to in other Commission documents, has not as yet been made publicly available.

11 Although DGs IV, X and XIII all commissioned consultant's reports on the implications of convergence the reports produced for DG XIII from Coudert Brothers in 1994, KPMG in 1996, NERA in 1996 and Squires, Sanders and Analysis in 1997 were noteworthy for their focus on the need for regulatory change.

12 KPMG predicted revenue increases of 40 per cent by 2005 for France, Germany, Italy, Netherlands and the UK if moves were made to promote convergence. Regulatory reform was only one part of such promotional activities but as KPMG put it 'this analysis does show the magnitude of loss that could result from a misdirected policy' (KPMG, Summary Report 1996: 9). While this prediction was hedged around with caveats and referred to *all* the growth that might occur up to 2005 in traditional and converged services, the Convergence Green Paper made a huge logical leap, citing the KPMG study as indicating 'that revenues in the relevant sectors could suffer by some 40 per cent by the year 2005 if the market does not develop in a direction which takes full advantage of convergence' (EC 1997d: 10).

13 A similar proposal had been made to the UK Government Peacock Committee in 1986. This had suggested that public money, rather than being spent on public broadcasters as such, should be spent on an Arts Council of the Air which could then finance 'public service programmes' (Peacock 1986).

14 In reality the 1989 Television Without Frontiers Directive had (together with the Cable and Satellite Directive) already provided a way of reconciling national licensing systems and trans-frontier satellite services.

15 Principally the API or applications programming interface, which provides the operating system within the box (akin to MSDos or Windows on a computer) and which dictates whether interactive systems work or not. See Chapter 4 above.

16 The Green Paper asked whether there should be a move towards creating:

> a coherent framework for both public and private broadcasting organisations, for example so that different organisations are allowed to bid to undertake such obligations, including organisations from outside the traditional sector. Where specific support in the form of industry or even public funding is available for the provision of such services, the issue arises, *inter alia*, as to whether that mechanism would need to be open to any organisation willing to be designated as fulfilling public interest obligations.
>
> (EC 1997d: 28)

17 As the Green Paper put it, the aim was to 'remove inconsistencies, avoid discrimination within and across sectors *and* continue to ensure the achievement of public interest objectives' (EC 1997d: 34) (author's italics).

18 This was the approach favoured by companies such as Microsoft, Intel, and Olivetti. See also *Agence Europe* 16 April 1998 for a report of a similar view from Time Warner Europe and the EU Committee of the American Chamber of Commerce in Belgium.

19 See NERA 1997 for evidence of the lack of industry support for this idea.

20 In advance of publication of the draft directive Commissioner Monti spelt out its purposes, stating: 'we are currently considering the development of a transparency mechanism to make sure that regulation only takes place where strictly necessary and in a coherent pan-European fashion' (speech at the University of Bonn, reproduced in *Agence Europe* 2 October 1996; see also Commission Press Release IP/96/695 24 July 1996).

21 See *Official Journal* C/110/1 8 April 1998 for the Council's Common Position on this Directive. Also see *Official Journal* C 62/48 26 February 1998 Annex III for a list of services included in the scope of the Directive. The following are listed as excluded on grounds that that they are not supplied on the individual request of a recipient:

- television broadcasting services (including near video-on-demand services)
- radio broadcasting services
- (televised) teletext.

22 *European Report* 29 October 1996

23 Interview with German Federal Government Official, Bonn 19 August 1997. According to this interviewee, while the Germans were not opposed to greater communication of national laws, the Commission's insistence on a Directive fuelled suspicions in Bonn that their real aim 'was an increase in EU competence'.

24 The definition was also prefaced by the words 'any service normally provided for remuneration' so as to exclude free services.

25 An addition to Article 9 para. 2 of the Directive stated that:

> with regard to draft rules on services, detailed opinions from the Commission or Member States may not affect any cultural policy measures, in particular in the audiovisual sphere, which Member States might adopt in accordance with Community Law, taking account of their linguistic diversity, their specific national and regional characteristics and their cultural heritage.

See *Official Journal* C62/53, 26 February 1998.

26 For Carole Tongue's views see her submission on the Green Paper itself posted on the Green Paper web site http://www.ispo.cec.be. (This web site also includes the other responses referred to below.) Kuhne was the rapporteur for the report from the EP Culture Committee.

8: Convergence: new approaches

1 PC/TVs may have an appeal in offices. In the domestic market the model seems more likely to involve enhanced TV, where the digital TV set will be used as a cheap way of accessing the Internet, and where Internet-delivered information will link to the TV programmes that the viewer is watching.

2 Where there are monopolies of distribution to the home – namely, through a cable system – and where the content that is being distributed has some influence on the public, even where that system includes, say, five hundred channels, there may still be public policy issues involved in how those channels are allocated.

3 The following statements are illustrative of this approach: 'It remains valid under convergence for governments to promote culture, although we believe that the objective is more likely to be self fulfilled as product differentiation occurs', 'quality and diversity objectives should be increasingly self-fulfilling as product differentiation develops' and 'removal of scarcity means that plurality of opinion will more readily occur. It will therefore become less of a concern to regulators' (KPMG 1996 Summary Report).

4 There is a consensus on this amongst UK industry consultants. KPMG expect

traditional channels to 'retain the lion's share of viewing' in the UK over the next ten years. This accords with the BBC's forecasts that traditional channels will have between 65 and 75 per cent of viewing by 2005 (BBC 1996).

5 No serious attempt has been made at quantifying any potential gains from regulatory reform. KPMG offered some preliminary ideas on this but their findings were then misquoted by the Commission's Green Paper on Convergence (see note 12 in Chapter 7). While many of the OECD's recent studies urge the need for regulatory convergence, none have provided any economic analysis of this kind (OECD 1997a and 1997b).

6 The British have generally succeeded in preventing the reception of foreign satellite pornography channels. However, other countries (notably in Scandinavia) have been less successful in preventing their territories being targeted by satellite channels that have based themselves in the UK to circumvent national legislation on, for example, advertising aimed at children. The 1997 revisions to the Television Without Frontiers Directive will make it more difficult for satellite broadcasters to fly 'flags of convenience', since they will be regulated according to the territory in which they have their head office, and in which the bulk of their economic activity takes place.

7 As long as governments do not seek to prohibit reception of channels licensed elsewhere in the EU, other than for reasons related to the 'protection of minors' or the enforcement of national protection for the televising of major events, they will not contravene the 1997 Television Without Frontiers Directive.

8 In addition, the weakest link in most parental control systems is frequently the parents themselves, particularly when it is their children who are the most technically adept users in the household.

9 According to the ITC the right approach – subject to the need to protect minors – is 'the more a programme enters the home on the basis of a conscious and specific decision on the part of an adult' then the less need there should be for the regulation of programme content to impose requirements which are over and above the general law of the land' (ITC 1997a).

10 The point is not to create the broadcast equivalent of *The Economist*, but rather to ensure that the widest possible number of people are exposed to programming that meets the objectives determined by policy-makers.

11 One consequence of this approach is that it would prevent governments or broadcasters themselves from restricting distribution of public service channels to a single distribution system, in an attempt to drive take-up of that system, as has happened in France where the digital programmes of France TV were initially only available on the TPS satellite system.

12 Two classic cases here concern dissemination on the Internet of material that was banned from publication. In the French 1997 legislative elections the ban on publishing opinion polls in the last two weeks of the election campaign was breached through publication abroad, and the subsequent posting of the results on the Internet. Similarly in England the contempt rule, under which a minor who was the subject of court proceedings (the Home Secretary's son, William Straw) could not be named in the English press, was circumvented by publication first on the Internet, and then in the Scottish press. Both cases highlight the difficulties involved in enforcement, but it would be false to draw the conclusion either that all rules on opinion polls are pointless, or that the Scottish legal system should immediately be merged with that operating in England and Wales.

13 For instance, in 1994–5 when the Advanced TV Standards directive was being framed, few were aware of the role that would be played by the API, the Verifier and the EPG, in acting as digital gateways. It is only a matter of time before new gateway technologies emerge.

14 As with a bank account, if users cannot get their customer information transferred readily to a new service provider, they will feel locked in to their current provider.

15 The Internet provides an example of some of the problems that might arise in terms of impersonation and false information on digital networks

16 Commissioner Oreja recognised this fact when, in his speech to the Birmingham Audiovisual Conference in April 1998, he suggested that investment obligations might replace broadcast quotas (Proceedings 1998: 75).

17 Cf. the recommendation that under convergence the EU's approach should 'be based primarily on competition law and should minimise regulatory intervention and avoid market distortion' (KPMG 1996 Summary Report: 26).

18 See *Financial Times* 11 February 1998 for an account of overload in DG IV. See also Green (1997: 21–3). Murroni and Irvine (1998: 54) offer a less pessimistic assessment of the efficacy of competition policy in this area.

19 Murroni (1997: 7) argues that 'getting rid of unrepresentative and unaccountable traditions of regulation is far more urgent than merging agencies and quangos [and that] . . . Without accountability we'll be better off with separate agencies arguing with each other in the public domain'.

20   We will . . . need to . . . design a European Communications and Media Act bringing together legislation on the provision of infrastructure, services, content (IPRs, privacy, data protection, digital signatures, harmful content) and on conditions for access to that content (via TV, computer, or telephone networks).

(Bangemann 1997a)

21 Because some kinds of content (e.g. holocaust denial) are illegal in some countries (such as France and Germany) whilst legal in others (such as the US and the UK).

22 Although it is interesting to note that in the NERA survey of fifty-two telecoms operators, regulators, policy-makers, telecoms competitors, and users, across nine EU countries, very few had strong views on how Community and national regulatory institutions should be structured to deal with convergence, and only 'a small number expressed the view that some reform of regulation would be necessary' (NERA 1997: 43).

9 Regulation, the state and the EU policy process

1 EU support schemes have naturally been vigorously defended by their beneficiaries, both current and potential, but whilst the sums of money involved have been important to their recipients, they have been insufficient to make any substantial impact on the industry. One of the most obvious benefits of EU support schemes has been the creation of a policy network that can be accessed, and on occasions mobilised, by the relevant part of the Commission.

2 Member State support for the 1997 Amsterdam protocol on public service broadcasting can be seen as much as evidence of support for subsidiarity in the broadcast field as for any necessary shared enthusiasm about public service broadcasting as such.

3 The rate of increase in the deficit grew from an 11 per cent increase in 1995 to 18 per cent in 1996. By 1996 the negative trade balance in films, television programmes and video reached a total 5.6 billion dollars in favour of the US (EC 1998a).

4 See Cram 1994 for a description of DGXIII's 's 'symbiotic relationship' with the IT industry.

Bibliography

Allen, D. (1996) 'Competition policy', in H. Wallace and W. Wallace (eds) *Policy-Making in the European Union*, Oxford: OUP: 160–83.

ANEC (1995) European Association for the co-ordination of consumer representation in standardisation, *Annual Report*.

Bangemann, M. (1997a) 'The need for an international charter. a new world Order for global communications', Speech to Telecom Inter@ctive '97 Conference (http://www.ispo.cec.be/infosoc/promo/speech/geneva .htm), Geneva, 8 Sept. 1997.

Bangemann, M. (1997b) 'Europe and the iInformation society: the policy response to globalisation and convergence', Speech in Venice, 18 Sept. 1997.

Barendt, E. M. (1995) *Broadcasting Law: A Comparative Study*, Oxford: OUP.

BBC (1996) *Extending Choice in the Digital Age*, London: BBC.

BBC (1998) *The BBC Beyond 2000*, London: BBC.

Begg, I. (1996) 'Regulation in the European Union', *Journal of European Public Policy* 3, 4 December 1996: 525–35.

Beltrame, F. (1996) 'Harmonising media ownership rules: problems and prospects', *Utilities Law Review*, October: 172–75.

Bennett, C. J. (1988) 'Different processes, one result: the convergence of data protection policy in Europe and the United States', *Governance* 1, 4: 415–41.

Bennett, C. J. (1991a) 'What is policy convergence and what causes it?' British *Journal of Political Science*, 21: 215–33.

Bennett, C. J. (1991b) 'How states utilize foreign evidence', *Journal of Public Policy* 11: 31–54.

Bennett, P. and Adamson, M. (1996) *Convergence in Europe: The New Information Infrastructure*, London: FT Telecommunications and Media Publishing.

Bertelsmann Foundation (1997) *White Paper: Communications Coordinates 2000: Criteria for Shaping Tomorrow's Communications*, Gutersloh:Bertelsmann Foundation.

Braun, P. and Schaal, A. (1998) 'Federalism, the nation state and the global network: the case of German communications policy', http://ksgwww.harvard.edui/iip/iicompol/Papers/Braun-Schaal.html.

Brown, C. (1996) *The Future of Film and TV Funding: Confrontation or Collaboration?* London: FT Telecoms and Media Publishing.

Brown, C. (1997) *The New Economics of Audio-Visual Production.*, London: FT Media and Telecoms.

Cairncross, F. (1998) *The Death of Distance. How the Communications Revolution will Change our Lives*, London: Orion Business.

Campbell, P and Konert, B. (1998) 'Building blocks for the information society' in J. Langham-Brown (ed.) *The Yearbook of the European Institute for the Media 1998*, Dusseldorf: EIN: 45–51.

Canal Plus (1995, 1996, 1997) *Annual Report*, Paris: Canal Plus.

Cathodon (1995) 'Broadcasting legislation in France over the past twenty years', *Réseaux* 3, 2: 263–90.

Cave, M. (1997) 'Regulating digital televisioin in a convergent world', *Telecom-munications Policy* 21, 7: 575–96.

Cave, M. and Cowie, C. (1996) 'Regulating conditional access in European pay broadcasting', *Communications and Strategies* 23, 3rd Quarter: 119–42.

Cave, M. and Cowie, C. (1998) 'Not only conditional access. Towards a better regulatory approach to digital TV', *Communications and Strategies* 30, 2nd quarter: 77–101.

Cave, M. and Crowther, P. (1996) 'Determining the level of regulation in EU telecommunications: A preliminary assessment', *Telecommunications Policy* 20, 10: 725–38.

Cawson, A. (1994) 'Business interests and the regulation of new technology in Europe: the case of television', *Business and the Contemporary World* 4: 68–80.

Chrocziel, P. and Dieselhorst, J. (1996) 'Multimedia legislation in Germany: what is 'broadcasting'?' *Computer and Telecommunications Law Review* 5: 194–7.

Clements, B. (1998) 'The impact of convergence on regulatory policy in Europe', *Telecommunications Policy* 22, 3: 197–205.

Coates, K. (1998) 'Commission notice on the application of the competition rules to access agreements in the telecommunications sector', *Competition Policy Newsletter*, 2 June: 45–6.

Coleman, F. and McMurtie, S. (1995) 'Red hot television: domestic and international legal aspects of the regulation of satellite television', *European Public Law* 1, 2: 201–14.

Collins, R. (1994a) 'Unity in diversity? The European single market in broadcasting and the audiovisual, 1982–92', *Journal of Common Market Studies* 32, 1: 89–102.

Collins, R. (1994b) *Broadcasting and Audio-Visual Policy in the European Single Market*, London: John Libbey.

Collins, R. (1996b) *Converging Media? Converging Regulation?* London: IPPR.

Collins, R. (1998) 'Locked in a mortal embrace. Les politiques audivisuelles du Royaume-Uni et de la France', *Réseaux* 87, Jan.-Fév. 1998: 137–62.

Collins, R. and Murroni, C. (1996) *New Media, New Policies*, London: Polity.

Commissariat général du Plan (1996) *Les réseaux de la societé de l'information. Rapport du Groupe présidé par Thierry Mileo*, Paris: Editions ASPE, europe: Editions ESKE.

Congdon, T., Graham, A., Green, D. *et al.* (1995) *The Cross Media Revolution: Ownership and Control*, London: John Libbey.

Conseil Supérieur de l'Audiovisuel (1997) *Les Risques de Position Dominante dans la Télévision à Péage par Satellite*, Paris: CSA.

Conseil Supérieur de l'Audiovisuel (1993) *Réglementation et Régulation Audiovisuelles en Europe*, Paris: CSA.

Conseil Supérieur de l'Audiovisuel (1998) *Réponse du CSA au Livrre Vert de la Commission Européenne*, Paris: CSA.

Convergent Decisions Group (1997) *Digital Terrestrial Television in Europe*, London: Convergent Decisions Group.

Coudert Brothers (1994) *An Overview and Analysis of the Regulatory Barriers to the Take-off of Mutlimedia Applications in Preparation for the Infrastructure Green Paper*, EC Contract Number 48246 London/Brussels/Paris: Coudert Brothers.

Council for Research, Technology and Innovation (1996) *The Information Society.Opportunities, Innovations and Challenges*, Bonn, Germany: The Federal Ministry of Education, Science, Research and Technology (BMBF).

Council of Ministers (1998) *Culture/Audiovisual Council No 12744/98, Press Release*, Brussels 17 November 1998.

Cowie, C. (1996) 'The evolution of digital television in Europe and the regulation of conditional access (1991–1995)', *Vierteljahrshefte zur Wirtschaftsforschung* 65, 4: 471–81.

Cowie, C. and Marsden, C. T. (1998) 'Convergence, competition and regulation', *International Journal of Communications Law and Policy* 1: htttp: www.digital-law.net/IJCLP/final/current/ijclp_webdoc_6_1_1998.html.

Cowie, C. and Williams, M. (1997) 'The economics of sports rights', *Telecommunications Policy* 21, 7: 619–34.

Crabit, E. (1995) '"Pluralism and media concentration": 10 questions and answers on the Commission's work', *IRIS*, Special Issue: Legal Developments in the Audiovisual Sector: 12–14.

Cram, L. (1994) 'The European Commission as a multi-organization: social policy and IT policy in the EU', *Journal of European Public Policy* 1, 2 (Autumn).

Cram, L. (1997) *Policy-making in the EU*, London: Routledge.

Craufurd Smith, R. (1997) 'Getting the measure of public services: community competition rules and public service broadcasting', in E. Barendt (ed.) *Yearbook of Media and Entertainment Law 1997/98*, Oxford: OUP: 75–95.

Craufurd Smith, R. (1997) 'Pluralism and freedom of expression: constitutional imperatives for a new broadcast order', in E. Barendt (ed.) *Yearbook of Media and Entertainment Law 1996*, Oxford: OUP: 21–44.

David, P. A. and Shurmer, M. (1996) 'Formal standards-setting for global telecommunications and information services: towards an institutional regime transformation?' *Telecommunications Policy* 20, 10: 789–815.

Department of Culture, Media and Sport and Department of Trade and Industry (1998b) *Government Response to 'The Multimedia Revolution'* (HC520–1), London: HMSO.

Department of Culture, Media and Sport and Radiocommunications Agency (1998a) *Television: The Digital Future. A Consultation Document*, London: HMSO.

Department of Culture, Media and Sport (1998a) *A Bigger Picture: The Report of the Film Policy Review Group*, London: HMSO.

Department of Culture, Media and Sport and Department of Trade and Industry (1998c) 'Regulating communications – approaching convergence in the Information Age', London: HMSO.

Department of Culture, Media and Sport (1998d) *Memorandum to House of Commons Select Committee on Culture Media and Sport*, London: DCMS.

Department of National Heritage (1995) *Media Ownership. The Government's Proposals*, London: HMSO.

Department of National Heritage (1997) *The BBC and the Future of Broadcasting. Memorandum to House of Commons National Heritage Select Committee*, London: DNH.

Department of Trade and Industry (1996a (November)) *The Regulation of Conditional Access services for Digital Television: Final Consultation Paper on Detailed Implementation Proposals*, London: DTI.

Department of Trade and Industry (1996b) *The Advanced Television Standards Regulations 1996 (SI 96/3151) and Conditional Access Services Class Licence*, London: DTI.

De Witte, B. (1995) 'The European content requirement in the EC television directive – five years after', in E. C. Barendt (ed.) *The Yearbook of Media and Entertainment Law. 1995*, Oxford: OUP: 101–27.

Dolowitz, D. and Marsh, D. (1996) 'Who learns what from whom: a review of the policy transfer literature', *Political Studies* XLIV (June): 343–57.

Doyle, C. (1996) 'Effective sectoral regulation: telecommunications in the EU', *Journal of European Public Policy* 3, 4 (Dec.): 612–28.

Doyle, G. (1997a) *Media Concentration in Europe: The Impact on Pluralism*, Stirling:

Council of Europe Committee of Experts on Media Concentration and Pluralism.

Doyle, G. (1997b) 'From 'pluralism' to 'ownership': Europe's emergent policy on media concentrations navigates the doldrums', *Journal of Information, Law and Technology (JILT)* 1997 3: http: //elj.warwick.ac.uk/jilt/commsreg/97_3doyl/ Refereed Article.

Doyle, G. (1998) 'Regulation of media ownership and pluralism in Europe: can the European Union take us forward?' *Cardozo Arts and Entertainment Law Journal* 16, 2/3: 451–73.

DVB (1997 10.12.) 'DVB takes major step towards harmonised multimedia home platform', Press release.

Dyson, K. (1992) *The Politics of German Regulation*, Aldershot: Dartmouth.

Dyson, K. and Homolka, W. E. (1996) *Culture First! Promoting Standards in the New Media Age*, London: Cassell.

Dyson, K., Humpreys, P. and eds (1990) *The Political Economy of Communications*, London: Routledge.

Economic and Social Committee (1991) *Opinion on the Commission Green Paper on the Development of European Standardisation: Action for Faster Technological Integration in Europe* (91/C 120/09 6 May 1991).

Esser, J. and Noppe, R. (1996) 'Private muddling through as a political programme? The role of the European Commission in the telecommunications sector in the 1980s', *West European Politics* 19, 3 (July): 547–62.

European Broadcasting Union, U. d. M., World Radio and Television Council (1996) *Freedom of Expression and the Financing of Public Broadcasting: A Commented Decision of the Constitutional Court of Germany*, Geneva: EBU/WRTVC.

European Broadcasting Union (1998) *Difficult to be Easy: The Electronic Programme Guide*, Geneva: EBU.

European Commission (1988) *The Audiovisual Media in the Single European Market*, Volume 4/1988 in European Documentation Series.

European Commission (1990) *Communication by the Commission to the Council and to the European Parliament on Audio-visual Policy*, COM (90): 78, 21 February 1990.

European Commission (1991) *Standardisation in the European Economy*, COM (91): 521, Final, 16 December 1991.

European Commission (1992) *Green Paper on Pluralism and Media Concentration in the Internal Market: An Assessment of the Need for Community Action*.

European Commission (1993) *Digital Video Broadcasting: A Volume of Technical Papers Accompanying the Commission's Communication*.

European Commission (1993–4) *Livre Vert de la Commission 'Pluralisme et Concentration des Medias dans le Marché Interiéur – Evaluation de la Necessité d'une Action Communautaire. Commentaires des Parties Interessées*.

European Commission (1993a) *White Paper on Growth Competitiveness and Employment*, (The Delors White Paper).

European Commission (1993b) *Communication from the Commission to the Council and the European Parliament. Digital Video Broadcasting: A Framework for Community Policy*.

European Commission (1993c) *Proposal for A Directive on the Use of Standards for the Transmission of Television Signals*, OJ C 341/18–19, 18 Dec. 1993.

European Commission (1994a) *Communication from the Commission to the Council and the European Parliament, Follow-up to the Consultation Process Relating to the Green Paper on 'Pluralism and Media Concentration in the Internal Market'*.

European Commission (1994b) *Green Paper on Strategy Options to Strengthen the European Programme Industry in the Context of the Audiovisual Policy of the European Union*.

European Commission (1994c, 26th May) *Europe and the Global Information Society:*

Recommendations to the European Council. ('The Bangemann Report').

European Commission (1994d) *Green Paper on the Liberalisation of Telecommunications Infrastructure and Cable TV Networks – Part I : Principle and Timetable.*

European Commission (1995) 'Pluralism and media concentration in the internal market: questionnaire no III concerning a possible initiative on media ownership'.

European Commission (1996a) *Regulatory Transparency in the Internal Market for Information Society services. Communication to the European Parliament, the Council of the European Union and the Economic and Social Committee,* 24 July 1996.

European Commission (1996b) *Communication. Universal Service for Telecomunications in the Perspective of Fully Liberalised Environment,* COM (96): 73.

European Commission (1996c) *Networks for People and their Communities. Making the Most of the Information Society in the European Union.* First Annual Report to the European Commission from the Information Society Forum.

European Commission (1996d) *Standardization and the Global Information Society: The European Approach,* COM (96): 359.

European Commission (1996e) *Draft notice on the Application of the Competition Rules to Access Agreements in the Telecommunications Sector,* December 1996, CEC 1996, COM (96): 649, final 10 December 1996.

European Commission (1996f) 25th *Report on Competition Policy* (1995), COM (96): 126, final 10 April 1996.

European Commission (1996g) *Green Paper on the Protection of Minors and Human Dignity in Audio-visual and Information Society Services,* 16 Oct. 1996.

European Commission (1997a) European Community Competition Policy: 26th Report on Competition Policy –1996.

European Commission (1997c) *Amended Proposal for a European Parliament and Council Directive Amending for the Third Time Directive 83/189/EEC Laying Down a Procedure for the Provision of Information in the Field of Technical Standards and Regulations,* COM (97): 601, final, 17 Nov. 1997.

European Commission (1997d) *Green Paper on the Convergence of the Telecommunications, Media and Information Technology Sectors, and the Implications for Regulation. Towards an Information Society Approach.*

European Commission (1997e) *The European Film Industry Under Analysis.* Second Information Report, Brussels: European Commission, DG X/C.

European Commission (1997f) *Communication on Illegal and Harmful Content on the Internet,* COM (96): 487.

European Commission (1997g) *Action Plan on Promoting Safe Use of the Internet,* COM (97): 570, final 18 Nov. 1997.

European Commission (1997h) *Follow-up to the Green Paper on the Protection of Minors and Human Dignity In Audio-visual and Information Services,* COM (97): 570, final 18 Nov. 1997.

European Commission (1998a) *Audiovisual Policy: Next Steps,* COM (98): 446, final 14 July 1998.

European Commission (1998b) *Culture, the Cultural Industries and Employment.* Commission Staff Working Paper. SEC 98 837.

European Commission (1998c) *Proceedings of the European Audiovisual Conference,* UK, 6–8 April 1998.

European Commission (1998d) *The Digital Age: European Audiovisual Policy.* Report from the High Level Group on Audiovisual Policy.

European Commission (1998e) *Notice on the Application of the Competition Rules to Access Agreements in the Telecommunications Sector. Framework, Relevant Markets and Principles,* OJ C: 265, 22 August 1998.

European Commission (1998f) *Communication Concerning the Review Under Competition Rules of the Joint Provision of Telecommunications and Cable TV Networks by a Single Operator and the Abolition of Restrictions on the Provision of Cable TV Capacity Over Telecommunications Networks*, OJ C: 71, 7 March 1998.

European Commission (1998g) 'Notice concerning application for negative clearance for BiB – Case No IV / 36.539', OJ 98/C: 322/05, 21 October 1998.

European Commission (1998h) *Status Report on European Union Telecommunications Policy.* Update Oct. 1998.

European Commission (1998i) *Summary of the Results of the Public Consultation on the Green Paper on the Convergence of the Telecommunications, Media and Information Technology Sectors. Areas for Further Reflection*, SEC (98) 1284, 29 Sept. 1998.

European Commission (1998j) *Audio-visual Services And Production*, London/Luxembourg: Kogan Page/Office for Official Publications of the European Communities.

European Commission (1998k) *Communication on The Need for Strengthened International Co-ordination*, COM (98): 50.

European Commission (1998l) 'Commission opens in-depth investigation in the Bertelsmann/Kirch/Premiere case' *European Commission Press release* IP/98/77, 23 Jan. 1998.

European Commission (1998m) *Third Comunication from the Commission to the Council and the European Parliament on the Application of Articles 4 and 5 of Directive 89/552/EEC.*

European Commission (1998, undated) *1st Report on the Consideration of Cultural Aspects in European Community Action. Communication from the European Commission to the European Parliament, the Council and the Committee of the Regions.*

European Council (1994) *Common Position (EC) No 48/94 Adopted by the Council on 22 December 1994. (On Digital Broadcasting)*, OJ C 384/36, 31 December 1994.

European Institute for the Media. (1994) *Transparency of Media Control. Study for the European Commission DG XV*, Dusseldorf: European Institute for the Media.

European Publishers Council (1995) *Media Regulation in Europe. The Facts, the History, the Anomalies*, London: Hydra Associates.

Eurostat (1998) 'The audio-visual sector in the European Economic Area in the 1990s', *Statistics in Focus* 98/2, 10 Feb. 1998, Luxembourg.

Farr, S. (1996) *Harmonisation of technical standards in the EC*, London: Wiley.

Federal Trust. (1995) *Network Europe and the Information Society*, London: Federal Trust.

Fraser, M. (1996a) 'Television', in H. Kassim and A. Menon (eds) *The European Union and National Industrial Policy*, London: Routledge: 204–25.

Fraser, M. (1996b) *Télévision sans Frontières: Décryptage d'un 'Grand Projet' Européen*, Paris: Doctorat.

Fuchs, G. (1994) 'Policy-making in a system of multi-level governance – the Commission of the European Community and the restructuring of the telecommunications sector', *Journal of European Public Policy* 1, 2: 177–94.

GAH (1994) *Feasability of Using Audience Measures to Assess Pluralism*. Position Paper prepared for DG XV European Commission.

Garnham, N. (1996) *Convergence Between Telecommunications and Audiovisual: Consequences for the Rules Governing the Information Market*, Brussels: European Commission – Legal Advisory Board.

Genschel, P. and Plumper, T. (1997) 'Regulatory competition and international co-operation', *Journal of European Public Policy* 4, 4: 626–42.

German Government (1996) *Information and Communication Services Bill* (IukDG), Bonn.

German Government (1997) *IukDG – Information and Communication Services Bill.*

Brief Outline, http://www.iid.de:

Goldberg, D., Prosser, T. and Verhulst, S. (1998) *Regulating the Changing Media: A Comparative Study*, Oxford: OUP.

Goldberg, D. and Verhulst, S. (1996) *Legal Responses to Regulating the Changing Media in the UK*, School of Law, University of Glasgow (unpublished paper).

Goodwin, P. (1998) *Television under the Tories. Broadcasting Policy: 1979–1997*, London: British Film Institute.

Gourgey, N. (1997) 'Pornography and freedom of speech', *Entertainment Law Review* 3: 89–93.

Graham, A. and Davies, G. (1997) *Broadcasting, Society and Policy in the Multimedia Age*, Luton: John Libbey Media.

Grant, C. (1994) *Delors. Inside the House that Jacques built*, London: Nicolas Brealy.

Green, D. (1997) *Regulating Media in the Digital Age*, London: European Media Forum

Green, D. (1998) *Do convergent media need convergent regulation?* London: European Media Forum.

Grimme, K. (1997) 'Business strategies and regulation of digital pay-tv services in Germany', *Communications and Strategies* 27, 3rd quarter: 133–49.

Harcourt, A. J. (1996) 'Regulating for media concentration: the emerging policy of the European Union', *Utilities Law Review* 5, 7: 202–10.

Harcourt, A. J. (1997) 'Limits to technocratic regulation in the European Union: the case of media ownership regulation', Political Studies Association Conference, Belfast 7–10 April 1997.

Harcourt, A. J. (1998a) 'EU media ownership regulation: conflict over the definition of alternatives', *Journal of Common Market Studies* 36, 3: 369–89.

Harcourt, A. J. (1998b) 'The European Commission and the regulation of the media industry', *Cardozo Arts and Entertainment Law Journal* 16, 2/3: 425–49.

Harcourt, A. and Radaelli, C. (1999) 'Beyond technocratic regulation? Single market policy-making in the EU', *European Journal of Political Research*, January.

Hickethier, K. (1996) 'The media in Germany', in A. Weymouth and B. Lamizet (eds), *Markets and Myths: Forces for Change in the European Media*, London: Longman.

High Level Group on the Information Society, B. G. (1994) *Europe and the Global Information Society*. Recommendations to the European Council, Brussels.

Hills, J. and Michalis, M. (1997a) 'Digital television and regulatory issues. The British case', *Communications and Strategies*, 27, 3rd quarter: 75–101.

Hills, J. and Michalis, M. (1997b) 'Technological convergence: regulatory competition. The British case of digital television', *Policy Studies* 18, 3/4: 219–37.

Hitchens, L. P. (1994) 'Media ownership and control: a European approach', *Modern Law Review* 57, 4: 585–601.

Hitchens, L. P. (1997) 'Identifying European Community audio-visual policy in the dawn of the information society', *Yearbook of Media and Entertainment Law* 1996: 45.

Hoehn, T., Koboldt, C. and Parr, M. (1997) *Competition Policy in Dynamic Markets: The Case of Convergence*, London: London Economics.

Hoffmann, S. (1966) 'Obstinate or obsolete: the fate of the nation state and the case of Western Europe', *Daedalus* 95, 3: 862–915.

Hoffmann-Riem, W. (1996a) *Regulating Media: The Licensing and Supervision of Broadcasting in Six Countries*, New York: Guildford Press.

Hoffmann-Riem, W. (1996b) 'New challenges for European multimedia policy: a German perspective', *European Journal of Communication* 11, 3: 327–46.

Hoffmann-Riem, W. (1996c) 'Regulating for cultural standards: a legal perspective', in K. Dyson and W. Homulka (eds), *Culture First!*, Cassell: 92–107.

Hoffmann-Riem, W. (1997) 'Public service orientations in broadcasting – current state and prospect of regulation in Germany', *Studies of Broadcasting* (NHK – Japan Broadcasting Corporation): 33.

Holznagel, B. (1998) 'The right regulatory framework for a creative media economy in a democratic society', Paper to Birmingham Audiovisual Conference.

House of Commons, *Culture, Media and Sport Committee (1998) The Multi-Media Revolution Volume 1 (HC 520–I)*, London: Stationery Office.

House of Lords Select Committee on the European Communities (1995) *European Film and Television Industry. Volume II – Evidence.*

Humphreys, P. J. (1994) *Media and Media Policy in Germany: the Press and Broadcasting since 1945*, Oxford: Berg.

Humphreys, P. J. (1996) *Mass Media and Media Policy in Western Europe*, Manchester: Manchester University Press.

Humphreys, P. J. (**1997**) 'Power and control in the new media', ECPR Workshop 'New Media and Political Communication', Bern.

Humphreys, P. J. (1998) 'The goal of pluralism and the ownership rules for private broadcasting in Germany: re-regulation or de-regulation?', *Cardozo Arts and Entertainment Law Journal* 16, 2/3: 527–55.

INA (1998) *Le Soutien Européen à l'Industrie de l'Audiovisuel et du Multimedia*, Paris: INA.

ITC (1997a) *The Case for a Single Regulator.* Memorandum to the National Heritage Select Committee 11.2.97, London: ITC.

ITC (1997b) 'Code of Conduct on Electronic Programme Guides', June 1997, London: ITC.

ITC (1998a) 'ITC Confirms End of Minimum Carriage Requirements', July 1998, London: ITC.

ITC (1998b) 'ITC Issues Consultation Document on Interoperability and Open Access', May 1998, London: ITC.

ITC (1998c) 'ITC Announces Results of Consultation on Interoperability and Open Access', September 1998, London: ITC.

Johnstone, C. (1998) 'Media moguls escape harsh new regulations', *European Voice* 4, 5: 1.

Kaitatzi-Whitlock, S. (1996) 'Pluralism and media concentration in Europe: media policy as industrial policy', *European Journal of Communication* 11, 4: 453–83.

Kaitatzi-Whitlock, S. (1997) 'The privatizing of conditional access control in the European Union', *Communications and strategies* 25, 1st quarter: 91–122.

Kassim, H. and Menon, A. (1996) *The European Union and National Industrial Policy*, London: Routledge.

Koenig, C. and Roder, E. (1998) 'Converging communications, diverging regulators? Germany's constitutional duplication in Internet governance', *International Journal of Communications Law and Policy*, htttp: www.digital-law.net/IJCLP/final/current/ijclp_webdoc_1_1_1998.html.

KPMG (1995) *Investing in Infrastructure for the European Information Society.* Report to DG XIII, January 1995.

KPMG (1996) *Public Policy Issues arising from Telecommunications and Audiovisual Convergence.* Report for the European Commission, London: KPMG.

Kreher, A. (1996) *The New European Agencies*, Conference Report, Florence: European University Institute.

Kuhn, R. (1995) *The Media in France*, London: Routledge.

Kuhn, R. (1996a) 'Broadcasting and the state: the Mitterrand era and its aftermath', *Intermedia* 24, 1 (Feb./March): 27–9.

Kuhn, R. (1996b) 'France', in V. Macleod (ed.) *Media Ownership and Control in the age of convergence*, London: International Institute of Communications: 49–63.

Kuhn, R. (1997) 'The media and politics', in P. Heywood, M. Rhodes, and V. Wright (eds) *Developments in West European Politics*, London: Macmillan: 263–80.

Labour Party (1995) *Communicating Britain's Future*, London: The Labour Party.

Lamizet, B. (1996) 'The media in France,' in A. Weymouth and B. Lamizet (eds) *Markets and Myths: Forces for Change in the European Media*.

Larouche, P. (1998) 'EC competition law and the convergence of the telecommunications and broadcasting sectors', *Telecommunications Policy* 22, 3: 219–42.

Levy, D. A. L. (1997a) 'The regulation of digital conditional access systems: a case study in European policy making', *Telecommunications Policy* 21, 7: 661–76.

Levy, D. A. L. (1997b) 'Regulating digital broadcasting in Europe: the limits of policy convergence', *West European Politics* 20, 4: 24–42.

Llorens-Maluquer, C. (1998) 'European responses to bottlenecks in digital pay TV: impacts on pluralism and competition policy', *Cardozo Arts and Entertainment Law Journal* 16, 2/3: 557–86.

London Economics (1994) *The Economic Impact of Television Quotas in the European Union*: a report for Sony Entertainment, London: London Economics.

Long, M. (1997) 'Entering the digital age: the promise of pluralism and the danger of monopoly control', ECPR Workshop 'New Media and Political Communi-cation', Bern.

Machet, E. and Robillard, S. (1998) *Television and Culture. Policies and Regulations in Europe*, Düsseldorf: European Institute for the Media.

Macleod, V. (1996) *Media Ownership and Control in the age of Convergence*, London: International Institute of Communications.

Maggiore, M. (1990) *Audiovisual Production in the Single Market*, Brussels: European Commission.

Majone, G. (1996) *Regulating Europe*, London: Routledge.

Majone, G. (1996b) *Temporal Consistency and Policy Credibility: Why Democracies need Non-Majoritarian Institutions*, Florence: European University Institute.

Marsden, C. T. (1997) 'The European digital convergence paradigm: from structural pluralism to behavioural competition law', *Journal of Information, Law and Technology (JILT)*, http: //elj.warwick.ac.uk/jilt/commsreg/97_3mars/, 3.

Mazey, S. and Richardson, J. E. (1993) *Lobbying in the European Community*, Oxford: OUP.

McCallum, L. (1999) 'EC competition law and digital pay television', *Competition Policy Newsletter* 1, Feb.: 4–16.

McGarvey, P. (1997) *Current Trends in European Media*, London: FT Media and Telecoms.

McGowan, F. and Wallace, H. (1996) 'Towards a European regulatory state', *Journal of European Public Policy* 3, 4 December 1996: 560–76.

Meyn, H. (1994) *Mass Media in the Federal Republic of Germany*, Hamburg: INTERPRESS.

Michel, H. (1994) *Les Télévisions en Europe*, Paris: Presses Universitaires de France.

Middleton, B. (1997) 'Conditional access: looking forward', *Consumer Policy Review* 7, 6 (November/December): 201–5.

Middleton, B. (1997) 'Towards a communications act', *Consumer Policy Review* 7, 3.

Ministry of Education Culture and science and NOS (1997) 'Experts meeting on public service broadcasting in Europe' Amsterdam.

Morgan, J. P. (1998a) *The European Pay-TV Industry*, London: J. P. Morgan.

Morgan, J. P. (1998b) *British Sky Broadcasting plc*, London: J. P. Morgan.

Morgan, J. P. (1998c) *Canal Plus*, London: J .P. Morgan.

Murroni, C. (1997) 'One little, two little, three little regulators?' *Bulletin of the European Institute for the Media* 14, 3: 6–7.

Murroni, C. and Irvine, N. (1998) *Access Matters*, London: IPPR.

National Economic Research Associates and Denton Hall (1997) *Issues Associated with the Creation of a European Regulatory Authority for Telecommunications*, Report for the European Commission, DG XIII, London.

National Economic Research Associates and Smith (1998) *A Study to estimate the economic impact of Government policies towards digital television*, London: DCMS.

Nihoul, P. (1998) 'Competition or regulation for multimedia?' *Telecommunications Policy* 22, 3: 207–18.

Noam, E. (1991) *Television in Europe*, New York: OUP.

Nolan, D. (1997) 'Bottlenecks in pay television. Impact on market developments in Europe', *Telecommunications Policy* 21, 7 (August): 597–610.

OECD (1993) *Competition Policy and a Changing Broadcast Industry*, Paris: OECD.

OECD (1997c ????) *Communications Outlook 1997*, Paris: OECD.

OECD Committee for Information, Computer and Communications Policy (1997a) *Global Information Infrastructure – Global Information Society (GII-GIS): Policy Recommendations for Action (OCDE/GD (97)138)*, Paris: OECD.

OECD Committee for Information, Computer and Communications Policy (1997b) *Information Infrastructures: Their Impact and Regulatory Requirements* (OCDE/GD(97)18), Paris: OECD.

OECD Committee for Information, Computer and Communications Policy (1997) *Webcasting and Convergence: Policy Implications* (OCDE/GD(97)221), Paris: OECD.

Office of Fair Trading (1996) *The Director General's Review of BSkyB's Position in the Wholesale Pay Tv Market*, London: Office of Fair Trading.

OFTEL (1995) *Beyond the Telephone, the Television and the PC*, London: OFTEL.

OFTEL (1996) *Conditional Access*, Consultative Document on Draft OFTEL guidelines, London: OFTEL.

OFTEL (1997) *The Regulation of Conditional Access for Digital Television Services*, London: OFTEL.

OFTEL (1998a) *First submission to the Culture Media and Sports Select Committee Inquiry into audio-visual communications and the regulation of broadcasting. Beyond the Telephone, the Television and the PC -II*, London: OFTEL.

OFTEL (1998b) *Second submission to the Culture Media and Sports Select Committee Inquiry into audio-visual communications and the regulation of broadcasting*, London: OFTEL.

OFTEL (1998c November) *Oftel's Response to the European Commission's Working Document Summarising the Results of the Public Consultation on the Green Paper on the Convergence of the Telecommunications, Media and Information Technology sectors*, London: OFTEL.

Oreja, M. (1997) 'European trump cards in a game with global players: EU audio-visual policy', Speech in Munich, Medientage, 14 October 1997.

Ostergaard, B. S. (1992)'*The media in Western Europe: The Euromedia Handbook*, London: Sage.

Panis, V. (1995) 'Politique audiovisuelle de l'union et identité culturelle Européene', Bruges, College of Europe (thesis).

Papathanassopoulos, S. (1990) 'Broadcasting and the European Community: the Commission's audiovisual policy' in K. Dyson and P. Humphreys (eds) *The Political Economy of Communications*, London: Routledge: 107–24.

Pappas, S. (1997) 'Digital television: 500 channels of junk video?' Speech to 4th Annual CEO Summit on Converging Technologies, 3 June 1997.

Peacock, A. (1986) *Report of the Committee on Financing the BBC, Comnd 9824*, London: Home Office.

Peterson, J. (1993) *High Technology and the Competition State: An Analysis of the Eureka Initiative*, London/New York: Routledge.

Peterson, J. (1995a) 'EU research and development policy: The politics of expertise', in C. Rhodes and S. Mazey (eds) *The State of the European Union: Integration in Perspective*, Boulder, Colorado/Essex: Lynne Rienner/Longman.

Peterson, J. (1995b) 'Decision-making in the European Union: towards a framework for analysis', *Journal of European Public Policy* 2, 1: 69–93.

Peterson, J. (1995c) 'Policy networks and European Union policy making: a reply to Kassim', *West European Politics* 18, 2 (April): 389–407.

Pollack, M. A. (1996) 'The new institutionalism and EC governance: the promise and limits of institutional analysis', *Governance* 9, 4: 429–58.

Pons, J.-F. (1996) 'La politique de Concurrence Européenne dans le domaine audiovisuel', *Competition Policy Newsletter* 2, 3, Autumn/Winter: 6–9.

Pons, J.-F. (1998a) 'The future of broadcasting', Speech to the Institute of Economic Affairs, 29 June 1998.

Pons, J.-F. (1998b) 'The application of competition and anti-trust policy in media and telecommunications in the European Union', Speech to International Bar Association. Vancouver, 14 Sept. 1998 .

Prosser, T. (1992) 'Public service broadcasting and deregulation in the UK', *European Journal of Communication* 7: 173–93.

Prosser, T., Goldberg, D. and Verhulst, S. (1996) *The Impact of the New Communications Technologies on Media Concentrations and Pluralism*. A study prepared at the request of the Committee of Experts on Media Concentrations and Pluralism of the Council of Europe, Glasgow, School of Law, Glasgow University.

Puttnam, D. (1997) *The Undeclared War: The Struggle for Control of the World's Film Industry*, London: HarperCollins.

Richardson, J. (1996) 'Policy-making in the EU: interests, ideas and garbage cans of primeval soup', in J. Richardson (ed.) *European Union: Power and Policy-Making*, London, Routledge: 3–23.

Ridder, C.-M. (1996) 'Media politics, diversity and the gatekeeper debate', *Intermedia* 24, 4 (August/Sept.): 24–6

Robillard, S. (1995) *Television in Europe: Regulatory Bodies*, London: John Libbey.

Rose, R. 'What is lesson-drawing?' *Journal of Public Policy* 11, 1: 3–30.

Rousseau, P.-O. (1996) 'The Regulation of New Services in France', IIR Conference London, 30 Oct. 1996.

Scharpf, F. (1996) 'Democratic Policy in Europe', *European Law Journal* 2, 2: 136–55.

Schaub, A. (1998) 'EC competition policy and its implications for the sports sector', Speech to World Sports Forum, St Moritz, 8 March 1998.

Scheider, V., Dang-Nguyen, G. and Werle, R. (1994) 'Corporate actor networks in European policy-making: harmonizing telecommunications policy', *Journal of Common Market Studies* 32, 4: 473–98.

Schlesinger, P. (1995) *Europeanisation and the Media: National Identity and the Public Sphere*, Oslo: Nordicam.

Schlesinger, P. and Doyle, G. (1995) 'Contradictions of economy and culture: the European Union and the information society', *Cultural Policy* 2, 1: 25–42.

Schoof, H. and Brown, A. W. (1995) 'Information highways and media policies in the European Union', *Telecommunications Policy* 19, 4: 325–28.

Schreiber, K. (1991) 'The new approach to technical harmonization and standards', in Hurwitz and C. Lequesne (eds) *The State of the European Community: Policies, Institutions and Debates in the Transition Years*, Boulder, Colorado: Longman: 97–112.

Schulz, W. (1992) 'European media systems in transition: general trends and modifying conditions. The case of the Federal Republic of Germany', *Gazette* 49: 23–40.

Scott, C. (1998) 'The proceduralization of telecommunications law', *Telecommunications Policy* 22, 3: 242–54.

Screen Digest (1996) 'Digital television : start of the worldwide lift-off', *Screen Digest*, August 1996.

Screen Digest (1997a) 'Consuming movies: pay TV eats into film spending cake', *Screen Digest* January 1997.

Screen Digest (1997b) 'Europe's "other" channels: numbers double every three years', *Screen Digest* March 1997.

Screen Digest (1997c) 'Television sports rights: a seller's market', *Screen Digest* April 1997.

Senat and Hugot, J.-P. (1997) *Rapport Fait au Nom de la Commission des Affaires Culturelles*, Paris: Senat.

Senat – Service des affaires Européennes (1997) *Les Instances de Regulation de l'Audiovisuel et la Déontologie des Programmes*, Paris: Senat.

Service Juridique et Technique de l'Information et Communication (2 octobre 1996) *Etude d'Impact du Projet de Loi Modifiant la Loi no 86–1067 du 30 Septembre 1986*, Paris: SJTI.

Skogerbo, E. (1996) 'External constraints and National Resources. Reflections on the Europeanization of communications policy', *Nordicom Review of Nordic Research on Media and Communication*, 1: 69–80.

Smith, C. (1997) Speech to the Royal Television Society Cambridge Convention – 18 Sept.1998, Department of Culture, Media and Sport.

Smith, C. (1998) *Creative Britain*, London: Faber and Faber

Smith, G. J. H. (1996) 'Internet law and regulation', London: *FT Law and Tax*.

Spectrum Strategy Consultants (1996) *Development of the Information Society: An International Analysis*, London: HMSO.

Squires, S. Sanders and Dempsey and Analysys (1998) *Study on Adapting the EU Regulatory Framework to the Developing Multimedia Environment. Summary Report*, Brussels and Luxembourg: European Commission.

Steemers, J. (1998) *Changing Channels: The Prospects for Television in a Digital World*, Luton: John Libbey.

Temple Lang, J. (1994) 'Defining legitimate competition: companies' duties to supply competitors, and access to essential facilities', in B. Hawk (ed.) *International Antitrust Law and Policy 1994* (Annual Proceedings of the Fordham Corporate Law Institute), New York: Juris Publishing.

Temple Lang, J. (1996a) 'European community antitrust law: innovation markets and high technology industries', in B. Hawk (ed.) *International Antitrust Law and Policy 1996*, New York: Juris Publishing.

Temple Lang, J. (1996b) *The Principle of Essential Facilities and its Consequences in European Community Competition Law*, Oxford: Regulatory Policy Institute.

Temple Lang, J. (1997) 'Media, multimedia and European Community antitrust law', Fordham Corporate Law Institute. 24th Annual Conference. International Antitrust Law and Policy, October 16–17, 1997.

Thatcher, M. (1996) 'High Technology', in H. Kassim and A. Menon (eds), *The European Union and National Industrial Policy*, London: Routledge: 178–203.

Thompson, I. (1997) *Convergence in Television and the Internet. Web TV or TV on the Web?* London: FT Media and Telecoms.

Tongue, C. (1998) *Culture or Monoculture? The European Audiovisual Challenge*, Ilford, Essex: Carole Tongue MEP.

Tracey, M. (1998) *The Decline and Fall of Public Service Broadcasting*, Oxford: OUP.

Trautmann, C. (1998) 'Audiovisuel, des règles plus claires, plus équitables', Communication en conseil des ministres présentées par Catherine Trautmann, ministre de la culture et de la communication (28.01.98). See http://www.cul-ture.fr/culture/actuel/conferen/audiovisuel.htm.

Tunstall, J. (1992) 'The United Kingdom', in B. S. Ostergaard (ed.) *The Media in Western Europe. The Euromedia Handbook*, London: Sage: 238–55.

Ungerer, H. (1995) *EU Competition Law in the Telecommunications, Media and Information Technology Sectors, New York.*

Ungerer, H. (1996a) 'Clarifying how recent EU policies and decisions will foster effective competition: who should be Europe's digital gatekeepers?' Talk to European Cable and Satellite Conference, Paris, 20 March 1996.

Ungerer, H. (1996b) 'Competition in the information society-multimedia', Speech to Annual General Meeting of the European Multimedia Forum, 19 November 1996.

Ungerer, H. (1998a) 'The arrival of competition in European telecommunications', Speech to 3rd European Forum on the Law of Telecommunications, Infrromation Technologies and Multimedia: Towards a Common Framework, Luxembourg 19 June 1998.

Ungerer, H. (1998b) 'Ensuring efficient access to bottleneck network facilities. The case of telecommunications in the European Union', Speech in Florence 13 Nov. 1998.

Van Miert, K. (1995) 'The competition policy of the new commission', Speech to EG – Kartellrechtsforum der Studienvereinigung Kartellrecht – Brussels, 11 May 1995.

Van Miert, K. (1997a) 'The impact of digital technologies on the telecommunications and television sectors', Speech in Rome, 12 June 1997.

Van Miert, K. (1997b) 'Europe 2000, the challenge of market and competition policy', Speech in Florence, 26 September 1997.

Van Miert, K. (1998) Statement by Commissioner van Miert. Commission Press Release IP/98/916 21.10.1998.

Vasconcelos, A. (1994) *Report by the Think-Tank on the Audiovisual Policy in the European Union*, Brussels and Luxembourg: European Commission.

Vedel, T. (1996) 'Les politiques des autoroutes de l'information dans les pays industrialisés: une analyse comparative', *Réseaux* 78: 13–27.

Vedel, T. (1996) 'The French policy for information superhighways: the end of high-tech Colbertism?' Paper to Conference on National and International Initiatives for Information Infrastructure, 25–7 January 1996, John F. Kennedy School of Government Taubman Conference Center.

Verhulst, S. (1997) 'Public service broadcasting in Europe', *Utilities Law Review* 8, 2 (March/April): 31–3.

Wachtmeister, A.-M. (1998) 'Broadcasting of sports events and competition law', *Competition Policy Newsletter,* 2 June 1998: 18–28.

Westcott, T. (1997) *All to Pay for: Pay-per-view Sport in Europe*, London: FT Media and Telecoms.

Weymouth, A. and Lamizet, B. (1996) *Markets and Myths: Forces for Change in the European Media*, London: Longman.

Wilks, S. (1996) 'Regulatory compliance and capitalist diversity in Europe', *Journal of European Public Policy* 3 (December): 536–59.

Williams, R. (1996) *Normal Service won't be Resumed. The Future of Public Service Broadcasting*, St Leonards, Australia: Allen and Unwin

Winsbury, R. (1996) 'How Bavaria sets its media policy', *Intermedia* 24, 4 (August/Sept.): 27.

Young, A. R. (1998) 'European consumer groups: multiple levels of governance and multiple logics of collective action', in J. Greenwood and M. Aspinwall (eds) *Collective Action in the European Union: Interests and the New Politics of Associability*, London: Routledge.

Index